MACHINE HEAD

INSIDE THE MACHINE

HEAD

MACHINE HEAD
INSIDE THE MACHINE

JOEL McIVER

OMNIBUS PRESS

London / New York / Paris / Sydney / Copenhagen / Berlin / Madrid / Tokyo

This book is dedicated to my wife, Emma, and to my children, Alice and Tom.

Contents

Foreword by Chris Kontos

Welcome to the first biography of Machine Head, of which I was a member between 1992 and 1995. Over the years, I have had some of the best people come into my life due to my time in Machine Head. The album I made with them, *Burn My Eyes*, has made a lot of people very happy and has inspired many young players to make music.

The music we made was outstanding: to this day, *Burn My Eyes* is still revered as one of the most accomplished metal records of all time – and I'm very proud of that.

I still struggle with my feelings about how it all ended, but I've been able to find respect for the other band members thanks to what we did together. After all, the only thing that really matters is the music, and the people who love it.

This book goes deep into why the music we made means so much to the metal community: you'll enjoy every step of the way.

Chris Kontos, 2012

Introduction

Sometimes it's hard to believe that heavy metal musicians ever find the strength to persevere. The array of obstacles that stand in the way of any metal band, even an averagely good one, is enough to make most sane people weep. For every bunch of headbangers who make it onto your TV or radio, a hundred other groups fail, falling victim to the machinations of the music business, the indifference of the public or simply the difficulties that crop up between getting out of bed each morning and getting back into it the same evening.

Machine Head, the Oakland heavy metal band, have come close, unbelievably close, to that fatal point on more than one occasion. Theirs is a classic rise, fall and rise again story, but that doesn't man it's ever been predictable. Bad luck in many forms has always battered the band, not into submission – never that – but often into a position of extreme difficulty. But they've come back, and come back, and come back yet again. After two decades of struggle, Machine Head are close, nail-bitingly so, to the very top of the metal scene. Sure, a handful of older groups occupy a more successful position, but that handful is diminishing fast, and a few years into the future, Machine Head may well have taken the step they need to be the biggest metal band in the world.

Don't believe me? Take a look at their story. Bands with this much drive to succeed come along only a few times in a generation, and in an industry where the giants of yore are being slowly undermined by age and wealth, that same drive is going to be what makes Machine Head winners in the epic battle to come. That sounds dramatic, right? Then again, this is a story that redefines 'dramatic'...

Joel McIver
2012

Acknowledgments

Emma, Alice, Tom, Robin and Kate, Dad, John and Jen, James, Tim, Moss, Naomi Alderman, Carlos Anaia, David Barraclough, Scott Bartlett, Charlie Benante, Jacqui Black, Paul Brannigan, Tom Bryant, Alex Burrows, Max and Gloria Cavalera, Dino Cazares, Chas Chandler, Chris Charlesworth, Ian Christe, Monte Conner, Ben Cooper, Tony Costanza, Joe Daly, Phil Demmel, Helen Donlon, John Doran, Jason Draper, Adam Duce, Mark Eglinton, David Ellefson, Robb Flynn, Lisa Gallagher, Matthew Hamilton, Sara Harding, Charlie Harris, Matt Higham, Glenn Hughes, Joseph Huston, Bill Irwin, Patrik Jensen, Michelle Kerr, Chris Kontos, Tina Korhonen, Borivoj Krgin, Brian Lew, Dave Ling, Frank Livadaros, Craig Locicero, Daniel Lukes, Corinne Lynn, Rachel Mann, Glen Matlock, Patrizia Mazzuocolo, Dave McClain, Alex Milas, Sir Patrick Moore, Eugenio Monti, Bob Nalbandian, Harald Oimoen, Martin Popoff, Mario Rimati, Nick Robbins, Elliott Rubinson, Adam Sagir, Ralph Santolla, Jonathan Selzer, Kirsten Sprinks, Wes Stanton, Jeff Stewart, Perry Strickland, Tom

Trakas, Dan Travis, Sue Tropio, David Vincent, Jeremy Wagner, Mick Wall, Alex Webster, Chris Williams, Ian Winwood, the staff of *Bass Guitar Magazine* and the families Arnold, Bhardwaj, Bowles, Cadette, Edwards, Fraser, Freed, Harrington, Herbert, Hogben, Jolliffe, Knight, Lamont, Legerton, Leim, Mathieson-Spires, Mendonça, Metcalfe, Miles, Parr and Woollard plus the visitors to www.joelmciver.co.uk and www.facebook.com/joelmciver.

Chapter 1

Before 1992

No book has ever been pretentious enough to include both the names Philip Larkin and Machine Head in its opening sentences before now, so let's establish that precedent, shall we? 'They fuck you up, your mum and dad / They may not mean to, but they do,' advised the late poet Larkin in one of his more noted couplets, relevant in this case because Machine Head's remarkable career has hit some low psychological points over the last couple of decades. In those bleak times, both singer Robert 'Robb' Flynn and bassist Adam Duce have talked about the mental scars they carry from their early lives. From tragedy comes creativity, thankfully, and some of Machine Head's finest music has been inspired by those black times. Of course, many other factors have made this remarkable band what they are, namely a love of the music for its own sake and a practically spiritual connection with the fanbase that makes other groups look aloof in comparison. But without that dark side, Machine Head's lyrics, musical aggression and perhaps even career trajectory might have been rather different.

There's a geographical factor in the rise of Machine Head, too. In the eighties, the decade in which Machine Head's roots lie, one of the most fertile places to be if you were a musician in an American heavy metal band was the eastern end of the Bay Area. Home to various creative communities for many years, the towns of Oakland, Hayward, Berkeley and others have been hot spots for musical, literary and other artistic endeavours since the fifties. In the timeframe that concerns us here, the renowned Bay Area thrash metal scene coalesced in the early eighties, when Robb Flynn was in his mid-teens.

He was born in Oakland on July 19, 1968 to unknown parents, although he revealed in later years that his birth name was Lawrence Matthew Cardine. Adopted and raised in Fremont, a relatively peaceful suburb in Alameda County, Flynn has revealed little about his pre-teen life, despite being asked about it in hundreds, perhaps thousands of interviews. We do know that he was a good student, especially in his early years at American High School in Fremont – and that an obsession with heavy metal struck him at an early age, specifically at the hands of the genre's founders, Black Sabbath.

Figuring out Sabbath's complex history was a reverse process for this budding headbanger. "When I got into Black Sabbath, both [sometime Sabbath singers] Ronnie James Dio and Ozzy Osbourne were already recording solo albums," he explained. "The first Sabbath album I ever got was *Heaven And Hell* [1980]. My friend Lori had a copy of it, and until that point I had never really heard Black Sabbath. I didn't even know there had been an Ozzy period. Later, I dug back, and the first Ozzy-era record I heard was *We Sold Our Souls For Rock 'N' Roll*, the compilation record. I heard 'Paranoid' and I thought the lyrics were just awesome. Then I heard 'Iron Man' and I was just... terrified! So I got totally into that era, too. But really, I love both [Ozzy and Dio] eras.'

By 1982, thrash metal was beginning to make its presence felt in the Bay Area, although no-one had given it that name yet. Hardcore punk co-existed with metal, although not always peacefully thanks to the clashes between the followers of the different movements: the length of a concert-goer's hair could literally determine whether he went home with or without his teeth after the show. "If it wasn't for those bands," recalled Flynn, "there wouldn't be a Machine Head. When I was a kid, Exodus was my favourite band of all time. [Their 1985 album] *Bonded By Blood* was my life. I once punched some kid in the face for saying that [Exodus guitarist] Gary Holt sucked."

It was only when Los Angeles thrashers Slayer emerged that the two cults of punk and metal were united. While Slayer, who appear in this book at several pivotal points, weren't the first Californian thrash metal band – that honour goes to Metallica, and just behind them, Exodus – they shed their influences faster than any of the other thrash metal groups, refining a relentlessly malevolent sound over a matter of months. Flynn and his metal buddies saw Slayer doing this and ideas began to form in their teenage minds, with particular relevance to kids who – like Flynn – had taken up the guitar.

The appeal of the new thrash metal scene for such kids was immediate and obvious. Even the average teenager craves an annihilation of the senses from time to time as part of the maturing experience, and troubled teens doubly so. The rebellion, the volume, the tribal belonging, the adrenaline, the sense of adventure... all these were present in thrash metal by its very nature.

"It was amazing then," Flynn told *Kerrang!* writer Tom Bryant two decades later. "Bands like Poison Idea, the Dead Kennedys, Metallica, Exodus, Possessed and Death Angel were all playing. I don't think any of us realised what an incredible musical thing was happening. My first couple of shows meant so much to me.

I had finally found somewhere that I fitted, a place where I could connect to everyone there." If Flynn was looking for catharsis, thrash provided it in abundance. "Oh man, it was violent then, incredibly violent," he continued. "I'd come out of shows with my nose and ribs broken. I remember seeing someone in a circle pit with a cow's leg bone. He was just smashing people round the head with it. Elsewhere there'd be people breaking glass and rolling in it. It was fucking crazy, man. There was no security, no insurance and no barriers – anything went."

"I was fortunate to be 14 years old and growing up in the golden age of thrash," Flynn recalled later. "In LA the musicians acted like rock stars. In the Bay Area, people were accessible. When I first saw Metallica, James Hetfield was hanging around outside the auditorium. You could get his autograph and talk to him. To a young kid, that made a huge impression. The Bay Area sound always had more evil notes than other styles of metal."

Two of Flynn's earliest friends were a drummer, Jim Pittman, and a guitarist, Jeff Stewart. The latter remembers: "I met Robb in junior high, at American High School: I was a couple of years older than him. I was in a band called Deep Freeze – we were playing kinda AC/DC, Judas Priest stuff. Robb and his friend Jim Pittman would come and watch us play."

When Flynn and Pittman formed their first band, a duo called Inquisitor, they practised staples from the Bay Area repertoire at Stewart's studio. As Flynn told Tom Trakas of *Midwest Metal* magazine, "Me and [Jim] were jamming, and we'd just discovered the joys of drinking a six-pack and listening to Metallica. So we started off just trying to emulate Metallica, just covering *Kill 'Em All* stuff: we liked Sabbath and all that. We'd play at a friend's party or something, playing Slayer or Metallica stuff and a bunch of older, biker kind of guys would be like 'Play Zeppelin'... And, of course, we'd be like 'Those guys suck'!"

Jeff Stewart continues: "In around 1984, I got in a thrash metal band called Annihilation, which was a little heavier than Deep Freeze. Annihilation had a rehearsal spot called Fast And Furious Studios, and that was the place to be. Robb was in Inquisitor, and he'd come to our studio and watch us play. We'd jam and I'd show him how to play arpeggios and hold his pick like Eddie Van Halen. We used to hang out quite a bit: we were pretty close. I used to go over to his house in Fremont all the time. It was a great, suburban area: very well kept. Definitely not the hood."

Stewart adds: "Robb's guitar chops were great, even then. He was a hell of a guitar player and he had a phenomenal ear. I was blown away by how quickly he learned. I introduced him to Uli Jon Roth's solo album, *Earthquake*, and he learned the solo from the title track and played me the licks. I'd say, 'Damn, dude!' He'd learn [Dokken guitarist] George Lynch's solos too. He was very quiet, but he had a vision. I always told him to follow his heart."

Soon the community of metal bands began to spread, Stewart remembers: "Inquisitor would do 'Motorbreath' by Metallica and other covers. I'd go and watch them in the garage and tell them they were doing good. It was good, we all felt like we were going somewhere. In fact, Annihilation was *the* band for a while, but we lost a lot of members and it never really worked out for us, even though [Bay Area DJ and inventor of the name 'Metallica'] Ron Quintana used to interview us a lot for his show on KUSF."

Another of Flynn's early allies was a kid called Craig Locicero, who also played guitar but – at two years Flynn's junior – was still some way behind him as a musician. As Locicero remembers, "I first met Robb in 1984 when I was a freshman in high school, a couple of months after I started playing guitar. At the high school I went to in Fremont, I was literally the only kid walking around wearing Venom shirts and carrying Mercyful Fate records: there was nobody else at that school who knew anything about metal.

But there was a Chinese kid named Clement in my class, and he walked up to me one day and said, 'Dude, I know another guy who likes that same crap that you like. It's my friend Robb: you should come with me after school and we'll go meet him, he lives right by me.' So I went over to his house and met him, and we started talking about music. He had all these records wrapped in plastic: he was very organised."

He continues, "Me and Robb – who spelled his name with one B at the time – hit it off right away. He was a super-fan of metal: I was a step below him, because I was still learning and he was a couple of years older than me, but we had that in common. I really wanted to play with the guy but that took some work before I earned my way into doing that. Robb's drummer, Jim Pittman, thought I was too evil to play with because of my Venom T-shirts. Robb sure ripped on guitar: he was already a good lead player at this early stage. John Tegio played bass and Leroy Munoz played guitar before me, and they advertised for a singer in the paper."

After initial jamming sessions, a singer called Russ Anderson was recruited to the new band. As Locicero recalls, "Robb called me, all excited, saying, 'We've found this singer, you should come down and watch!' So I went down to Leroy's garage where they rehearsed and heard Russ sing. Wow, he was great! I made the decision right away that there was no way that I was going to walk out of that garage without being a member of the band. The other guys went to get some cigarettes and beer while Russ and I stayed behind. While they were away I picked up a guitar and played 'Balls To The Wall' by Accept. Russ said, 'Dude, you're way better than Leroy' – and within a few days they were playing in my garage. Things move fast when you're young. The band didn't have a name: we had a load of stupid ideas like War Witch. Eventually we became Forbidden Evil, which was Jim Pittman's idea."

Forbidden Evil's early shows were that Bay Area staple event of the Eighties – backyard 'keggers', where a party would revolve around a keg of beer. "Thrash metal was just beginning to move into Fremont at this point, because we had brought it in," says Locicero. "When we chose the setlist for the parties we played in back yards, our set would be obscure to anyone who didn't know about thrash. We were playing 'A Lesson In Violence' by Exodus before the *Bonded By Blood* album even came out, because we had the demos. We did 'Violence And Force' by Exciter and 'Am I Evil?' by Diamond Head. Metallica had put out *Ride The Lightning* so we did 'Creeping Death'. When we played these songs, people lost their minds. They didn't know what they were hearing. We slipped in a couple of originals too: 'Legions Of Death' and 'Egypt Has Fallen' were the first ones, I think. Those were Robb's songs."

It hadn't taken long for Flynn to make his mark as a songwriter, remembers Locicero. "At first, Robb was definitely in charge. I was trying to improve my guitar playing and I'd play the odd solo here and there. At the first few shows we did, although they were parties rather than shows, we did his songs. The first thing we wrote together was 'Forbidden Evil', which was a conglomeration of both our riffs that he'd found a way to put together. One thing that Robb did better than anybody else was take an arrangement and put his riffs into it – the intro, the verse, the pre-chorus, the chorus and so on. He had that down. Later I started writing too, and the songs that appear on the albums we recorded, we wrote together."

Songwriting and arranging were definitely among the teenage Flynn's skills, recalls his sometime guitarist. "I have fond memories of writing music with Robb," says Locicero. "I learned a lot from him: he was something of a mentor to me, musically. He was a really nice kid. Everyone liked him and he joked around a lot.

He wasn't a ladies' man at the time, although he was trying. I remember one of the later Ruthie's Inn shows, he'd got a leather jacket and he wore it on stage and found a persona. He met a girl before the show and she really liked him, and they were an item after that. That was when Robb found himself and became a man. He was still shy, though: a lot of people don't know that about him. It changed his life. And more power to him."

Along with the long nights of metallic debauchery there came drugs, specifically speed – a cheap, nasty way to guarantee being able to stay up all night. Flynn has long been open about his use of this filthy-but-fun stimulant back in those early days: the drug was so commonly used in the Bay Area thrash scene that an early name for the music, speed metal, was often used before the more conventional 'thrash' label began to be applied in around 1984.

"Me and my friends would get a bunch of crank – speed – and the cheapest beer we could find, three dollars for a 12-pack," remembered Flynn. "Then we'd go to Berkeley and get wired and drunk before seeing a show. Afterwards, we'd drive home blaring the bands we'd just seen from the stereo. Then, because I was still so wired, I'd sit up playing guitar until dawn, trying to work out the riffs I'd just heard the bands playing."

Although Flynn's performance at American High School in Fremont is said to have been exemplary until his mid-teens, he only scraped through graduation – and his behaviour continued to deteriorate to the point where, in 1985, his adopted parents asked him to leave their home. "They kicked me out because I was too crazy," Flynn told Tom Bryant. "Their attitude was, 'You're 17 years old and you think you've got everything all figured out. Fine, go figure it out.' I totally resented that back then. But now, looking back, it was probably a good thing. Now that I'm not a skateboarding, fighting, speed-freak, 17-year-old asshole, I can see that being kicked out helped me learn some responsibilities."

Poverty was no fun for this teenage hellraiser: Flynn was tough enough to brave a certain degree of squalor (this was thrash metal's garage-level heyday, remember) but the crunch point came when he began to emit a certain odour. "Not having any money and not having any food sucked," he sighed. "Once I couldn't afford a new pair of shoes, and the pair I had stank. Man, it was a satanic stench. I was so embarrassed that I couldn't take my shoes off."

Nonetheless, the partying continued. Locicero recalls, "Back then our weights would fluctuate depending on what drugs we were doing at the time! That's what Bay Area metal was about. Speed kept us going. That's why they called it speed metal: we were literally playing as fast as we could." In fact, the drug soon became a form of employment as well as of entertainment. While switching between sleeping at friends' houses, Flynn began dealing speed to keep afloat. "There were a lot of crack dealers," he observed. "You'd look at them making a living and realise, 'I could do that'. I thought, 'I do speed, I may as well sell it too'. It turned out that I had quite a knack for it. I made pretty good money."

This may sound pretty desperate, but Flynn later looked back on this period as one of the best times of his life. "They were great times," he told *Rock Sound*. "[Drugs were] not a self-destructive thing; we were just partying a lot and I was doing a lot of speed. We were 17-year-old kids going to thrash shows and everyone did speed there: it gave you the balls to go crazy and go stagedive. All our idols and all the bands were doing it, and it got to a point where it became bad for me, but it didn't ruin my life... I just look back on those times as crazy."

"Somebody was probably getting low while we were high," he reflected, aware of the potential downside. "I know we fought a lot when we were taking speed, but it was always someone at a show who was on speed wanting to fight us back, so it wasn't like

9

we were hurting people who didn't want to get hurt already. The one thing about speed that I used to think was a bad thing, but have now come to realise was a good thing, was that I was never a person that could stay up for days and days on speed. I had friends who would stay up for a week on speed and not sleep."

Fortunately for Flynn's career, he had no such stamina. He added, "I could never last more than two days on speed. I would start at 9pm one night, party all night, and then by 6pm the following day my body was shutting down and narcolepsy would set in, and I would fall asleep mid-sentence for three hours, then wake up and perfectly continue the sentence I was in the middle of before I passed out. I think to a large degree that was beneficial for me, as I couldn't get that much into it."

In any case, music was now calling and Flynn couldn't spend too much time out of his mind: Forbidden Evil demanded the maximum from his evolving guitar skills. As any metal guitarist will tell you, playing thrash riffs accurately requires a picking hand of almost inhuman precision or the music will sound muddy: the only way to achieve this level of picking accuracy is to spend hundreds of hours practising, rather than being wall-eyed with amphetamines. Jeff Stewart recalls how quickly Flynn's guitar skills improved: "I was taking lessons in classical and jazz, and I would jam with everyone around town and show Robb things. He would learn stuff by ear, because his ear was phenomenal, and he kept practising, and I'd show him how to double-pick and what scales to practise, and picking techniques. He got up to where I was at. Me, Craig and Robb always had some healthy competition."

With the musicians fully dedicated to the band, Forbidden Evil began to make some progress. "After not too long we started getting out there and playing better gigs," says Locicero. "Our first was with Metal Church, the day before they supported

Metallica. They weren't very popular at the time, but I thought they were good. It was at Ruthie's Inn on January 30, 1985: that gig was recorded for a live album called *At The Eastern Front*."

One early witness to the new band's onstage antics was budding photographer, manager, bassist and all-round 'Bay Area banger' Harald Oimoen, who was later immortalised in the song 'The Ballad Of Harald O' by the Metallica side project Spastik Children. Oimoen, who compiled his pictures and memories of the early Bay Area thrash scene alongside those of fellow metalhead Brian Lew in a 2011 book, *Murder In The Front Row*, recalls: "Forbidden Evil were basically just drunk teenagers at that point. I never thought they would go very far, which is amazing because they're more popular than ever now. Craig Locicero is one of the most dedicated musicians I've ever met: to this day, music is his life. From the moment he joined Forbidden Evil, you could tell that it was going to be his career. He's the heart of the band."

At the same time, a second thrash metal band called Vio-Lence was making their presence felt in the Bay Area. Oimoen remembers the emergence of Vio-Lence, saying: "The first Vio-Lence show was at Ruthie's Inn. They had a different singer, Jerry Birr, and they didn't look like contenders: they were almost like a parody of thrash. Then Sean Killian came in and made it a bit more serious: they started singing about social issues and got a bit more hardcore. I hung out with them all the time. I was in a band called Terminal Shock at the time, which was the band that the bassist Deen Dell was in before he joined Vio-Lence."

Guitarist Phil Demmel was the glue that held Vio-Lence together. His history was similar to Flynn's in that he had paid his dues in covers bands before his first shot at success. As Demmel explained in a 2001 interview with *Midwest Metal*, "I was with a group of friends I had grown up with, you know, and bounced back and forth with them in a band called Betrayal. That band

11

was a little more instrumental, like Savatage or Accept, but it broke up and I was looking for something to do. So I joined Death Penalty, which was pretty established at the time: it was Jerry Birr, Troy Fua, Eddie Billy and Perry Strickland – and they were looking for a guitar player. I joined them, we played a party and before the next party we did, Perry changed the name to Vio-Lence. We were Vio-Lence for about three months, then we lost Eddie and brought in Deen Dell. It's funny, a lot of people think I formed the band and got everyone together, which isn't the case, but I just slowly took over. The songs we were playing at the time were a culmination of stuff which friends of the band had written, stuff from past members and all that."

Demmel was one of the most committed 'bangers' in the band, as he later recalled: "I'll give you a *Spinal Tap* moment. I've got a scar on my shin; you can barely see it now. We were playing Pittsburgh. I was jumping off the monitors, so I ran across the stage and leapt off the wedge and it gave in. I fell backwards and ploughed the whole drum set. The songs stopped and the next day, we wore peg pants back in the day, so the peg pants were all tight, and you could see this huge lump that came across [his entire shin]. It hurt but I'll never forget it."

The guitarist also recalled his first encounter with Robb Flynn, saying: "We shared a studio with a band called Annihilation. It was their place, so we set up in front of them and we paid them a little rent. Forbidden Evil practised around the corner, and we'd go and check them out: it was really our first introduction to another scene besides our own. We saw Robb play, and Troy and I thought he was killer."

Although Forbidden Evil were making some progress, Flynn wasn't happy with them, and Vio-Lence provided him with an exit strategy in 1986. Flynn recalled meeting the members of Vio-Lence for the first time, telling *Midwest Metal*: "They started practising in the same building as us, [and] we may have done a show together. But they were playing by us and I met Phil and we became drinking friends, pretty much, and one night he invited me to check them out. I was checking them out and they went into the middle riff of 'Eternal Nightmare', the bass line part, and I was just like 'Fuck!' I was blown away. That was one of the heaviest things I'd ever heard at the time. So from there I was a fan."

Demmel added: "Disaster Records was into us and wanted to put us into the studio and we were kind of freaking out: our first label talk. So we approached Robb and said, 'We're not looking for a guitar player, we're not going to audition people' and all that. If Robb didn't want to do it, we would've kept Troy, but he wanted to do it."

As Locicero recalls it, Flynn's switch to the other group was unexpected – even though he had been asked to join Vio-Lence himself. "Two of the guys in Vio-Lence showed up at my house and asked me to join the band, a couple of months before Robb joined," he tells us. "I said no because I didn't like their singer. Right after that they got a new singer, Sean Killian, and we saw them play and Robb really liked them. He liked Sean's live delivery and he was into it, whereas I wasn't."

He continues: "We were getting ready to record a demo, and Robb showed up to practice with his arm in a sling. We were like, 'Fuck, dude, what happened?' and he said, 'Yeah man, I stole some beer from a store and the cops started chasing me and I jumped over a fence!' and he told us this whole story. We were like, 'Man, that's hardcore. Are you going to be able to record the demo?' and he said 'No, I'm gonna need a couple more weeks' and we were like, 'Ah, crap!' So the time to record the demo comes and he shows up to practice the day before we record without a sling. We said, 'Are you going to be all right?' and he said, 'I think

I got it'. He starts playing and he's insane: we were like, 'Wow, dude, you're amazing!' without a clue what was going on. So we recorded the demo and then he disappeared for a couple of weeks afterwards. We all went over to his house and played the demo for him, but he didn't say too much."

Locicero adds that a line-up change occurred at about this time, with drummer Pittman and bassist Tegio replaced by new blood: "This was when Paul Bostaph and Matt Camacho were in the band, which was the line-up – minus Robb – that put out the *Forbidden Evil* album in 1988. Anyway, Robb called Russ back the next day and they went and had a meeting, with pizza and beer that Robb had bought. So I show up to practice that night and we were all standing there, and Russ was like, 'Robb's got something to tell us'. Then Robb told us words to the effect of, 'I'm quitting this band because it's going nowhere. The vocals suck. You guys can't play. It's not what I'm into. You guys kind of suck!' and we were like, 'What? So what are you going to do?' and he said, 'I'm joining Vio-Lence'."

Stunned, Locicero found no coherent response. "In my head I was thinking, 'Vio-Lence just asked *me* to join, not even two months ago...' but I couldn't think of anything to say. I couldn't believe it. I was only 16, and I couldn't articulate a rational thought. So these words came out of my mouth: 'Mark my words. One day I will take a shit on your head!', and Robb fired back, 'Thanks, Craig, for making my decision even easier'. He had faked the broken arm to go and work with Vio-Lence for a couple of weeks. It felt like the ultimate betrayal."

Note that all this juvenile stuff is long past: as Locicero tells the tale, he adds: "When I tell that story about Robb, I have no ill feelings towards him: those things are what kids do to be passive-aggressive about how to deal with things."

Flynn's departure fuelled a mutually competitive edge between the two bands which lasted some years, Locicero explains. "The beginning of the Vio-Lence and Forbidden Evil rivalry was right there. We'd been friends with those guys, but after that we had a problem. We had an issue with them because of this guy – and they went on to become Bay Area kings. They were huge around here, but they couldn't get anything going anywhere else. You had to see them live to understand them. They were the cockiest of all the bands, just legendary assholes. I liked them and looked up to them, though, and we're friends to this day despite the rivalry. They were winning the race, until we came out with *Forbidden Evil*."

Vio-Lence were at their strongest when they were on stage, recalled Flynn later: "I knew the chemistry of what we were trying to do was right. The five of us would walk into a room and we had to be the centre of attention – it had to be all eyes on us, and our chemistry just ended up working like that. And we just wanted to be the craziest, the fastest, thrashiest band we could, and we had Phil. If it wasn't for that guy, then half of the shit that happened wouldn't have, and that's the fucking truth. He carried this band a lot... When I first joined the band, Phil, Perry and Sean pretty much called the shots, but if you really wanted to get technical about it, it was Phil. He was the man: he could talk to people, he could talk business, and everyone was OK with it because he did it so well."

Jeff Stewart recalls, "I was good friends with Phil Demmel. Vio-Lence was his baby. He'd been in a band with Steve 'Zetro' Souza [also of Legacy and Exodus] and Perry Strickland called Death Penalty: they played kind of AC/DC stuff. I became friends with him because I was in the studio once, playing some Randy Rhoads riffs, and we got to talking about Randy."

Among the new line-up's first priorities was to record a demo, titled *Mechanic* after the subsidiary of the major MCA label which had offered Vio-Lence an album deal. The young band-members were clueless about the music industry, admitted Flynn: "We went in and did the demo and it garnered a lot of interest, I think, because we were offering up something different. Nobody sounded like Vio-Lence at all. Sure, riff-wise it was total Bay Area [with] a lot of Slayer mixed into it, but we had Sean and no-one sounded like Sean. That, plus the fact that he had an attitude and so did the rest of us, seemed to really help. But getting signed, we really didn't know too much of what was going on, that was [down to] our managers."

Vio-Lence had two capable co-managers, one of whom was Joseph Huston, a college student who worked tirelessly to promote the metal cause. "Joey was our original manager," said Flynn, "and we hooked up with him soon after I joined. Joey was just our friend, he was like 18 or 19 and he had one of those fancy college educations, ha ha! The rest of us were just out of, or dropping out of, high school, but he was a few years older and considerably smarter."

He added: "We were stoked to be signed. I know [Mechanic] was a brand new label, there was only one other band on it, and they totally sucked – so we were the best thing they had. And they were just hell into it. [Mechanic A&R exec] Steve Sinclair was the man and he was really into Sean and Phil, he really got off on their attitude and charisma. Then there was the demo giveaway: in every magazine we picked up, there was a full-page ad, giving the demo to any and everyone. I don't remember all the bands that got signed or the order they were signed in, but I do know we were signed before Forbidden. They were our arch rivals, so we always kept an eye on them!"

The band's other co-manager was the late and much-missed Debbie Abono, a legendary local figure who had begun her career as a heavy metal manager when she took on the black metal pioneers Possessed. Abono, who was in her late middle age, also managed Forbidden. "When Robb left, I was on a mission," says Craig Locicero, "and I scored Debbie Abono to manage us. As soon as we had her, Vio-Lence sent Joey Huston over to convince her that she should manage them. They literally stole our manager! Still, she had us doing shows together everywhere, even though we had all this silly kid rivalry going on." Of Abono, who passed away in 2011, Locicero remembers: "She was the coveted manager that everybody wanted, because she had a lot of connections. She was a beautiful person. She was always super-proud of me, Robb, Larry Lalonde [guitarist with Possessed, Blind Illusion and Primus] and Paul Bostaph, of all the Bay Area guys."

Huston was an essential cog in the workings of Vio-Lence from day one, said Demmel. "Joey was there from the beginning: he'd help us get shows and make flyers and he was like the sixth member of the band. We had him with us for a while, and Perry and Sean decided he wasn't going to 'take us to the next level', which will become a recurring theme later in the story. But that's what they thought... Debbie had just started working with Forbidden. So we went and met with Exodus' manager Toni Isabella, who was pretty powerful. We tried to one-up Forbidden with her, and all she spoke about was percentages and money and really turned us off her, quick. I had met Debbie and we totally hit it off, and she didn't mind handling both bands. She was really nice and was a fan, so it worked out great."

Harald Oimoen also got involved in the battle of the two thrash bands, recalling: "I actually used to manage Forbidden right after Robb left, when [replacement guitarist] Glen Alvelais joined in around 1987. I did it for about six months: they played a couple of really good shows with Suicidal Tendencies and other bands. There was some competition with Vio-Lence there for a little while: they kept going pretty strong even after Robb left. They were determined."

Things moved fast, said Demmel. "Maybe a month after [Flynn joined] the band, we played our first show at the Stone, which was really an established club at the time. We opened for Heathen and got a really good response: our demo was out and we started getting mail from overseas. [British writer] Steffan Chirazi got interested and wrote our first *Kerrang!* article and that was like, wow!"

At the time the members of Vio-Lence were eking out a living doing menial jobs – the lot of novice musicians since rock music was invented. "In 1986 I was working at Subaru," said Demmel. "I worked there with Sean, Deen, Zetro, Eric [Peterson] from Testament, Deen's brother... there was a good 15 of us working this union job, making good money. It was an import place, so my job was driving these brand new cars off the boat onto a pier. We'd be out there just beating the shit out of these cars. But we managed to fuck that up and we all lost our jobs! Let's see... Perry was driving a street sweeper, and Robb really wasn't doing anything. I think he'd get little construction jobs if he needed some money. I remember he'd be like, 'I was picking up wood in the rain today and it fucking sucked!'"

Meanwhile, the offstage fun and games continued. Oimoen and Flynn were close friends and shared more than a few escapades. One adventure occurred at a show by the notorious punk GG Allin, whose stage act often involved his own faecal matter. Oimoen recalls: "Me and Robb and a couple of friends went to see GG Allin when he played a show in San Francisco. It was so crazy. He was famous for finding somebody and smearing crap on them, it was horrible. You'd think people would beat him up, but he got away with it. There was a real sense of danger in the room. We hid up in the balcony because we didn't want to get crap on us. He threw all this crap out in the audience. All of a sudden he runs out towards the balcony with this big turd in his hand, ready to smear it on somebody. We ran for our lives, downstairs from the balcony, but GG Allin turns around and all of a sudden he's running towards us. I thought we were going to be trampled to death. It was one of the craziest things I've ever seen. The opening band was coming from the same place as GG Allin was, and this girl was getting fisted on stage when we came into the club."

He continues, "After the show, Robb had left a bag of speed in our car, and he called up and said, 'Harald, this is Robb, call me back right away. I left something in your car'. So we called him back right away and said, 'No, we haven't seen it' and making sniffing noises, ha ha! We would refer to that stuff as 'Dave'. That was the code word: 'Dave' was a roommate of his. When he finally got popular enough with Machine Head and he didn't have to do that any more to support himself, he came up to me at a show one time and said, 'Dave's finally moved out'. Essentially, Dave was a roommate that they didn't really want to have around, but they had to have him around in order to make the rent every month..."

Deep Freeze, Vio-Lence and Forbidden were one of a small number of Bay Area bands in the late Eighties that gave several key musicians their start in the business. In the early-to-middle years of the decade, the same could be said of Exodus, Legacy, Metallica and still earlier bands such as Trauma, and while most of the characters in this book were too young to have been active musicians before the middle of the decade, Jeff Stewart is old enough to have witnessed both generations. "My band Deep Freeze opened for Trauma at the Keystone in Berkeley, where I met Cliff Burton before he was in Metallica," he says. "I encountered all these dudes: down the road I met this guy called Ben Avery, who became our second singer in Deep Freeze, and he knew Chuck Billy – who was later in Testament – and Perry Strickland, who went on to play drums in Vio-Lence after he was in Deep Freeze."

Metal was everywhere, says Stewart: "We went to Exciter's SF show on their first tour. We saw Mercyful Fate too: we were

19

totally into them, they were one of our favourite bands. We saw Iron Maiden, of course, and Metallica... we went to see Exodus all the time. Later, when I met Robb, I introduced all these guys to Venom and Holocaust and Angel Witch."

Flynn himself remembered this unique environment with affection, saying: "As a kid growing up in the Bay Area, pretty much the golden era of thrash, I got to see some incredible bands and I got to see some crappy bands, too. There's a lot of crappy metal out there, [but] there was a lot of good metal, and for me and my friends, we started getting into punk rock and we started getting into hardcore and metal and rap and all these things were coming out right at that time, and for us, [it] was just kind of very *Beavis And Butthead*. [Music either] kicked ass, or it sucked, and it had more to do with the attitude and the spirit. You could see that some people really believed in what they were doing and were trying to push things to be new and different, and that was always more exciting, and then there was the people who just tried to do things the same way and never pushed it far enough, and we didn't get into it."

Vio-Lence's music was just as powerful as that of Forbidden (who dropped the 'Evil' after Flynn left), and the lifestyle of the musicians was similarly chaotic. "They were probably the craziest days of my life," Flynn told interviewer Tom Bryant. "I was fighting every weekend. We would go out drinking just so that we could have a fight. I wouldn't say I regret those days. Ninety-five percent of the people we were fighting were drunk and looking for trouble too... It was about then that I stopped smoking speed – smoking, by the way, is the connoisseur's way to do crank, it's a little more gourmet. But I looked at where I was heading and thought, 'I'm not going down this route'. I still don't know if that was shrewd business or dumb luck."

Flynn's arrival gave Demmel the impetus to improve his songwriting. "The first month, or month and a half, we were working on stuff he had brought with him, and that was really refreshing to me – but also kind of threatening to me," he said. "I was like, 'Oh cool', but I knew I had to come up with more music. It really got me off my ass for a while." The group half-heartedly attempted to rework the Forbidden song 'Chalice Of Blood', but soon let that drop, he added. "This will show you how petty we were! We really liked 'Chalice Of Blood' a lot, [and] it was Robb's music, so we started playing it and called It 'Calling In The Coroner'... But we couldn't do it any more, it was really bad."

Harald Oimoen remembers that Vio-Lence had the upper hand, at least in the early days of the rivalry. "Vio-Lence were huge in the Bay Area," he says. "They'd play the Stone and it would be a huge, chaotic, wild show, the wildest you've ever seen. It was funny when they first started playing, because they didn't have wireless guitar systems, they used guitar cables – so after one song there would be this huge spaghetti of guitar cables everywhere because they ran around on stage so much. When they got wireless units, it was a huge relief. But they were never very big outside the Bay Area, even though their shows here were legendary. They commanded the stage. A lot of it came down to Sean's vocals: they were unique. You either loved them or hated them. Also, Phil Demmel was amazing. He's like Craig, in that his path was set from the get-go. After Vio-Lence split up and got different line-ups, he was the Craig of that band. He held it together."

The friendship between Flynn and Locicero was soon resumed, despite the public rivalry between their respective bands. As the latter explains, "Later on, Robb and I became friends again when he was dating Debbie Abono's daughter Gina and the *Forbidden Evil* album had taken off. He knew we were having problems with our guitar player, Glen, whose head got huge after the record. Robb actually asked me in 1989 if we would be interested in having him back in the band. I said, 'Robb, it's awesome that you would say that, but I've just recruited this guy who's really, really good'. I didn't mean to insult him or anything, and we hung out that night. It wouldn't have been the right thing anyway: he had moved on to his own style by then and I had mine. He was looking for something, though: a short cut back into music with guys that he knew. Nobody knows that it happened, although it's not a big deal, and I don't take it too seriously."

Locicero remembers that by that point, Flynn had had enough of Vio-Lence. "He wasn't happy: he didn't get along with all those dudes, although he loved Deen Dell and he liked Phil. He really hated Perry Strickland and he hated Sean, because they were flat-out mean in those days – teasing him and whatnot. They picked on him even though he was the talent: he was the reason they were so killer.'

Jeff Stewart confirms this, saying: "Perry Strickland and Sean Killian were always picking on Robb, always fucking with him. They were just mean. They were assholes, basically, just saying, 'You're a fag!' and being childish. I knew Perry very well, and he's grown out of that now, of course, but back then he was mean. Phil Demmel was always the mediator: he was the balance in that band." Tracked down for an interview, Perry Strickland says: "I was the one who found and took Robb from Forbidden Evil. Why? Because he was bad-fucking-ass! I let Robb move into my house and got him a job. I pushed Robb. Sean and I were very, very high-strung people: Robb, Phil and Deen were much more laid-back. I dig all my Vio-Lence brothers. Our struggle was one of growing up, more than us disliking each other – at least, that's how I feel. All is fair in metal, love and life!"

Despite the harsh treatment, Flynn stuck it out until 1992, when thrash metal both in California and worldwide had waned significantly. Along the way Vio-Lence recorded and released three albums with various record labels and managers attached, but never with any significant success. In an extensive interview with Tom Trakas of *Midwest Metal*, Flynn recalled that the group's trajectory had been far from smooth at any point. "There were a lot of phenomenal highs," he said. "I mean, if I want to really think back, I could get hella pissed, because we got fucked, dude. To this day we don't own our own publishing, no-one even knows who owns it, for all the records. I saw $5,800 in six years and that was due to an advance publishing deal before [third LP] *Nothing To Gain* came out. I got $4,000 up front and $300 [a month] for six months, that was it. For all those years and three records, that was the only money I saw. Shit like that will make you think differently: it's brutal to get taken like that. But on the other hand, those were my wildest times, I was just out of my mind... It was an unbelievable learning experience and I learned a lot, and I'm proud of everything we did. We carved a niche in history: it may have not been the biggest, but we made our mark. I mean, any band where there's no middle ground... you were either a fucking die-hard Vio-Lence fan or a 'fuck off' type person. Some of the reviews were so bad I couldn't believe I was reading them, and we wanted to kill journalists! I think we were one of those bands that made enough of a statement that the people we touched, we really made an impact [on]. I was bitter about the situation for a long time, but when I look back, they were definitely good times."

Vio-Lence had started out with all the optimism in the world, Flynn recalled, as well as a singular determination to experience as much debauchery as possible. A high point of their career was a US tour in support of Bay Area thrashers Testament, who had broken through in the late Eighties. To put this into perspective, along with Exodus, Testament had the best claim to a possible 'Big Fifth' slot, should the ruling Big Four of thrash metal (Metallica, Megadeth, Anthrax and Slayer) ever expand their ranks. It looked highly plausible at this point: little wonder that Vio-Lence wrung every moment of enjoyment out of the Testament shows. "That tour was my introduction to everything!" confessed Flynn to Tom Trakas. "I'd already done drugs and tons of drinking, but at that point [I hadn't been] on tour [adding] groupies and more drugs and more drinking into it all. We were all like 19… crammed into the van, no hotels, crashing out on people's floors and shit like that. Debbie came out with us for a few dates and those ruled, because we'd get to eat at [diner chain] Denny's. We'd just eat as much as humanly possible and hopefully we'd eat at the show, but we had absolutely no spending money. We weren't making anything, that's for sure – maybe we made $50 a night. We'd pull up, have to unload our stuff, play for a half hour, I'd stop playing, put my guitar in its case and start loading everything again. The drives could suck, but if you were in the back seat of the van, you were in heaven because there were only two people back there."

It wasn't all high jinks, he noted. "Halfway through the tour, as soon as we entered Texas, middle of the summer mind you, the air conditioning broke! So for the next week and a half, it's 115 degrees out, and we're driving and everyone's dying and crabby, and all you hear is 'Stop sweating on me'… Testament were really big at the time… they were on fire! [But] we went out on that tour and we were like, 'You know, this tour wouldn't be doing half as good if it wasn't for us', that kind of shit. We thought we were Led Zeppelin, the biggest and best thing since sliced bread."

"Man, that sucked!" said Demmel of the air-conditioning episode. "Actually, on that tour, during the Texas leg, Testament flew back to New York to play the Megaforce anniversary party with S.O.D., Anthrax and Overkill. So when they did that, we got to spend a night or two on their bus, which was pretty cool. But once we got back in the van, it was bad news. With Perry wiping his boogers on the ceiling. It was just bad."

Demmel added that the off-stage debauchery sometimes went too far: "I got a little too out of hand one too many nights. I remember one night in Baltimore, Chuck [Billy, Testament singer] dragged me down some stairs because I was drunk and acting stupid. As he's dragging me down the stairs, my head's hitting everything and he's dragging me through the mud saying, 'All right, he's had enough!' I woke up the next day all scarred up."

A later tour with Canadian metal legends Voivod, whose touring budget was a fraction of Testament's, was a wake-up call for Vio-Lence, however. "The Voivod tour, we go out and reality really smacks us in the face," said Flynn. "That tour was pretty dismal, not a lot of people at the shows, still loading and unloading ourselves, in a van, but with a trailer... [and] between the two tours I got hit by a car while skateboarding. I fucked up my back, so that tour I just thrashed my back, bad. I couldn't get enough pills or booze to try and control the pain. So I was doing it up hella hard, still lots of girls. We started having contests at that time who could get the most girls... Phil [won]. Come on, he was the social butterfly of the band, he could talk to anyone convincingly. And back then, Phil was also the mediator of the band. It was me and Deen on one side and Perry and Sean on the other, and Phil had to toe both lines."

When Mechanic released the first Vio-Lence album in 1988, *Eternal Nightmare*, it was a relative flop and the band was promptly dropped. Fortunately, a home in the form of Megaforce, the New York label that had launched Metallica's career five years previously, awaited. "For a major label, *Eternal Nightmare* did horrible," mused Flynn. "At the time MCA had tons of bands selling millions and we sold 30,000 worldwide, so it was like 'Later'... One minute we're with them and the next we were on Megaforce. [But] Vio-Lence, in the Bay Area, was pretty fucking huge. I was 20 and it was great, drinking, doing speed...

So [that time] is a bit of a blur, and in that blur we got dropped, and we're now on Megaforce, and I was like, 'Cool'."

Hindsight tells us that thrash metal was on its last legs, commercially speaking, by the end of the decade. Nonetheless, Flynn savoured the opportunity to record Vio-Lence's second album, *Oppressing The Masses*, with the acclaimed producer Alex Perialas. "We went to Ithaca, New York, to record with Alex at Pyramid Studios and I was in heaven. I mean, he had done so much: he did the first S.O.D. album [*Speak English Or Die*]... I thought, and still think, that guitar sound was just retarded! Heavy as hell. But at the same time we fired Debbie, and it was my job to do it because I was dating her daughter. They elected me to do it and I did it. So the recording of the album was a lot of ups and downs. Cool because we're with Alex, and the down because we had the personal stuff with Debbie hanging over us. But the recording of it was ragingly fun. [We were] still doing speed and living like maniacs every night, and we made a ton of friends."

"We got to New York and it was great," added Demmel. "It was snowing, we were up there isolated and we were totally ready to do the album. The band was getting along pretty good too... well, there'd be plenty of times where Perry would wake everyone up by smashing a mallet into the medicine cabinet of the hotel room. The rooms were connected by the medicine cabinet, and he never slept. That dude was so high-strung, he'd be up at like four in the morning banging on the fucking thing, screaming 'Wake up!'"

The songwriting partnership between Flynn and Demmel had matured by that point, he added. "Phil and I totally complemented each other. I remember writing 'I Profit', Phil and I writing 'Officer Nice' and the title track. I remember hating 'Engulfed By Flames', that was written very fast... When the album came out, I think we felt we were hitting our stride. We were shooting a video for 'World In A World', and it was like, 'Wow! We're shooting a video, we've got a new manager'."

As is so often the case, it was the band's decision to fire their old manager and go with a big name that proved to be their undoing. Jeff Stewart comments, "They got big heads and they let Debbie go, and they lost it after that. They wanted to get bigger management, because they thought they were bigger than where they were at, so they let her go – and all the connections they had liked Debbie, so that fucked their whole touring in the USA and they got shitty shows and a dumbass manager. Sure, Joey was co-managing them, but he was going to school at the time and he couldn't be there for them [full-time]."

"Firing Debbie was really, really hard, especially for Deen, Robb and I," said Demmel. "The other two were just like, 'Fuck it, fire her,' you know? 'Get some other dude, be huge'… I did what was going to try and make the camp happy, dude, that was my whole downfall. Instead of trying to make people happy I should've just stood up for myself and said, 'This ain't right'. Firing her blew everything for us… We started losing contact with people because she was and still is so respected and liked. We couldn't get a tour. The whole Suicidal Tendencies thing happened at this time, [and] we were up for the Danzig/Soundgarden tour that ended up going to Corrosion Of Conformity. We couldn't get on shit, so what do we do? We go out and fucking headline! We did what Testament did, but they pulled it off. It was cool being on a bus and the tour itself was fucking great, but we weren't winning over anyone new. We were supposed to get off that tour and go straight to Europe to hook up with Flotsam And Jetsam. During the headlining tour, our booking agent, who was a friend of Debbie's, drops us. In the middle of the tour, which was unheard of! And we went into this lull which we never recovered from."

Flynn explained of the new manager: "[It was] this guy who played like he was some Hollywood hotshot [but] was actually the worst scumbag on earth. But when the album came out, we played and sold out two back-to-back nights in our hometown at the Omni and the Stone. We then went out on a headlining tour with Defiance in support, which was real cool. We had a bus, our first bus, which was great. We were able to get more girls with that, so we still had some good times on that tour. I think I'd stopped doing speed for that tour... [but] that tour was basically the beginning of the end. We had then realised our big Hollywood manager was nothing but a scam artist, and we were spending money that we didn't even have, hand over fist. No-one was making any money in the band."

According to Flynn, a tour booked with highly inappropriate tourmates Alien Sex Fiend – goth idols to a man – simply exacerbated the already desperate situation. "It was a headlining thing, we should've had a bus, but we find out at the last minute it's an RV with a few friends following us in a van with the equipment. So [our manager] tells us, 'I've got you guys doing some stuff, but the first show is with Alien Sex Fiend', and we're like, 'What, who, why them'? and he's like, 'They're huge, it'll be good'. So he tells us the tour begins on the 25th, so we have to leave on the 20th to get to Florida. We wanted to fly, but no go. So it's like the 19th and he calls in a panic, 'Oh my God, I made a mistake, the tour starts on the 23rd!' And now we've got three days to get from San Francisco to Florida, so all of us just pile in and go... three days straight, four-hour shifts, get to the gig, clean up and go on stage."

Despite their efforts, Vio-Lence failed to make an impression on the goth crowd, he added. "Dude, the whole place just stood there – they were all total Alien Sex Fiend fans and didn't want to hear any of what we had to offer. We'd finish a song, and you could

28

hear them whispering in the corner. We make it three shows later to Miami, and the RV is basically melting. We lift the hood and all the plastic, rubber gaskets and clamps and whatever else was plastic has now melted and moulded together. So we play the show and rent a car to get to the next show in Atlanta. So we're in Atlanta, play the show, it was cool [but] something was wrong with the rental car. So we call the place and they're like, 'You're where? You can't leave the state with that car! That's stealing – we're calling the cops!' And we're like, 'What the fuck?'"

Crushed by this failure, Vio-Lence prepared to return home, only to find themselves left high and dry by their manager. "The tour's over, we have no money, [he] has cut all communication with us – dude, he didn't change his number, he disconnected every phone he had! Our booking agent drops us that same day and we're in Tallahassee, Florida, stranded. We had $159 each to get home and eat for however long it took to get home. Those guys all took a bus home, five days on the road back. I borrowed money from Debbie Abono, actually: I swore to God to pay her back if she'd just loan me $300. She did, and I paid her back with my first royalty cheque from Machine Head years later."

"Robb flew home after he borrowed some money from Debbie," said Demmel. "The rest of us planned on getting on a bus. In the morning, Deen and I just said, 'No fucking way are we going to travel across the country with those two assholes [Strickland and Killian]!' so we left in the middle of the night and got a 12-hour head start."

Demmel recalled, "That was a dark period. When we got [that manager] we were just rolling with the punches, we were getting a little money at the time, we had gotten a merchandising advance, he puts us on this stupid tour and he didn't know what the hell he was doing. We'd get to clubs that had been shut down, club managers that didn't even know we were coming, and so on. The whole Alien Sex Fiend shit, the RV breaking down… So he quits, we start getting managed by [new manager] Alexis Olsen and Megaforce said, 'Alright, enough tour support for you, go write another album'."

That third album, *Nothing To Gain*, was turned down by Megaforce. "I think they just wanted to shelve us," said Demmel of the label. "There was no money being put into us, we got minimal support for that tour, and I really think they thought they were getting something other than they did. We then start pre-production for *Nothing To Gain*, which took forever! We were doing demos and when [Johnny Z, Megaforce owner] heard the tapes he wanted us to change this and change that, and we just got fed up. We go into Fantasy Studios and thought everything would go good. In that time Megaforce lost its distribution deal with Atlantic, and we just sat and sat. Robb's a guitar head, man, he's got to be playing, he's got to be doing stuff and he went stir crazy."

Flynn was beginning to move away from the traditional thrash metal direction by this point (as he said, "That's right when I was getting into downtuning. There was a lot of collaborating with Phil, I remember we were trying to stay away from writing fast"), but this clashed with the vision of the other band-members, who had noticed that alternative rock and grunge was on the rise and wanted to move in that direction. "We're all just fighting like crazy, like every single day, and no-one can see eye to eye," said Flynn. "Perry and Sean started becoming more and more the shot callers. Phil was kinda getting beat down, because the two of them were always ganging up on him. Don't get me wrong, everyone was still looking to him for final decisions, but at that point those two thought they knew best, so they started steering the ship. We'd gotten a new manager… and we had this new deal for *Nothing To Gain* pending, and it seemed pretty solid and I was waiting for that to happen. But at this point I was quite unhappy and I was just like, 'Whoever's steering the ship now is an idiot!' But there was a lot of fighting, more than before."

Demmel added that the situation had become more or less impossible to manage. "You had two people being quiet, two people ranting and raving and one guy trying to bridge the gap, and pretty soon I just couldn't do it any more. It got to the point where pride became my motivation. I still felt this was my band, and I was keeping everything together, trying to make it work with the guys we had. I could never kick Perry or Sean or anyone out of the band. I mean, there'd be times when Perry and Sean would be talking like, 'Oh Robb's not doing this, or Robb's not doing that' and I was like, 'Fuck you guys, when's my time gonna come'... They'd say the same thing about Deen, and Sean would say it about Perry and vice versa... It was all personality shit: there were a couple of ruthless motherfuckers in the band that would say shit. We were the biggest dysfunctional family there was! All we ever did was just talk shit to and about each other. Everyone would be doing it: it was just ruthless shit that I would never even repeat here or anywhere. But that became the norm: touchy subjects, personal shit, everything. [Once] Perry and Sean went at it pretty good... one time they just went at it and brawled on the bus. I thought it was one of the road crew, then I saw it was them and I was like, 'Yeah, beat the shit out of each other!'"

A few months into 1992, tensions escalated to breaking point. The new deal for *Nothing To Gain* fell through, although it was ultimately issued the following year, and Flynn began to consider his future. When two of his new songs, 'Blood For Blood' and 'Death Church', were rejected by the other members, he told them that he planned to start a side project.

Flynn explained to Trakas how the last straw came about: "Right about that same time I ended up getting into a fight with this pretty bad gang, they were from our neighbourhood and used to hang out at this club we'd go to. For some reason I got accused of stabbing someone, and I had nothing to do with a stabbing. I was in a fight, but I didn't do that shit. But it was a rumour and these guys wanted to kill me, literally. Vio-Lence was supposed to do a show, and this gang was calling up the club and were doing bomb threats and just fucked-up shit. So the day after I tell them I'm doing this side project, this shit happens! The show was the next day and I said, 'I'm not doing the show', it just wasn't gonna happen. So we got into this big fight and I just quit. And it was weird. It was a crazy ending and I was out on my own. They'd changed the locks on the rehearsal studio and I talked my way into there to get my stuff out. They were hella pissed... we all hated each other for fucking ever, lots of shit talking and all that."

Jeff Stewart and Craig Locicero, Flynn's metal brothers-in-arms, were watching from the sidelines: the former describes him at this point as "optimistic but angry... very angry. He was very articulate about what he wanted". Locicero recalls, "Robb was really fucking pissed: he was really begrudging against all those guys for a long, long time. He took my friend Eddie aside, who was teching for them at the time, and said, 'I'm gonna fucking show these dicks. I'm gonna start my own band, and I'm gonna call it Machine Head'."

Chapter 2

1992–1993

The basic point that thrash metal was at death's door in the early Nineties has been made many times before – in fact, so often that the actual facts have been obscured – but let's reiterate this point in a way that is free of agenda or wishful thinking.

The year 1992 was definitely not an ideal one to form a band, not if your musical upbringing was based on thrash metal anyway. The genre had peaked in commercial terms in 1989 and 1990, when a tour called Clash Of The Titans (variously featuring Slayer, Megadeth, Anthrax, Testament and Suicidal Tendencies) had swept through Europe and the USA. Just a year later, Nirvana released their second album, *Nevermind,* and suddenly grunge was the buzzword of the day: the larger record companies swept their roster clean of thrash metal and glam metal, the two polar extremes of heavy music, as they became deeply uncool almost overnight. At almost the same time, Metallica – the band who had first made thrash metal a commercially viable form – released their self-titled fifth album, a giant-selling behemoth which abandoned thrash beats for mid-tempo grooves and sharp-edged riffs that eschewed speed for impact.

American thrash metal in the committed, Forbidden and Vio-Lence sense went underground and stayed there until late in the decade. In the larger, more commercial sense of the term, thrash beats and riffs appeared now and again in songs from the Sepultura and Pantera albums released in the early nineties, but those bands used other styles in their songwriting as well, and the thrash elements were minimal. Only Slayer continued to make the original fast-paced sound their primary method of attack. Testament flirted briefly with the slowed-down commercial sound that Metallica had established, while in Europe, former thrashers such as Kreator went in other, experimental directions.

Even mainstream heavy metal bands who would never dream of inserting a thrash beat into a song suffered from audiences' sudden switch in loyalty to grunge. Titans such as Iron Maiden and Judas Priest both lost their iconic frontmen in the early Nineties. Motörhead came close to splitting up due to public apathy. Def Leppard had already gone in a pop direction. Later bands such as Korn had yet to emerge. In this hiatus, plenty of metal bands were filling clubs, but the only group that received major attention was Pantera, a four-piece who came out of Texas in 1990 with the *Cowboys From Hell* album and consolidated that position two years later with their masterpiece, *Vulgar Display Of Power*. Their secret? Grooves. Lots of them.

This was the point at which Robb Flynn decided to form Machine Head. Inspired by Metallica's performance at San Francisco's Day On The Green event in October 1991, he had left Vio-Lence by early '92. In the interim, he had begun writing songs with a friend, Adam Duce, who played bass. "We always hung out," said Duce later on. "We actually lived in the same apartment towards the ass-end of the Vio-Lence thing. I lost my apartment, so he let me stay on the floor in his apartment and we started writing songs. We wrote 'Death Church' and 'Blood For Blood' in that apartment, sitting on the floor and jamming without amps."

While Flynn was looking for a guitarist and drummer for his new band, Duce jammed with a trio. "It was kind of rock fusion," he told the author. "I laid down the bass tracks with that band in return for studio time: I thought it would be a great opportunity to get some experience. Even though Robb and I had already started Machine Head, we hadn't yet put the whole band together yet. But the guitar player in this band was a full-on heroin addict, and a Guitar Institute of Technology graduate – a total shredder. He called everyone that, too, it was hilarious – 'What's up, shredder?' Ha ha! It was a three-piece, all instrumental. You can probably guess what it sounded like. It was guitar-dork-driven. I ripped off a lot of stuff from Joe Satriani's bass player, because it seemed to fit. Anyway, I quit after that – I said, I can't take your heroin habit and your bullshit, I'm done with this."

Duce's bass playing was informed by the heavy metal greats. As he explained, "My heroes were Geezer Butler, Cliff Burton and to a certain extent Steve Harris, which is funny because they're all fingerstyle players, which doesn't work with what I'm doing. But the sheer aggression that those guys played with is what I'm all about as a bass player. I punch a ridiculous amount of aggression into that instrument every night! It's kind of a punk rock idea, but played tightly. Seeing those old videos of Cliff when Metallica were opening for Ozzy in 1986, you think, 'Look at that dude attack that bass!' and that's what it's all about to me." Unlike many of the alternative rock bands whose heyday was approaching, he had no intention of inserting any slap bass into Machine Head's grooves: "I haven't mastered that style by any stretch. I've messed around with it a little bit, just playing some Primus or some Red Hot Chili Peppers. I admire it, but it just isn't one of the things I ever learned. I think it sounds great when Billy Gould from Faith No More plays slap, though."

As well as an incredibly robust bass style, Duce also brought a wide taste in music to Machine Head, an asset which would prove invaluable as the band honed an individual style. His influences vary from classic stoner rock ("I used to listen to a lot of Kyuss. I used to go wakeboarding all summer long, and that was the only tape we had in the truck") to the music pumped out on radio all day long: "I listen to a lot of radio stuff too, especially the crap they play down at the gym – I sweat so much that I fill my ears up and my headphones don't work, so I have to. To me, music in general is a representation of freedom. If I didn't have that kind of freedom, it would be completely against the reason why I'm doing it in the first place. This is an arena where you get to do whatever you want to, wherever the song wants to go. You have the freedom to get yourself out of the way and let the music do whatever it wants."

Like Flynn, Duce had spent some of his formative years exploring many a chemical high. As he told *Absolut Metal* in 1997, "Drugs on the overall are evil. But I like 'em anyway... Every drug that I've ever done, I've ended up doing so much of it, that I can't do it any more, except for fucking pot. Heroin, I tried it, I didn't even like it. I tried it a bunch of times just to give it a chance, but I just don't like it. Ecstasy is fun, but it has a brutal fucking downside. I get into this depression hella hard. Special K [ketamine]? Yeah, that's a fun drug to do, but it's a dangerous one too. I mean it's just dangerous. Speed... can't do that. I can't handle the comedown off of it, and it tweaks my mind, it makes me want to punch holes in myself."

An old friend of Duce's, a Canadian guitarist called Logan Mader, was recruited to be Machine Head's second guitarist. Although Mader was far from being a guitar virtuoso – "I didn't get a guitar until I was 15 years old," he told interviewer Sheila Rene, adding: "Before Machine Head I had never played lead guitar" – he was a dyed-in-the-wool metalhead and possessed a picking hand of great precision as well as a sense of groove, essential for the new songs. Asked about his friendship with Duce, he explained: "We grew up together. Adam and I were maybe 10 years old, and we decided after listening to Black Sabbath and AC/DC that we wanted to play in a band. One of us will often be thinking the same thing the other person is verbalising, even down to where we want to have dinner. We hang out a lot together. We like to go fishing on his boat when we can, and we go snowboarding together. We're pretty close."

All that remained was to recruit a drummer. When a sticksman of Flynn's acquaintance failed to commit to the band, Machine Head were contacted by a Las Vegas-based drummer called Tony Costanza, who had played in a hardcore act called Papsmear (not to be confused with a near-contemporary project of the same name formed by Slayer guitarist Jeff Hanneman). Costanza recalls, "I knew Robb because I used to go see Vio-Lence back in the day. I heard they needed a drummer, but the guy that was supposed to come out there was basically not coming through. I called Robb and told him that I wanted to try out for them, and I sent him a videotape. They liked it, waited two months for me to move from Vegas to the Bay Area, and then I was in the band. I started rehearsing the next night, right after I got there."

The new band began practising in April 1992. A style was gradually forming which focused on heaviness and urgency rather than speed and adrenaline. It's significant that at around this time, Flynn and his old comrade Craig Locicero jammed in a Black Sabbath tribute act – Sabbath being the band who first pioneered the idea of elephantine riffs performed in a lower tuning than standard E. "When he was just starting Machine Head, one of the things I did with Robb was to form a band called Slack Babbath, where we played all of Sabbath's rare songs," says Locicero. "He had just started Machine Head but he hadn't done a demo yet: people were just seeing them. Robb wanted to do his own arrangement of 'Electric Funeral'. He tuned it really low and I played it with him, and I was thinking, 'You're on to something here' because the way he did it was different. It was a Machine Head version. Even way back then, I knew it was really good."

"Robb was obviously the director of the band, but he treated us all equally," says Costanza. "It wasn't like there was some boss telling you what to do. The vibe was really great: as soon as I heard the songs, I knew they were going to be huge, and I was right. I don't think any of them were complete, from what I remember: they were all at the beginning of their formation. We had 'Death Church', 'Blood For Blood', 'Fuck It All', 'I'm Your God Now' and 'Thousand Lies', plus a couple more like 'Rage To Overcome'."

Rehearsals progressed quickly, but finding gigs was a problem. "The scene was dead then," said Flynn. "We had to play in tiny, shit-hole punk clubs alongside bands like Rancid just to get a gig. The punks sort of accepted us. They'd see a bunch of long-haired dudes, realise we'd fight people just for looking at us the wrong way, and thought, 'We'll just leave them alone'. The funny thing was, we were these tough dudes who would secretly listen to The Cure. I could sing all the lyrics to 'Careless Whisper' by George Michael..."

On August 15, a debut gig of sorts took place at the house of a roadie, Mike Rivera, on Woolsey Street in Oakland. Harald

Oimoen was there, and he remembers: "I'll never forget the first gig that Machine Head played. It was at a house party of one of the roadies, Mike, whose nickname was 'Scum'. He was my neighbour in my apartment." Duce added, "It was at our friend Mike's house. He just fucking walked past, [this] big guy with no shirt. He was getting kicked out of his house because he'd been squatting for like six months and not paying rent, so we came in and fucked the house up. That was our first show." Costanza recalls, "There were a lot of people there and we tore it up. It was a little rented house and people were going nuts. It was great: I felt on top of the world."

A passing opportunity came up for Flynn to audition for the industrial rock act Ministry, then in need of a guitarist. In preparation for this, and to show the members of Ministry what he could do musically, Flynn enlisted Costanza's drum tech Chris Kontos to help him record some songs. As Kontos recalls: "I knew Robb from Forbidden Evil with Craig Locicero, and later Vio-Lence from playing in town at Ruthie's Inn and other gigs around the Bay Area. This was right when the crossover [between punk and metal] happened. You had Death Angel, Vio-Lence, DRI, Attitude Adjustment and Sacrilege, who would play on Tuesdays, Wednesdays and Sundays – the nights when the Big Four weren't playing! These little B-bands would all do the crossover thing. The big hardcore bands would come and play, and the metal bands would show up on those bills."

He continues: "By 1989 I'd been in a couple of bands that played overseas, like Verbal Abuse and Death Angel, but Vio-Lence hadn't done much touring at all. At this time I guess Robb started to think about music in a new way. He had downtuned the guitars and there was more of a rhythmic, percussive thing going on, rather than the generic thrash overtones which still existed in the Bay Area at the time. He had found something cool that he felt Vio-Lence could not pull off. It was the same kind of groove that Pantera found."

Kontos and Flynn had first struck up their acquaintanceship in the previous year or two, recalls the former. "It really solidified in 1991 to '92, when I was in a band called Grinch, which played kind of Melvins-influenced music with maybe a Tool kind of vibe. Robb was really enamoured with what I was doing: there were a lot of tribal beats and lots of hypnotic double bass, just a lot of musical vibe from the drums. He started coming to gigs and standing in the front watching our every move. I could see his wheels spinning, so I asked him, 'Robb! What's happening?' and he said, 'I really dig the band'. We were doing three-part harmonies and he was really tripping on it. At the time he was still in Vio-Lence, but he was cataloguing new ideas about tuning and rhythmic riffs. I also knew Logan, from when he used to come out with my band Attitude Adjustment on a couple of tours up and down the West Coast as a guitar tech."

Kontos continues, "Robb wanted to do a quick demo of where his head was at right then, to send to Ministry. He asked me, right before I was heading out to New York for a few months, if I would come in and drum on these four songs. They were great songs: 'Blood For Blood', 'Death Church', 'Fuck It All' and 'Old'. He had an old Panasonic boombox that he borrowed from a friend of ours, which had two stereo condenser mics, and if he stuck it in the middle of the room, it could make a pretty audible, pretty listenable tape. That's how he wanted to do it. We did that recording and then I took off to New York for six months. The Ministry thing didn't come to pass, though."

A black-and-white video for the song 'Fuck It All' (later retitled 'Block') was shot in mid-'92 and was a typical performance clip for the era, focusing on Flynn's uncompromising scowl, a depressed urban environment (at one point the band are seen near a railtrack as a train passes) and the obvious three-word chorus. It's Costanza's sole video appearance with Machine Head, and a document of the young, hungry band that works, despite the evidently meagre budget.

In 1992, Machine Head also recorded at least two further demo tapes on portable four-track machines to use to persuade promoters to give them gigs, featuring Costanza on drums. Gigs were still few and far between, however, and it wasn't until 29 August that a 'real' show took place. This time it was no house party, but the Huntridge Theater in Costanza's home town of Las Vegas. Asked if the crowd were into Machine Head's music, the drummer laughs: "Kind of! They got into it when we did a cover of Poison Idea's 'Alan's On Fire', more than anything. It was basically a punk crowd, and I don't think they really knew what we were, musically. We were just different. No-one knew where to put us. Marco Barbieri from Metal Blade told me that we sounded like thrash, and we were like, 'No we're not!'"

Sadly for Tony Costanza, the Vegas show was his second and also his last for Machine Head. He felt unable to cope with the band's gruelling lifestyle and was also facing problems of his own, as he explains. "I quit the band, I wasn't fired," he says. "I never, ever wanted to quit, but I had a major problem with depression and anxiety, and I had moved to a city where all these bands lived: Exodus, Testament, Forbidden. Here I am, an equal all of a sudden, because I'm in Robb's band, and I hadn't been playing very long. We rehearsed four days a week, six hours a day. I was working a job and it was rough. This was basically why I ended up leaving the band, because I couldn't survive any more. My double bass wasn't up to par, and I basically self-destructed. I ended up going back to Vegas and taking medication."

He adds: "I was fine within a week. I guess I just needed a break from the pressure of it all, but it was too late. They had to move on, and I understand that. I didn't know any better. Nowadays I know my limits and I'm secure in my playing, but it really hurt at the time. Basically, because of my own personal demons, I had to leave my favourite band ever. I had to watch them climb the ladder and be what I always wanted to be." All these years later, however, Costanza is still friends with his sometime bandmates, so for once here's a rock 'n' roll tale that doesn't have a grim ending.

Costanza's tech Chris Kontos was keen to take over the drum stool, and indeed, he was the most obvious choice for the job. "I really wanted to get the drum spot," he recalls, "so I talked to Logan and Adam and Robb about it. It felt like a good mission. I thought Joseph Huston was a stand-up guy: he'd worked really hard to promote the music scene here in California, and I knew he'd take a real professional crack at shopping the band. He was investing some of his own money in the band and he was really behind it. They said they would talk about it, and soon they approached me to be in the band."

Things began to move more quickly towards the end of 1992, with Kontos debuting at a November 21 show in Pleasant Hill and another eight days later in Santa Clara in support of Testament. Into 1993, and gigs continued to come, albeit in small numbers and largely in Berkeley, Oakland and San Francisco: at this point Machine Head were still just another local band, although their reputation preceded them thanks to Flynn's previous membership of Vio-Lence and Forbidden. However, a major leap forward came with the *Fuck It All* demo, named after its most abrasive (but also catchiest) song. As Kontos remembers, "When we recorded the demo, there was something special there: it felt as if I did thrash beats behind the riffs, it wouldn't be special, so I began to reach into some of my old funk and funk-rock influences and go in the opposite direction with that. That was how we ended up with songs like 'Old', which had that kind of danceable, body-sway tone to it. Once we had the demo we could get it out there: Robb and Joey had a list of people."

Kontos explains: "I had a pretty good feel for what was going to be the formula for those songs, after finishing the songs that Robb and Logan were writing. I was listening to Soundgarden and it was scaring the hell out of me, with drummers like Matt Cameron. I said to myself, 'My hi-hats have got to kick in. I want to do this kind of drumming to metal'. Drummers out here hadn't stepped on their hi-hat pedal in 10 years, but it can give the songs so much swing and groove. I also brought a lot to the table when it came to arrangements: I hummed out riffs that become bridges, and there's a bunch of those on the record. One of my little tricks on that album which is real simple happens when the guitar riff doesn't change, it just goes on for 32 measures: in that time I play three different textures. This builds pressure in the riffs. The fast hands that I did come from [jazz legend] Billy Cobham, and the punk influences from all the bands I grew up on, who all had really tasty fast stuff going on. I just collided all that with what Robb and Logan had going on. We were so pumped up and self-aware: we were on a mission to do something that would really turn heads."

New Californian bands looking for a deal at this time always visited an annual music-industry convention called the Foundations Forum in Los Angeles; and, demo in hand, Flynn did exactly that. However, his trip would have been wasted had it not been for his old jamming buddy Jeff Stewart, who was also at the Forum. Stewart remembers: "He was being a bit of a recluse at the time when he did the demo, but I saw him at the Foundations Forum in LA afterwards. He didn't have the money to get in, but he had all his stuff with him, so I gave him one of my passes and said, 'Go in there and take care of your demo, dude'. I was 100 percent behind Machine Head, because I knew he was good." In retrospect, Stewart's act of generosity was pivotal: what might have become of Machine Head without this gesture is unknown.

Flynn was utterly motivated to get Machine Head signed at this point, and evidently not in the mood to play games. As Craig Locicero recalls, "When he recorded the *Fuck It All* demo, I was fully into it. I was fucking blown away! I was giving it to everyone and trying to hype him up as much as I could to help him out. So in late '93 I'd gotten a gig with Death, and I was out in Europe playing with them on the *Individual Thought Patterns* tour. I'd called [Forbidden bassist] Matt Camacho and he told me that Robb was flipping out on me, pissed. Before I'd left I had done an interview with the local music rag, *Bam* magazine. The interviewer had asked me if I cried at movies and I'd answered, 'Sure, I cry manly tears all the time. Even Robb Flynn cries at *The Sound Of Music*' as a joke. So I called Robb and I was like, 'Hey Robb, what's happening brother, how's everything going?' and he was all quiet and saying, 'It's cool man, it's going good'. I said, 'Everybody loves your demo, I'm totally pumping it up out here on tour with Death', but all he said was, 'Cool man'. We ended the conversation unresolved."

Locicero continues: "When I got home, Robb called me up and said, 'Don't ever mention that we played together again. I want nothing to do with Forbidden ever again. You did that interview with *BAM* magazine!' He took it to mean that we were all laughing at him. The other Machine Head guys really laid it on him because of that. They all said, 'Robb... *The Sound Of Music*?' and he was like, 'Fucking hell!' He was so mad about it, but I never take this shit seriously, myself."

Record labels began to express an interest in late 1993. As Kontos remembers it: "What was cool about the demo to me was that it was on cassette, and steeped in the whole roots vibe. Robb was offered a couple of deals by some guy in Germany, and another guy in the UK, and there was real pen-pal communication going on. It had all the features of a band coming up through house parties and local shows. We played with Possessed, who hadn't played in a while, and we really took our time picking the shows that we played on, and it all worked out organically. It just happened so fast that when [journalist, renowned talent-spotter and now owner of the Blabbermouth news portal] Borivoj Krgin passed the demo on to Roadrunner, who signed us unseen, that was heavy."

Roadrunner Records was a hard rock and heavy metal label that had expanded from its original European roots in the Eighties to become one of the major players in the American independent market. Its A&R guru Monte Conner had made a name for himself after signing the Brazilian thrash metal band Sepultura, and by this point in the label's history it boasted a large roster of metal acts, ranging from Danish black metallers King Diamond to the gothic New York act Type O Negative. When Conner offered Machine Head a deal, the band and management were ecstatic – but after so many years in the industry, neither was prepared to sign anything but the very best contract. Kontos recalls, "We revised that record deal 10 times, and when we were done Roadrunner said, 'We will never sign another record deal like this again'. We knew what we wanted, and we weren't going to be just folding on the first contract put in front of us. It was going to have longevity, with tour support built in, and time lines that Roadrunner had to follow. This and that had to be changed and fixed and tweaked. Joey and our lawyer Jeff Saltzman really worked that contract, because if we were going to sign ourselves away like that we had to cover our asses: remember, Roadrunner wanted a slice of the publishing and the merchandise too. It was going to be a big deal, and it was unique for its time."

Flynn later told Tom Bryant at *Kerrang!* that he celebrated the signing of the Roadrunner deal with a night out that was almost his last. "It was October 9, 1993, and my friend and I went out and got absolutely fucking trashed. We'd just signed a deal, man. It was amazing! I had been dabbling with heroin at that point but, luckily, I just didn't enjoy it that much. I'd shoot it, throw up for two hours, and think, 'This sucks'. That night, though, drunk at two in the morning, we were like, 'Let's go score!' We went to the dealer's house and, because I was scared of needles and afraid of messing up, he shot me up."

Flynn continued, "I overdosed on the spot. They told me afterwards that I turned blue, so they dragged me in the bathroom, got me breathing again and just left me there. I woke up in that bathroom six hours later thinking, 'What the fuck?' The dealer, who was half nodded-out, said, 'Oh my God! You're alive'. I thought, 'Oh my God, I'm alive? What the fuck are you talking about? You just dumped me in the bathroom after I OD'ed? Fuck you guys!' I called my girlfriend [Genevra], who's now my wife, and she went crazy. I felt so stupid. So stupid. I was incredibly ashamed of myself. I was so embarrassed that I cried. What the fuck was I doing? Why am I so self-destructive?'"

After recovering from this close call, Flynn regrouped the band and rehearsed the songs which would comprise the first Machine Head album, set for release in 1994. Titled *Burn My Eyes*, the album was recorded at Fantasy Studios in Berkeley, California. Chris Kontos, who knew the studio through the work of his musician father, remembers: "My dad was a songwriter who had come up through the industry – Thomas Jefferson Kaye was his name – and he was working with Steely Dan's producer before Steely Dan was big. I was always around how it happens, and I knew the things that have to happen at home, and the things that have to happen abroad [to make an album work]. The recording was at Fantasy Studios and that was great, because I'd been there when my dad was working there when I was a kid. Now to be actually there recording a big-budget record, and seeing all the old Jefferson Starship, Santana, Journey and Y&T gold albums on the wall as you walked down the hall was amazing."

The band was aware of the impact that their album could make if it was recorded correctly, at least to an extent. When Kontos notes, "It was a critical moment for metal bands," he is obviously speaking with the benefit of hindsight; but on the other hand there was a real mood of change in the air which was evident to any working musician of the day. He correctly ascribes this state of flux to the two biggest metal bands of the moment: "You had some bands following the Metallica 'Black Album' lead, and others following the Pantera lead. A lot of the musicians admitted later that they dabbled in ballads becouse of the hair bands, and then after the Black Album, they went more for a radio-rock vibe. They were chasing what the record labels wanted. Even Gary Holt of Exodus, who is one of my real good friends and also one of my all-time favourite guitar players and writers, told me that there were records that he wished Exodus hadn't done."

He continues, "We weren't going to do the really palatable thing that was happening to a lot of metal bands, and which I dreaded. The Machine Head sound was raw, and really potent and punishing. Robb really had a connection with people from the stage: he had that powerful frame and Charles Manson look and mindset, which is always good when you're playing live."

Monte Conner of Roadrunner flew over to California from his New York office to see how the album was progressing, but he didn't interfere. As Kontos explains, "Monte come out while we were recording a few times, but he never really pushed us in one way or the other. He was a fan of the songs and the band: you could tell. Monte is a stand-up guy in my book." Instead, the shape of the songs was determined by producer Colin Richardson, a veteran who had produced a stellar list of albums. Kontos: "Colin pushed Robb's vocal performance one-on-one more then he did with the rest of us, but I don't really need that shove over the edge when I'm recording. There were times when he'd look at me and I knew he wanted another take. So we didn't spend too much time listening back to takes: if it wasn't the real-deal take, we'd just do it again till it was right. It was definitely a team effort."

The drummer adds: "I think Vincent Wojno brought a lot to the table as an engineer, a really hyper 'let's get it done!' attitude. He was using lots of miking techniques and actually being willing to go in and move the mic, as opposed to just turning a knob on the console first. This was one of the last albums to be made like a Van Halen record, but without the midgets and champagne and green M&Ms, ha ha! It was still recording to two-inch tape and no cutting between multiple takes, like you can do nowadays with Pro-Tools. We were doing long takes and punching in if we had to. We broke out the razorblades a few times – and those times were classic, old-school hold-your-breath moments while we made an edit."

Kontos recalls that the mixing of *Burn My Eyes* was far from straightforward. "When we started to mix the record at Fantasy Studios, it wasn't going well at all," he remembers. "We couldn't get control of the low end, and the drums weren't right. We'd think we had it close, but it would sound like shit at home, and it wasn't going to meet the standards that we and Roadrunner wanted. At the same time, we went through some fighting and arguments that almost resulted in me leaving the band – just due to stress – but we decided to remix the record in LA at Scream Studios, which was known for big killer mixes. Robb took over as the person in the room with Vinny and Colin: we would go in and listen back to the songs, and give our input here and there. Once we got to Scream Studios, the mix went really well, but this was when I started not to gel with Robb at all."

Once *Burn My Eyes* was complete, the band and label held their collective breath to see what impact it would make. Kontos sums up what lay ahead: "The year before this, we had snuck into the Foundation Forums before we were signed. The next year, Roadrunner was taking us out to dinner there. The year after that, we were the main support band playing there. It was that fast."

Chapter 3

1994–1995

Apart from a period of intense flux in 2007 and 2008, the most pivotal years of Machine Head's career to date have arguably been 1994 and 1995. In this brief period of time, the band went from being local wannabes to a group with a classic album under their belts, together with an international presence, the backing of a leading record label, several months of world touring experience and the support of the media. That's not bad going. Now imagine how Robb Flynn, Logan Mader, Adam Duce and Chris Kontos must have felt, given that all of them – but Flynn and Kontos in particular – had been struggling for years in the face of apparently insuperable odds to make it in the music business.

Burn My Eyes was set for release on August 9, 1994. Before then, Machine Head was about to embark on their first tour in April alongside Roadrunner stablemates Obituary and British grindcore pioneers Napalm Death, both older and more experienced acts. Machine Head's music was nothing like these two bands: while

Flynn and his comrades specialised in slow to mid-tempo riffs, tuned down for maximum heaviness and with a touch of booty-shaking groove, the others played straight-ahead death metal and grindcore that alternated thrash and blastbeats. Machine Head also played more melodic songs with singable choruses, making for an expert combination of accessible and brutal music that was the key to its popularity.

Not that anyone had analysed Machine Head's songs with this cold an eye yet. What the band really needed was more exposure than the simple release of the album could provide: a chance to prove to people, not just club audiences but arena crowds, that they were doing something new and worthwhile.

The obvious opportunity in 1994 came from Slayer, the Los Angeles legends whose adherence to a fast, graphic style of thrash metal was unique at this time. As we've already seen, in the wake of key early-Nineties albums such as Nirvana's *Nevermind*, the Red Hot Chili Peppers' *Blood Sugar Sex Magik* and Metallica's all-conquering 'Black Album', most of the biggest names in heavy metal had lost their focus. Slayer either didn't care about all that, or didn't know any other way to be. They continued to play world-class extreme metal – even if their current album, *Divine Intervention*, divided fans with its curious production. Slayer's 1994–5 world tour, dubbed 'Divine Intourvention' by some wag in their record label's marketing department, was the most extensive tour of the year by a band of this nature, and a support slot would yield enormous dividends to any band lucky enough to be awarded it. Machine Head and Roadrunner duly entered negotiations with Slayer's management and waited to hear the verdict.

Chris Kontos describes this period as highly surreal, because both Obituary and Napalm Death had also taken a shot at the Slayer support slot: "It was very strange, because both of those bands were also fighting to get the support slot on that Slayer tour. We didn't think we had a shot at all to go out with Slayer." When the news came in that Machine Head had won the Divine Intourvention support alongside East Coast act Biohazard, the band-members had to finish off the Napalm/Obituary tour without mentioning it. "It became a reality," says Kontos, "and we had to tour with Napalm and Obituary for the rest of the dates, knowing that we were going out with Slayer. We had to hold it in the whole tour: it was tough to do because I love those guys. We shared the bus with them, and it was painful. It added to the tensions that you feel on the road with bands when you're on the same bus."

Burn My Eyes was a revelation: an album that genuinely sounded different to most of the contemporary metal releases of the day. Even nowadays, the crushing, almost doom-metal riff that ends the opening track, 'Davidian', is a highlight of Machine Head's live set. It, and many other riffs on the album, possess a funky, hypnotic quality that attracted a wider audience to the band than the standard headbanger crowd. It isn't going too far to pinpoint this album, along with Pantera's *Vulgar Display Of Power* from 1992, as the record that began the process of widening heavy metal's appeal, a process which continued through the decade.

'Old' and 'A Thousand Lies' continue along similarly groove-heavy lines: it isn't until the midsection of the latter that Machine Head's heritage as a thrash metal band raises its violent head, and even then this is only a precursor to a final riff which slows down further and further for maximum heaviness. The thrash elements are taken to their logical conclusion with 'A Nation On Fire' and 'Blood For Blood', although an important distinction is that the fast riffs were influenced more by hardcore punk than thrash metal, per se. As Flynn put it in an interview with Earth Dog: "Machine

Head was never thrash, period. After Vio-Lence, I wanted to move away from that... All the breakdowns off the first two records were all very groove-oriented and influenced by bands like Biohazard. Machine Head's fast stuff was way more influenced by hardcore bands like Poison Idea, Attitude Adjustment, Sick Of It All, Discharge, and definitely not thrash bands."

Other songs such as 'None But My Own' introduce an arrangement alternating between clean vocals and melodic hooks in the choruses and more abrasive vocals in the verses: this went on to be a much-emulated songwriting trick. Without meaning to sound too musicologically pedantic, it's interesting to note that the album contains several other future Machine Head trademarks, such as staccato, triple-picked riffs with pinch harmonics, atmospheric song sections with 'tribal' beats played on floor toms, and lyrics that address social ills such as religious corruption, substance addiction and the decay of society. The penultimate song 'Real Eyes, Realize, Real Lies' is particularly vitriolic on the subject of how low we as a species have sunk, a sentiment echoed by 'Block', the retitled version of 'Fuck It All'. The album is still a thought-provoking piece of work, almost 20 years later.

Burn My Eyes became Roadrunner's bestselling debut album until the emergence of Slipknot nine years later – a hell of a feat for any band in the confused musical environment of the early to mid-Nineties. The album's success is at least partly attributable to the extensive touring, both in support of Slayer and as a headline act, which followed. Flynn explained in later years that Machine Head's method, like Vio-Lence before it, was to spread the message gig by gig – and it was this ethos which characterised the band's activities through late 1994, through the whole of 1995 and into 1996.

ob Flynn (left) and Phil Demmel (right) kicking out the jams, Bay Area-style, in the pre-Machine Head thrash metal band Vio-Lence.
nn would soon take his music in a heavier, more considered direction. HARALD OIMOEN

Vio-Lence had their moments, for sure. Their stage show was second to none and the musicians could play, especially Flynn and Demmel—but thrash metal was on the wane... HARALD OIMOEN

Although public attention was wandering elsewhere and the strain of living on zero budget was taking its toll, the two headbangers knew how to enjoy themselves on stage. HARALD OIMOEN

Vio-Lence (from left): Dean Dell (bass), Phil Demmel (guitar), Sean Killian (vocals), Perry Strickland (drums), Robb Flynn (guitar). Pissed-off, broke and tight of trouser, the lot of them. PRESS

Flynn and guitarist Logan Mader (left) in the brand-new Machine Head, which took Flynn's concept of metal in a direction more focused on downtuned groove. MICK HUTSON

Machine Head's success rests on the band's live show: here's Robb Flynn doing what he does best, converting the masses to the message, one show at a time. MICK HUTSON

oducing Adam Duce, bass player extraordinaire and the man who keeps Machine Head grounded. JOHN MCMURTIE/RETNA UK

Duce in full flow. Flynn recalled one onstage collision: "Adam was playing a bass with a razor-sharp headstock, and he came flying past me—and t headstock literally ploughed into my temple. I was pretty much unconscious for a second." MICK HUTSON

By the late 90s, Machine Head—pictured here with Mader's replacement Ahrue Luster (far right)—were flirting with a then-fashionable urban loo with the notable exception of Duce. MICK HUTSON

e and drummer Dave McClain, who replaced original sticksman Chris Kontos, form a mighty rhythm section. Fast, tight and uncompromising, al runs through their veins. LEFT: JO HALE/GETTY IMAGES, RIGHT: ROSS HALFIN

n left, Duce, McClain, Flynn and Demmel: the current and most accomplished line-up of Machine Head, performing at the peak of their iderable powers. MICK HUTSON

Phil Demmel sharing the love with an ecstatic audience. MICK HUTSON

And yet it all could have been so different. Here's Luster and Flynn, in the *From This Day* era. Critics tend to dismiss the albums MH made in their rappin', frontin' days, but there were some musical gems there. PAUL BERGEN/GETTYIMAGES

The 'Divine Intourvention' dates kicked off on November 6 in Dublin, Ireland and passed rapidly through Northern Ireland, England, Wales and Scotland: the United Kingdom has been a safe haven for American metal bands since the Eighties and the rise of Metallica, but Machine Head were especially welcome here. The tour moved on to France, Spain, Portugal, Switzerland, Italy, Slovenia, Austria, Hungary, Poland, the Czech Republic, Germany, Holland, Belgium, Norway, Sweden and Denmark before landing back in England for a final show at Nottingham's fabled Rock City. After Slayer departed for the US, Machine Head remained for one extra show, a legendary headliner at London's now-defunct but once beloved Astoria venue.

Supporting Slayer took serious courage, even for as committed a band as Machine Head. Stories have abounded since the mid-Eighties of support acts forced off stage by audiences screaming for the headliners: the humiliation of having to slink off to the dressing room, shrieks of 'Slayer' ringing in one's ears, must be close to absolute. It's a testament to Machine Head's on-stage presence, not only that they survived the experience but that they converted gig-goers to their cause. As Flynn told the author, "Supporting Slayer was the hardest-core crowd ever. In a lot of ways, it was the best tour we could ever do. It was literally the second tour that we did – five months with Slayer! We really cut our teeth. It didn't really happen too often. Truth be told, we held our ground really good: we didn't really get a super-Slayering like some bands have."

Kontos adds: "I'm an old-school Slayer fan, I'd seen them play in the Bay Area as a kid. I hung out with the people that told them not to wear make-up [in 1982]. I've been in the audience booing Slayer's support acts before, and knowing that I was walking full-bore into that gauntlet and that the audiences might shout 'Kill! Kill! Kill!' at us, or they might raise the horns to us and let us live, was quite scary to say the least."

The drummer attributes some of this positive reaction to the marketing spin which had placed Machine Head as a band of tough guys from the ghetto: "We went in there so over-the-top confident as a band, and Roadrunner riding it so hard on the hype of the whole Bay Area thrash thing and the whole Hollywood image of the mean streets of Oakland." In fact, the image of the band was beginning to feel a little out of place to Kontos. He adds, "That always bothered me, by the way. The whole tough-guy perception and the whole 'gun-toting, mean streets of Oakland' thing – it was a bit prefabricated. I'm not saying that we weren't men ready to fight if we had to, or that Oakland is not a tough place, but the vibe was not like that in the metal scene. It was as schmaltzy a gimmick as any rapper taking on that 'gangsta' image."

The drummer continues, "Once an interviewer asked us, 'After wading through the crack vials and bullet shells to get to your studio, what's your mindset like?' and I just blew a raspberry fart sound with my mouth. I was like, 'Look man, we get burritos, we drive there, we go in and we rock out'. The whole Bay Area metal scene wouldn't have been able to exist if it was so dangerous and a kill zone. I told him that there is a very sad, depressed area here in Oakland called the Red Triangle, where 17- to 22-year-old young men kill each other over drug turf, and it's awful and perpetuated by poverty and liquor stores and gun stores and all the crap that happens in ghettos – but to couple ourselves with that, and try to gain some kind of street cred from it, I never really adhered to it, especially if everyone was going to stand there and look really, really upset and hard."

Image or no image, Flynn proved himself able to handle abuse from the crowd easily enough. Asked how he copes with hecklers, he said: "It depends on what the heckling is. Sometimes the best strategy is to ignore them. Other times it requires a good roasting – and I will roast the hell out of somebody. You just find something about them that you can laugh at. You just do that until they're put in their place. Sometimes you can say funny stuff, like, 'Yeah, I remember my first beer too'... The best thing about playing live is the instant self-gratification. You see people reacting. It's fun. We get to have a few drinks and make people go crazy, it's awesome. We have really, really intense fans. We saw this kid in the crowd once who was punching himself in the face through the entire show. I wanted to go up and say, 'Dude, chill out!' The worst part about playing live is having technical problems – because it throws your game when you're trying to create a rapport with the crowd, which is what it's all about. I've played shows where my guitar was down for five songs in a row."

Machine Head also took the opportunity, like all new bands do, to indulge in plenty of off-stage debauchery. Adam Duce recalled a time when they fired a home-made 'potato launcher' from their tour bus. "We have shot the spud gun out the top while we're rolling. One night we had this window [open], so you could see out. We had the potato launcher aimed out that way and we were watching to see what was going by, and then all of a sudden this huge car lot was out there... Couldn't see where the potato went, but there were so many cars out there, it had to have hit one of them."

The band also had no illusions about the glamour of the touring life. As Duce explained about the lavatory arrangements: "You're not allowed to shit on the bus, and usually the shitter in the venue has piss all over the seat... who wants to go in there? If we get here early, we go in there and use the women's bathroom, always. [But] if you have to take a shit and the club is packed, you can't just walk into the women's bathroom so you gotta fucking line the toilet in [the bus] with a bag, and then fucking take a shit in the bag, and throw it out in the parking lot."

Despite the often primitive touring conditions, Machine Head were young, hungry for the prize and in a position to grab it from the position they'd been given as Slayer's main support band. The first three months of 1995 were taken up with the Divine Intourvention's US leg, which wound up on March 12. The final show, at Mesa in Arizona, was filmed for Slayer's *Live Intrusion* home video, which was ultimately released after a four-year delay in 1999 and then reissued on DVD a decade later still. A riotous collage of the live set and Slayer's off-stage antics, the show features as one of its highlights a jam between Flynn, Kontos, Slayer singer Tom Araya and guitarist Kerry King. Together the foursome roar through a cover of 'Witching Hour' by Newcastle thrash metal pioneers Venom, an influence on both later bands.

Kontos recalls the run-up to the song, which comes at the end of Slayer's set. "I'd never seen a special guest at a Slayer show: they were like your big uncles of metal doing their thing, so being asked to play 'Witching Hour' was a total shock and really historic. I remember thinking that I didn't want to mess it up, and then we were told that we were also doing a 13-camera shoot with NFL Films. I'd been watching NFL Films my whole life. So now you had a completely pressurised situation!"

He continues: "I wanted to warm up a bit, so we ran through [the Slayer song] 'Seasons In The Abyss' and then we did 'Witching Hour' and it sounded amazing. So Machine Head did our set that night, with Robb and I totally preoccupied with what was about to happen. Remember that this was the last night of the tour for us all, so we had some stuff to trick Biohazard. We got some rubber poop, and then I got a goat mask and these branches from the parking lot and a big black cloak, and when Bio went on stage the poop was all over the place on the drums and the mics and stage – and I came out like this big hell goat! It was hella funny. They had the guys from Sepultura come up and play with them, and then Slayer went on stage. Robb and I went backstage and checked with each other a few times that we knew 'Witching Hour' – and then we were up there. By the time it was a reality and we were playing the song, we were off stage again. I will never forget that moment."

It's a sign of the speed of Machine Head's rise to the public eye that when the Slayer tour finished, the band was able to return almost immediately to Europe and headline many of the same venues that they had so recently played. Mader later recalled the intensity of the show in Belfast, Northern Ireland, saying: "We got there, and it was right after the ceasefire and after the border became open again. The kids were telling us there hadn't been a show there in nine months prior to our show. And let me tell you – you could tell! Those kids were starving. They gorged themselves on us and it was amazing! The energy was amazing. We were just blown away by those kids. Fucking amazing show."

"We finished the US leg of that tour," says Kontos, "and then right away we came back to Europe, and we were headlining something like 40 or 50 percent of the same venues that we'd playing when we were supporting Slayer. I know that the French kids and the English kids loved it all, and bought right into the marketing of Machine Head as street-tough guys from the hood. You know, we were playing Snoop Dogg when we were interviewed on MTV, as well as [nu-metal bands] Korn and Downset, right before the nu-metal and rap-metal thing went huge. I was not down for it at all."

Dates in Finland, Sweden, Norway, Denmark, Holland, Belgium, Germany, Switzerland, France, Austria, Italy and Spain followed, taking Machine Head as far as May 1995. A tour of this intensity and duration takes an enormous toll on anyone who participates in it, and this one was no exception: Kontos was the first to feel that he might be permanently damaged by the experience. By the time Machine Head arrived back in the UK, he was in trouble.

"It was a grand tour, lasting about 22 months," he says, "and with very little time off. For the last six months I was sick: I had kidney stones and a viral infection in my salivary glands. They weren't producing spit, they were producing pus. I had very painful flare-ups and my family and I were really concerned about it, but I battled on through Spain, Ireland and Scotland. I played the Glasgow Barrowlands with my airway partly blocked. It was really scary stuff. I was hammering myself with antibiotics, but they weren't working – I was also doing a lot of hard drinking and smoking a ton of marijuana at the time. I wasn't eating all that well, because I wasn't in my right mind and I feeling really bad – and tour food sucks."

Kontos ultimately bowed to the pressure after more UK dates and a five-date stint in Japan. "I finally got really sick when we went to Japan, and while we were there I pretty much had a breakdown from being scared of being sick for this long. I explained to each of those guys that I felt like I was going to die. I couldn't digest food. I had to go on and on to get them to say it was OK to come home."

Faced with an impending tour of Australia, a show in South America, major festival dates in the summer and North American dates stretching through to the end of 1995, Kontos recruited a pal to take his place as a temporary measure. "I found my dear friend Walter Ryan to replace me for the shows," he says, "and then I went home after a day in the hospital in Japan. I was put on a plane with my own row, and slept the whole way. It resulted in major operations when I got home: my spit glands were bored out and the crystallised stones in there were taken out, so I had really bad scarring in the ports under my tongue – it was really terrible. The infections re-occur for the rest of your life, because the boring operations enlarge the ports into your salivary glands, and food particles get in there as a result. So I came home from Japan and I missed out on going to Australia. It felt like a colossal fail. I really was hurt by how I had to beg to come home."

With Ryan now manning the drums, Machine Head played five dates in Australia and two more in Europe before a date in Buenos Aires, Argentina, for which Kontos returned. By now the rest of the band was in pretty poor shape too: as he says, "I had the operations, and I did South America with them. Robb had walking pneumonia, a slipped disc in his back and an eye infection, or some shit. He should never have gone on tour, but you can't stop Robb, so we went out. I should have waited to see how I really was, and if I was really better as well. We did that trip to Argentina, but then the whole left side of my face blew up when we came home. I had to have the same operation again."

Adam Duce was also feeling the ill-effects of a year and more of headbanging every night. As he recalled later, the early shows had actually reshaped his body: "I came home from touring *Burn My Eyes* for about a year and a half, and I didn't know anything about stretching. I played my bass in a super-low position. From holding my bass that low, and doing that repetitive motion which was wearing on one side of my back every night, I ended up with a slight scoliosis [curvature of the spine]. My back curves sideways a little, as if I'm dropping my shoulder to meet the strings way down by my knees. That's exactly how the curve follows. My spine was messed up, because on one side I was holding the bass up and with the other I was reaching down with the pick. I've changed my style since then, and I do regular maintenance on it. I go to the gym a lot and I see a chiropractor on a semi-regular basis and an acupuncturist. If I don't do the maintenance, it ends up hurting. I don't wear my bass as low any more – and to tell you the truth, I don't know why I had it that low. It didn't look as cool as I thought it did!"

Despite their injuries, Duce and Flynn, along with Mader and Ryan, then played the most prestigious festival of their careers to date: the famous Monsters Of Rock event at Donington in England. Donington '95 boasted a stellar line-up, as always: this time Metallica were headlining during a break from recording a new album (the ultimately disappointing *Load*), and as a result the event had been renamed 'Escape From The Studio '95'. Also on the bill were Slayer, Skid Row, Therapy?, Slash's Snakepit, White Zombie, Warrior Soul and Corrosion Of Conformity – an esoteric mixture of Eighties glam and Nineties alternative metal. No wonder Machine Head, one of the most exciting new bands to emerge in years, were on the bill. Sadly, Kontos was too ill to make the trip.

Mader recalled of the event, "Then we get to Donington, which I'm very proud of. A very prestigious thing for us to do. It was fucking huge [but] bittersweet [because] Chris wasn't with us. There were a lot of emotions going on that weren't so good around that time, although our friend Walter Ryan helped us out. It just wasn't the same, though."

Kontos says now: "I wanted to play Donington before I even knew who Robb was. Missing that show was colossal to me: I was gutted to say the least." However, his illness, terrible though it was, formed only a part of his gradual divergence from the other members of Machine Head. Flynn, by his own admission a man forever torn by inner conflicts, was driven by anger in the early days of the band, and while this undoubtedly made the band the success it is today, can hardly have made him easy company at times. "I had so much anger then," he told *Kerrang!*. "I was so angry at the world, at everything I saw. Part of me was pleased we were getting somewhere at last; part of me didn't think we deserved it. I'm never completely satisfied with anything. Perhaps I'm a perfectionist. Maybe that's what drives me."

Kontos found this difficult, he says. "It seemed to me that we were revolving too much about anger – too much anger. That started to become a bit of a turn-off to me. Robb had a real plan and a real vision and a single focus, which in the end was too narrow for me. I need to be involved in planning things, and I need people to be a little bit more open to discussion while making plans, and be open to different ways of thinking. I've been known to patch into a vision before, though: this was right in the Sepultura moment and the Pantera moment, and there were other great bands involved in the mix too, like Fear Factory – basically the whole Roadrunner movement, which seemed to be growing in a political way."

He admits that the differences between himself and the rest of the band were exacerbated by the hothouse environment of the tour bus. "Machine Head was more about grip-it-and-rip-it vodka and Red Bull racing and smoking pot than hard drugs, although we would and did do hard drugs at times. There wasn't much speed or coke in Europe, so it was mainly drinking and pot. Add sleep deprivation and no recovery days, and your judgement gets blurred and people get hurt and bottle it up with no communication; people get sick, people get upset easily and so on. Even after the first tour, I knew that we weren't the same as far as the values that we held, and what we felt about our families and upbringings, and we were stuck in a bus together to get to know each other. I realised that Robb and I didn't really connect on many levels at all, even though we had a great mission and a great band with great songs – and he is a great frontman. The things they said, without going into detail, were not what I felt at all. I felt used and left out of a lot of what was going on at this point."

The intra-band relationship soon became toxic, Kontos adds. "They would call me 'General Public' because I would go out and walk the line with the quote-unquote punters, a term I fucking loathe, because I'm a stage-diving punter to this day. I would meet the kids because I wanted to know where the killer old buildings were nearby, and McDonald's, the record shop, the cool coffee shop and all the other good stuff. Some of these fans turned into lifelong friends. That's how I've always rolled, because in punk rock, the kids at the shows are your connection with the town you're playing in. That was something I could never get across to them. Maybe it was too hippie for them. I would go out there, and they would sit on the bus and laugh at me."

Finally, financial issues raised their ugly heads. Kontos recalls: "I also had a lot of different ideas about how our money should be spent. We spent an exorbitant amount of money on lighting and sound: hundreds and thousands of dollars, and then we would take 300 dollars home a month. We weren't even making our rent at that point, and our girlfriends and wives would be at home, struggling, while these clubs were being lit up like something out of *Close Encounters*. I wanted to cut back on some of the spending that was creating our debt, and I think that started to pinch Robb and Joey. I wanted to be a little more realistic. We started getting into that, and respect lines weren't drawn early on in the relationship, so these arguments weren't executed with much respect or leeway or compromise."

The heaviest debt which the band carried had come from buying onto the Slayer tour, which Kontos estimates as a six-figure sum. "The Slayer tour was not cheap, and it cast Machine

Head into debt that was so huge they would have to sell [a certain number of] records to make that money back, but it was not possible and it got them dropped some years later. Just to put it into context, I think when I left the band they were in excess of $500,000 in debt to Roadrunner. The cost of the Slayer tour was upwards of a hundred grand for each leg in Europe and the USA. In the States it might even have been a little more expensive. With the next record the cost just went up, as they chased that money when it went out of the window."

In due course Kontos was inevitably fired. "They kicked me out on the phone," he says. "It got real ugly real fast. I never really got my say about how I felt in the press. I know that they've bashed me in the press, as did I when given the chance back then. It put me in a hard place for 10 years… It hurt my family more than it hurt me, really." Nowadays he understands the process that the band went through: "I love Joey Huston to death, but I think he was overwhelmed at the time and I don't think he knew how to play it when Robb and I got into it over things, nor when I got sick. It's not his fault, but I wish we could have retained our composure, because I think the band could have gone on to be a bigger entity with no member changes."

A final word from Chris Kontos, who went on to be one of the most in-demand drummers in the Bay Area and continues to tour today with Attitude Adjustment: "I really do like Adam Duce and [future member] Phil Demmel, and I've spent time with [his replacement] Dave McClain at shows a few times: we talk drum shop because we have common interests in the drums and in other players, so that's always fine. It's no secret that I feel that Robb is a dark person, but I won't bash him more than that: there's no sour grapes on my part, although it may sound like there are. I've been really happy with things in my life. After Machine Head I've done many musical endeavours with bands and family. I'm super proud of *Burn My Eyes*: if I end up doing a bigger record than that one, that will be great – but if not, I'll still be proud of what it did for me and my life."

A short summer break prefaced Machine Head's first American headline tour, with a Bay Area drummer called Will Carroll playing the drums for the duration. That small amount of off-time was essential for the band to recover from the huge demands of the previous year: Flynn in particular had acquired some impressive on-stage injuries. As the years passed, this turned into a veritable litany of damage, as he told the author in an interview for *Total Guitar* magazine a decade and more later.

"I've had a million injuries," he said. "I jumped off a drum riser and herniated one leg. I herniated a disc in my lower back. I've got permanent 'metal neck', because the bones and the muscles just get thrashed. If you think about it, I've got a 15-pound guitar around my neck, I'm hunched over a microphone and I'm headbanging – basically I'm turning myself into a hunchback. The back side of my teeth has been chipped off from people stage-diving and slamming the microphone into my face, and I've got a permanent upside-down U on my two front teeth too. I sprained my wrist from smashing it into the corner of my guitar. I broke a rib from stage-diving off the PA – two or three times. It was hella fun! I've given myself black eyes from headbanging into the microphone. I've smashed my nose into my guitar. Then there was this time that Adam was playing a bass with a razor-sharp headstock, and he came flying past me, head down, not looking where he was going – and this headstock literally ploughed into my temple. I was pretty much unconscious for a second there."

After the two-month tour, a jaunt with Stuck Mojo which covered several US states and also took in Canada, Machine Head returned home and began looking for a permanent drummer. Carroll, Flynn said, was a capable sticksman but not what they were looking for at the time, and so the hunt for recommendations began. When asked why Kontos had left the band, a variety of explanations were given: Mader told interviewer Sheila Rene that illness had been the root cause. "He's a great drummer, but it's just that we had some personal conflicts that we were unable to reconcile. We tried and tried. He got sick, but not that sick, and cancelled out of some very important shows for us. He left us hanging in a bad situation and soon after that, we got the Donington gig. It was a very prestigious show for us, in the sense that we felt we might not get that opportunity offered to us again. Chris didn't want to do it, and backed out only three days before the show." Duce added: "Basically he didn't want to tour… and so we threw him to the kerb. But he was hard to deal with, and he didn't want to fullfil comitments that we already had to tour… We'd given him an ultimatum. We told him he had one last chance, and pulling out of Donington was that chance, so we gave him a fair warning and he basically chose not to go, so there you have it."

After it became known that Machine Head were auditioning drummers, a phone call came to Flynn from Sepultura drummer Igor Cavalera and the music journalist Borivoj Krgin, who had sent their demo to Roadrunner. The two men told Flynn that Dave McClain, the drummer with the thrash band Sacred Reich, was a hugely talented musician and that he should be invited to audition at all costs. Flynn duly contacted McClain, who later recalled in an interview with Tom Trakas: "It's no secret that Sacred Reich weren't the hardest-working band in history, it was actually the opposite. Even when I first joined the band, before the Sepultura tour we'd only practised a few times! I'd say to [them], 'Hey, you want to practise?' and [they] just said, 'Ah, you know the songs', so they were pretty notorious for being lazy. So when I got the call from Robb, I went and talked to the Sacred Reich guys. I didn't tell them I had gotten a call, but I told them we needed to get serious and buckle down, and I wanted to know what we were going to do. And the guys were like, 'Yeah, yeah, yeah', you know? So I called Robb back, and I told him that I had to say no and that the Sacred Reich guys were going to turn over a new leaf here and be a little more serious, and he was like 'OK'."

Machine Head then auditioned other potential drummers – future Journey/Ozzy Osbourne percussionist Deen Castronovo, and Jason Bittner, soon to be a drumming legend in his own right with the band Shadows Fall, among them – but were soon contacted again by McClain, who had realised that the promises made by his colleagues in Sacred Reich would come to nothing. "Three weeks, maybe a month had passed and there was nothing," said McClain. "No practice, no this, no that, no nothing and I was like, 'Fuck this!' I knew I had to take a chance and I called Robb back again, and he was like, 'Cool, whatever, you know...'"

A meeting was scheduled in Oakland on December 16, where McClain jammed with the band. The pressure was on: he had to match up to Kontos's expert drumming, or there would be no point in recruiting him. "We knew it wasn't going to be easy," recalled Mader. "They were big shoes to fill, because Chris is a good drummer. We couldn't settle for anything less than what we had before. Dave came around and the try-out was so amazing. I was trying to keep from smiling once I heard him play. He was so cool to watch."

As McClain recalled, "I had learned the entire *Burn My Eyes* album, so I think we just went track by track in order. Once we did that, they had some riffs they'd been working on: I think they wanted to see if I could play what they were hearing. So then we played through the songs again. I knew I did good, I mean I learned the whole album. One thing I picked up from the Sacred Reich days was when a band loses its drummer and it was a good drummer, they want to hear you play the stuff pretty much how it was recorded. They don't want someone coming in and ad-libbing all over the place."

Machine Head had their new drummer, although Flynn – in a spirit of mischief – left it 10 days before he informed McClain that he'd got the job. On December 26, 1995 he made the call, recalled McClain: "It was the day after Christmas… they left me hanging for two weeks. Which wasn't too stressful!"

Once more a full band, Machine Head now had to prove that *Burn My Eyes* had not simply been a successful fluke. All the work they had put in, all the sleep they had lost, all the injuries they had sustained: all this now hung by the most fragile of threads.

Chapter 4

1996–1999

Fortunately for Machine Head, they had renewed fire in their engine room. Dave McClain was one of the few drummers with both the speed and the groove to be able to take Chris Kontos's place. When he joined the band, much of 1996 was already allocated to the writing and recording of the second album, the record which would demonstrate whether Machine Head had any staying power.

As McClain was born in 1965, his background – in San Antonio, Texas – was that of the classic Eighties metal kid, he explained to *Midwest Metal* interviewer Tom Trakas. "In the beginning it was Kiss," he said. "Kiss is what got me into drumming to begin with, so I'd have to say they were my introduction to metal. For about two years Kiss was the only band I listened to: it got to the point where my dad would take me to the mall and say, 'Go to the record store and buy something, anything but Kiss' – and I'd be like, 'Dammit!' Even though I had every album, it didn't matter. So the first 'real' metal band I got into was Judas Priest. I had a neighbour who not only had a drum kit but he also had a copy of [Priest's 1978 album] *Stained Class*, and this was right about the time *Hell Bent For Leather* [also 1978] came out. So for the first few years I drummed, it was to Priest and Kiss."

As with so many musicians of his age, McClain's attention was grabbed at the beginning of the Eighties by the New Wave Of British Heavy Metal, or NWOBHM. He continued: "Back in San Antonio there was a radio station [where] the DJ's name was Joe Anthony, and this guy would play the most underground stuff. One night I remember him saying he was going to play a new band from England called Iron Maiden, and I think he played 'Transylvania' and 'Phantom Of The Opera'... when Maiden came on, it was like, 'Fuck!' So Joe Anthony would be playing Angel Witch, Tygers Of Pan Tang, all the NWOBHM stuff. My friend and I were in a band at the time, it was a cover band playing Priest and Riot tunes and stuff, and we put out an ad in a paper looking for people into the NWOBHM bands – and the next thing you know we had a band."

The kids named their band Slayer, unaware of the band of the same name from Los Angeles. Asked if he knew that a rival group was forming, McClain laughed: "No idea at all! We were just kids with a kick-ass name and we started writing tunes: we had no idea about the music business, let alone another band called Slayer. It was funny though: a lot of magazines ended up reviewing both Slayer [debut releases] at the same time [*Show No Mercy* from the LA Slayer and *Prepare To Die* by the San Antonio version], but as far as us, we were blown away that our EP made it onto the *Kerrang!* charts. I mean we made it to the same magazine as Iron Maiden!"

In 1986 McClain left Slayer – or more properly S.A. Slayer, as they had inevitably become known when the California version's career took off – and played in a band called Murdercar alongside guitarist Ross Robinson, later famed for his production with Korn, Limp Bizkit, Slipknot and other nu-metal bands. After this, he joined the Arizona thrash metal band Sacred Reich, a genuine force in the late Eighties. "I really loved that band," he said. "I loved [the 1988 EP] *Surf Nicaragua*, it blew me away – so when I joined them I literally thought I was joining the next Metallica." At the time McClain was sporting the big hair look that was expected of any Eighties metaller, an amusing concept for many Machine Head fans accustomed to his shaven-headed look. "It was cool back then," he chuckled, in an interview with the author for *Rhythm* magazine. "It was what you did back then. Anybody who was in a band in the Eighties, that was what they did, I don't care who they were. I look at some of the styles now and I think, man... It's the same thing as we were doing back then."

McClain cut his teeth in the major leagues of metal by touring alongside Pantera on the Texans' *Vulgar Display Of Power* tour before making his next move. Sacred Reich were managed by Gloria Cavalera, who also managed Sepultura: hence the chain of events through which McClain was recommended to Robb Flynn by Sepultura drummer Igor Cavalera. By now an experienced and phenomenally talented drummer, he was the perfect choice to replace Kontos for the next album, which was recorded in late 1996 after a handful of tour dates to keep Machine Head in the public eye.

After so much early success, McClain knew as well as any of the other band-members how much pressure was resting on album number two. "I think [the other members] felt they had something to prove, because the first album had done so well," he said later. "But Robb and I worked a lot on the drum parts for the album and I think he wanted to prove people wrong about what could be done. I really think at the time, he wanted to prove to

Chris [Kontos] that the band had gotten a killer drummer capable of doing some cool stuff."

Mader added: "We didn't expect to be the biggest-selling debut act on Roadrunner ever! That was a shock to us, to say the least. It was good. As to writing the second record, our standards to ourselves as a band are very high. We write these songs to please ourselves. We know what we're capable of, and there was no way we were going to fall beneath what we had done before. So that put the pressure on for us. We knew there were a lot of expectations on this, not just from us but from the fans. We were challenged by that and also by the fact that we didn't have long to write all these songs. That really motivated us to focus, and really pushed us to bring the best out in us."

In traditional style, the members were feeling the pressure of coming up with an album in a few months that would outdo a previous album that had been a huge hit. It's a story that musicians signed to record companies have told for decades, but no easier to live through for all that.

It's not surprising that the second album failed to simply fall into place, given these pressures. Mader emphasised: "It wasn't easy. We got halfway through writing these songs and the pressure really hit, because we hit walls. Some of the songs were just fighting us. One song got written and then torn apart and then put back together and then torn apart... This riff's good and this riff's good, so keep those and we'll try again. And we'd put the song back together again and it still sucked."

While the creative process was difficult, actually laying down the tracks was relatively easy for the band, all of whom now had some studio experience under their belts. Mader heaped praise on McClain, saying: "Dave nailed a couple of songs in one take. I believe they were 'Blistering' and 'Take My Scars'. McClain really came through for us. It was really great working with him in the studio. We could push him in a constructive way to bring the best out of him. He was willing to work with us, while someone else might get defensive. We had great communications."

Mader's own performance was good, he felt: "I feel more confident all around. *Burn My Eyes* was the first album I recorded, so a lot of that was brand new. Going into this record, I have some experience to base my playing on and can put more into the performance. My improvisational skills are far better, and I'm more comfortable doing that now. There's stuff like that on this record: some stuff that was born in the studio, just little fills and licks. After touring so much, our abilities and confidence went way up as a band and individually. We did some things here that we wouldn't have done on the last record, musically and vocally. We pushed the limits a little bit."

Nonetheless, the overall experience of recording the album that would be released in March 1997 as *The More Things Change...* wasn't one that the band, and Flynn in particular, looked back upon fondly. "Everyone was stressing out and arguing," he said. "There were plenty of times I was totally depressed, thinking, 'This is never going to happen'. It was a fucking nightmare, I can't even begin to tell you just how much of a nightmare."

The album, produced by Colin Richardson once more, required no fewer than three mixes before Machine Head were satisfied with it. "Finally, the third time was the charm," said Mader. "A lot of crazy shit went on in the recording and mixing processes. We all learned a lot in the process and we all spent a lot of money! We're going to be paying for it the rest of our lives. It's worth it, because [we'd] rather throw in the towel than put out something that we felt was inferior... All these songs had to push the boundaries of our styles, so that we could break new ground and broaden our sound. But at the same time we had to stay true to what the core of Machine Head is, which is extreme groove-oriented, dynamically-oriented metal, with flavours of hardcore and rock, and even rap. Everything we like, all rolled up in there."

The More Things Change... is not radically different from *Burn My Eyes*, and it would be inaccurate to attribute to it the struggles which lay ahead for Machine Head. The immense presence of the downtuned guitars, together with Flynn's impassioned vocals and the muscular rhythm section, made the songs inescapable, whether they took their tone from a groove or thrash standpoint – or somewhere in between. 'Ten Ton Hammer', the album's opening track, is a huge statement of intent, while 'Struck A Nerve' is one of several songs which revisit the fast hardcore tempos that made Machine Head such a stirring band to see live. Subtleties abound in songs such as 'Spine', which begins with a simple but devastating bass riff from Adam Duce. In similar fashion, 'Down To None' and 'Blood Of The Zodiac' focus on atmospheric textures as much as sonic violence, making *The More Things Change...* a worthy second album, if not quite as startling as *Burn My Eyes*, which had the advantage of sounding entirely new at the time of its release.

It's interesting to note that in 1996, heavy metal was changing into a new form inspired by Korn, the Bakersfield, California quintet who had introduced the world to the concept of nu-metal, a hip-hop-inspired subgenre. There was no nu-metal on *The More Things Change...*, but in the spirit of exploration which had begun to seep into metal at the time, Machine Head recorded a cover of 'Colors' by rapper Ice-T for the expanded Japanese edition of the album. "It was experimental for us to try that, because we didn't do the typical metal rap crossover thing," said Mader. "We didn't incorporate metal into it. There's no hard guitars or real drums. It's basically a hardcore rap song redone by us, with six tracks of distorted bass, distorted vocals, drum machine loop, distorted kinda dirty-sounding. Like the East Coast hardcore rap style."

Flynn later described this period as a time of extreme stress during which he would go on "violent rampages" in which he'd "cry, scream, break chairs and tables, punch holes in walls. For a long time it just didn't seem as if anything was going to get better." Perhaps only the solace of releasing all his pent-up frustration on stage would solve this problem: fortunately, almost eight whole months of touring lay ahead. In April and May Machine Head rolled through Europe and the USA, in some cases playing cities where they'd performed twice or more already.

A major shot at serious exposure came with a slot on the very first Ozzfest, the rolling festival headlined by Ozzy Osbourne and organised by his wife and manager Sharon Osbourne after Lollapalooza had turned Ozzy down. To make the new festival more attractive, Ozzy's old band Black Sabbath had reformed and were also playing on the bill, making it the summer's must-visit attraction for metalheads. Wisely, Sharon Osbourne and her team had selected a range of bands from the traditional and new (not yet 'nu') genres of metal.

Dave McClain looked back on the first Ozzfest, saying: "I still remember getting the call from Robb and him saying, 'Main stage, Ozzfest!' That was really cool as it was the first big one, and we felt like this up-and-coming band, and the bill was incredible with Pantera and Sabbath. It definitely worked out for us: it got us the Pantera tour too. Phil [Anselmo, Pantera singer] was a big supporter during that time: he'd watch us a lot and we were doing 'Off-fest' dates. We were in Oklahoma and he came up to us and said, 'Mark my words, you'll be on the next Pantera tour' and I was like 'Cool!'"

The stories of Pantera and Machine Head overlap in many ways, and indeed had Pantera not split, it's likely that they would be touring together today. Both bands redefined American heavy metal in the early Nineties, adding a touch of groove to the traditional, square-edged riffing; both worked solidly at club level to establish a fanbase; and both came to prominence at a time when the only metal band doing really big business was Metallica, under whose long shadow few new bands flourished. In 1997 Pantera were approaching the peak of their powers, having released three major-label albums (note that the Texas-based band had honed their chops in the Eighties in glam-metal territory, before wisely toughening up their sound). It was the perfect time for Machine Head to be exposed to Pantera's audiences, a shot they were given after the release of the Texans' fourth album, *The Great Southern Trendkill*.

Flynn later wrote about the experience of being on the road with Pantera, by all accounts one of the hardest-partying bands ever to board a tourbus. Their guitarist, Darrell Abbott – known as 'Dimebag' Darrell – was renowned for his consumption of whisky, his prowess on his instrument and the remarkable ability for the former not to affect the latter. Labelling the tour "one of the funnest, craziest, greatest goddamned tours we have ever done", Flynn recalled several antics worthy of recognition by any self-respecting party animal – such as the time when Dimebag grabbed Flynn's backup guitar, ran on stage with it, played 'air guitar' during opening band Coal Chamber's set and then smashed it on the stage, shattering the neck. Reminded what had happened the following day, Dimebag gave Flynn twice as much money than the sum required to fix the neck and arranged for two of his signature guitars to be presented to Flynn and Mader on stage a few days later. That's the kind of man he was. His death on stage at the hands of a disturbed fan in 2004 remains one of heavy music's greatest tragedies.

The Pantera tour was only one of a relentless line of tours that filled 1997. As we've already seen, the pressure of delivering music as intense as Machine Head's, night after night and city after city, becomes colossal after months on the road – a fact which is often ignored, especially in the band's later career when they are superficially in a more comfortable position. It was this period of consolidation, from 1994 through to approximately 1998, which established Machine Head as a viable force in an industry which is notoriously unforgiving. But there were victims.

The first to snap was Logan Mader, whose indulgence in rock 'n' roll's traditional lifestyle had taken him to the limit. Resentments had built up and in mid-1998, he arrived at a band meeting in a frame of mind unsuited for polite negotiation. Dave McClain later remembered, "It was personality-wise... we were doing a headline run with Snot supporting, and things there just started to surface. He was hanging out with Lynn [Strait, Snot's mercurial singer] a lot and it all came to a head after the touring was done. We had a meeting and he just went off on people. Man, I can remember it like it was yesterday. We had done so much in support of the record and it all came down to one day, you know? Logan had gotten a lot of press with the band, he was a killer guitarist and had killer stage presence, and I think he thought there was more out there for him to do."

Mader has only hinted at the problems which led him to quit Machine Head the day after the meeting, but it came as a surprise to the fanbase, who weren't privy to the relationships inside the band. Some of this might have been due to Mader's openness about the important role which the music played for him: he once said, "Writing a song about something that makes you angry doesn't make the anger go away, [but] it's a healthy release performing it. I get everything out every night. I just sweat it out and try to break a hole in the stage flooring every night. It's a healthy thing to perform these songs." With that in mind, Machine Head must have been a crucial element in his life: it's telling that he went on to join Soulfly, an equally aggressive band, for a few months in

1998. By the middle of the next decade, Mader had conquered his demons and become a much in-demand producer, an outcome for which he is much respected.

In the meantime, Machine Head were once again short of a member. This time, Flynn, Duce and McClain sat down and talked in depth about what they wanted to achieve with their band, a conversation which significantly affected their choice of who to recruit in Mader's place. McClain recalled: "I remember having talks around the time after Logan left: it was about our goals as a band, and where do we see ourselves. What kind of band do we want to be? And the two bands that we all agreed on was Metallica and the Grateful Dead. And even though none of us like the Grateful Dead, obviously we liked Metallica... it was about a state of mind about how to go about doing your band. Some people may criticise Metallica now for certain things they've done, but there's no question they've got one of the greatest fan clubs. I mean they go so above and beyond what I've ever seen most bands do for their fans. Special shows, and letting them come to rehearsals, and both those bands are from the Bay Area, so it's a state of mind we've been steeped in... the Grateful Dead with the people following them around, and the involvement with everything, and the [live tape] trading. With us it was never about the rock star [element] of it. Granted, when we're up there, it's about being larger than life, but how you conduct yourself is definitely the most important thing."

Auditions for a new guitar player began, with the process made more difficult by the fact that Machine Head had completed the touring cycle for *The More Things Change...* and were beginning to consider a third album. There was some uncertainty about whether the right replacement for Mader could be found in time, recalled McClain: "We were auditioning guitar players [and thinking], 'All right, what do we want out of a guitar player?' He has to be cool. He has to be able to play the old stuff obviously. We wanted somebody to write. We wanted someone that's not a log onstage, someone that can actually have a stage presence. And it's like, 'Who are we getting, you know? We're going to get like maybe two out of five, or whatever."

After a number of auditions, Machine Head settled on a guitarist called Ahrue Luster, an acquaintance of Flynn's from the Bay Area. Although Luster had yet to play in a professional touring band, he had earned his stripes in the underground with a band called Horde Of Torment. He had moved around as a kid, he explained in an interview with the *Bay Area Music Scene* blog: "When I was 13 I was living in Hawaii, and I had a friend named Peter. I looked up to him; he was into electric guitar and could play a couple of AC/DC songs. We were best friends and we were trying to start a band called High Voltage. We wanted to do all AC/DC songs and dress like Angus Young. I ended up moving away from Hawaii and we were supposed to keep in touch, but we never [did], so I ended up getting a guitar and learned some Billy Idol songs. At 14 is when I started playing [and] I got into heavier and heavier music: by the time I was 15, I had Slayer's first album and Metallica's first album. I was into Venom and Mercyful Fate, and that's kind of where I got started. After that bands like Kreator came out, then Possessed. The Bay Area thrash scene started to break out. That's when I decided to move to the Bay Area. I was living in Las Vegas at the time with my mother... I ended up staying in the Bay Area, my band broke up and they went home, and I stuck it out and it paid off. [Horde Of Torment] played with Vio-Lence back in the day as well as Forbidden, Death Angel, Testament, Defiance, Skinlab and all sorts of bands. I knew Robb. [He] used to come to my house: he was good friends with my drummer when he was in Vio-Lence."

He continued, "At the time when Logan left Machine Head, I was playing in a band with Craig Locicero from Forbidden...

the band was Man Made God. I initially heard that Robb had a friend who was asking if I wanted to audition for Machine Head. At the time Man Made God just started to get going, so I tried out and thought about it for a while, then we played together and I saw how I gelled with the guys. It was better than just us playing together: there was this energy that I had never felt with anyone else before, and it felt really good, so I decided to do it. From then on I was in the band. I had known Robb for the longest time before I knew Adam or Dave: I quickly became friends with them as well. It was a great experience. Whenever I look back on those days, there were some of the most fun times of my life."

What was most interesting about Luster's recruitment into Machine Head, and which came with implications for the band's future direction, was that he was – by his own admission – not solely a fan of heavy metal. His tastes in music went in other directions as well. "When he came into the band, we knew he wasn't this metalhead guy," said McClain. "We knew we weren't getting another Logan in the band, and that's not what we were looking for. We also knew what he had done in his previous bands, what songs he wrote and they were different, but that's what we wanted at the time."

McClain concluded: "Ahrue is one of the last guys we auditioned. [He] walked in, put his guitar on, plugged in, and hit a couple notes. By the end of the audition, it just felt totally right. And then we wanted to see how he was, so me and Robb took him out drinking, and he was a really cool guy, he just fit in perfect. The whole time he was there we were trying to gel as people, which we were doing while we rehearsed... It [wasn't] the same as gelling with someone while touring, where you really get to know a lot about a person."

Although the Flynn/Luster/Duce/McClain line-up looked and felt right, tensions continued to run beneath the surface.

Flynn in particular was beginning to feel the strain, physical and psychological, of directing and maintaining his life in a successful metal band. As he later explained to Tom Bryant of *Kerrang!*, this period was a particularly low one for him. He recalled waking up after a night on ketamine, the infamous hallucinogenic tranquilliser, to find that he had carved the word 'Metal' into his chest with a knife. "I've got issues, man," he told Bryant. "I've got issues you can't imagine. There's always been an explosion of anger around me. At some point in my life, I stopped taking all that rage out on the world, and turned it on myself. There have been times when I've ripped myself apart. Ripped myself apart."

Destructive abuse of cocaine and booze wasn't helping, he added, and he had also developed bulimia due to a terrible self-image. He described the latter as "a way of trying to force control onto everything around me. If I could control my body, then I would be OK, I thought. That's what the bulimia was about, I think. I was in a bad way... There's this glamour about being the fucked-up singer in a rock band. Maybe I was playing up to that. But there's nothing glamorous about puking into a toilet because you thought you were fat. There's nothing glamorous about that puke splashing back into your eyes. There's nothing glamorous about having your wife walk into the bathroom and watch you as puke runs down your face. There's nothing glamorous about that at all. It's pathetic. Absolutely pathetic."

"For so long in my life, I had been fighting everything around me," Flynn added in an interview with writer Don Kaye in *Metal Edge* magazine, "and I couldn't fight everything around me any more. So I started taking it out on myself... After [Mader] quit, it just spiralled so hard out of control that it reached a point where I was just going to live or not live." Therapy was the obvious solution, and so Flynn began sessions with a counsellor.

Inevitably, a lot of this horrendous inner turmoil translated onto the next album, *The Burning Red*. Flynn told *Absolut Metal* that his songwriting has always come from a personal standpoint: "The music that's lasted with me for my life has been the music that's had some kind of connection to me, like whether it was an emotional connection or just something that I could completely relate to. Whether it was just like, 'Fuck, I know what that guy is going through', or what that girl is going through, or whatever. So I try and write from that perspective, and I can't say that it works every time but, you know, some of the stuff on the record is just stuff I need to get off my chest."

Perhaps not coincidentally, the producer of the new album was Ross Robinson, a specialist in eliciting the most impassioned performances from the bands he worked with. In 1994 he had done this with Korn, guiding singer Jonathan Davis through a deeply upsetting song about childhood abuse called 'Daddy', and he would do this again when Slipknot recorded their first album in 1999. At the same time, Machine Head were keen to try new songwriting and recording angles, and were equipped with the ideal guitarist in Ahrue Luster to enable these ideas. Put all these factors together and it's no surprise at all that *The Burning Red* (and to an extent, its successor *Supercharger*) sounded different from *Burn My Eyes* and *The More Things Change....*

"Looking back," said Dave McClain later, "*The More Things Change...* can be seen as almost a *Burn My Eyes Part II* – not as great, or whatever, but we still got some shit for staying the same. So when it was time to do *The Burning Red* there were a lot of conscious efforts to do things differently, from toning down the drum parts, to making the songs themselves a little more basic, and having Ross Robinson produce – which was the first time we didn't use Colin Richardson – so it was definitely going to be different. I know some people weren't happy that two of the songs had more of a hip-hop type feel, [but] while it can be looked at like a departure, sometimes you have to do things like that. Looking back on the record, though, there is some great stuff on there, and some stuff that wasn't as focused – but we did have new people around and we wanted to try some new things. At that point, the band and even the record company… wanted to see things keep going up – bigger this and bigger that – so we did have some songs that were catered to be on the radio, but at the same time it wasn't like we were writing a bunch of ballads or something."

The Burning Red was released on August 10, 1999. A single, 'From This Day', unnerved a few of Machine Head's older fans, not because the song was particularly out of character but because of the accompanying video clip, in which Flynn appeared with spiked hair, a curious range of leisurewear and brandishing the full range of hip-hop hand gestures. On listening to the album itself, the listener might have been slightly taken aback by the first full song, 'Desire To Fire', in which Flynn actually rapped for a couple of minutes. While the nu-metal movement was in full swing by the summer of 1999, with Limp Bizkit, Linkin Park, Papa Roach and literally hundreds more bands combining metal and hip-hop, somehow this hadn't been expected of Machine Head.

But hold on a second. The traditional critical response when discussing the late-Nineties and 21st century output of this band has generally been pretty savage. This is not necessarily a reasonable view. Firstly, if rap meeting riffs is not to your taste, the only track you really need to avoid here is 'Desire To Fire': the rest of *The Burning Red* doesn't include any fast-talking of any description. Flynn himself said, "There's a minute and a half of rapping on that album. The other 53 minutes of the record are like a giant scar being ripped open while I projectile-vomit through it. If all that people got out of that album was rap-metal, then they didn't fucking listen to it."

This is not to say that there aren't dated elements on *The Burning Red*, when viewed from this distance. 'The Blood, The Sweat, The Tears' has nothing less than a disco drum beat anchoring it, for example, and Flynn's croon of 'Ooh-ooh!' in 'Silver' is a little incongruous. Most oddly, Machine Head chose to pursue that fatal nu-metal cliché – a cover of an Eighties pop song, reinterpreted in metal style. There's nothing wrong with the song they chose – the excellent 'Message In A Bottle' by The Police – but their delivery was strangely ill-judged: the cover was neither as atmospheric as the original, nor sufficiently heavy to make it interesting. Of 'Message In A Bottle', McClain explained: "I guess it kind of stuck in Robb's head, and we were recording Robb's guitar tracks and he started playing it, singing along with it, kind of mellow, and someone goes, 'We should cover that' [because] we needed songs for B-sides. So, one day we were on a break, [and] Ross is like really spontaneous, he likes things to be really unrehearsed. For this song, we were all just kicking it out at the studio: there's like acres and acres of land, we were out there throwing oranges and stuff at each other, and Ross rounded us up, and was like, 'Let's go do this song'. We didn't know it, and I went out and bought the CD for it, so we could learn it… [We] had to figure everything out… so he was like, 'Great, you guys know the basic riffs, turn it into a Machine Head song, it'll be killer'. So I went in there and after an hour of working on it, we played it once through… And we wanted to use it on the record but we were kind of afraid to put it on the record, just because right now there's this whole trend [of covering Eighties songs]."

But there's great music on *The Burning Red* too: anyone who dismisses the album out of hand either isn't giving it enough of a chance or simply isn't a fan of the atmospheric, impassioned groove-metal that Machine Head were focusing on at this stage. 'Devil With The King's Card' has some immensely heavy, almost doom metal-indebted moments, as does 'I Defy', with its clear sense of stadium dynamics. The title track, which closes the album, is Machine Head's most experimental song to date, and whether you enjoy its distorted drums and freeform structure or not, you have to admire its ambition.

Flynn was at his most confessional on 'Five', a heartbreaking tale of his own abuse as a five-year-old by an unnamed perpetrator. It's too close to the bone to stand repeated plays, perhaps even for its creator. As he told Bryant, "I will never play that song onstage. Ever. That was a song ripped straight from the heart. I try to never think about what happened but it creeps in, though, it creeps in. When I'm alone in my bunk, lots of things I don't want to think about come into my head. I try to block them out, but they keep on coming."

Let's be clear about one thing. *The Burning Red* sounds different to Machine Head's earlier albums, not merely because the band was flirting with nu-metal dynamics at the time – and it *was* merely a flirtation, not a wholesale conversion to the form. The new sounds appeared because the group was digging deeper into their own songwriting, performing and recording abilities, honed over years of touring. Producer Robinson encouraged this, as all decent producers should, the audible result of which is that at times Flynn adopts a clean, Eddie Vedder-style baritone instead of his usual ursine roar and that both he and Luster often play plangent, picked guitar parts rather than incessant riffs. Even the album's artwork – a blood-red orchid, about as far from a traditional heavy metal image as you can get – implied a frame of mind other than the usual macho mindset.

Of course, the band was forced to defend this new, wider approach, and have spent the subsequent years doing just that in literally hundreds of interviews. "After *The More Things Change…*," said Flynn, "we told ourselves that we were going to try to bring in new elements to express how we feel at that moment. We're trying to make music here, and succeed or fail: if you try to limit what you do because of how someone else might react to it, then it's stifling. It's such a suffocating feeling. If we're going to be accused of anything, it's that we dared to fail, not because we played it safe or stayed complacent because it might affect our fanbase. We've thrown caution to the wind many times. Sometimes we won and sometimes we lost, but at least we tried something different to inject our sound with something new and fresh."

Elsewhere, he added with justifiable irritation: "I find that a lot of US journalists who kind of missed out on *Burn My Eyes* and *The More Things Change…* and who just started hearing us around *The Burning Red*, started seeing us as rap-metal, and that's just pure ignorance. So whenever they say we suddenly changed to play heavy music to suit the times, it's absurd to me. I just think we tried different things. We were kind of getting into this pattern of what we could and couldn't do, and we wanted to do different things. When a band does the same record over and over again, I lose interest. I'm not saying everyone's like this, but I have a short attention span, and when I hear a song that sounds like a song on the last record but only a crappier version of it, then it just doesn't do anything for me. But it's kind of a Catch-22 situation: if you bring in too many new elements, you're criticised for changing too much, but if you don't change, then you're accused of being predictable."

Dave McClain backed him up, explaining: "On this record we wanted to break down all these boundaries, like, 'Oh, this part sounds like The Cure, we can't do it' – well, screw it, let's do it. Robb's voice has evolved over the last record, he's got a really clean singing voice, and he's also still got his gravel voice. He wanted to be more melodic with his voice, and it's all good… We're a metal band, we're not going to deny that, ya know? We're a metal band but there are labels that can get put on you when you're a metal band, or a set of rules, things you're not supposed to do."

McClain also heaped praise on his old bandmate Ross Robinson's production style, saying: "Ross has a really good way of working. He makes it fun. He's pretty different from any other producer. He doesn't really go for total perfection, he goes for more of a vibe. And then he's sitting there in the room with you, with his headphones on, jumping around, probably jumping around probably more than anyone else who's there, and making you play hard, as hard as you can. Ahrue got whacked a couple times... he threw a water bottle at me. A flattened one, but a water bottle nonetheless. He usually told me, 'If I don't get goosebumps when you count that song off...' He's like a really good football coach."

As for the mixed reactions which *The Burning Red* received on its release from fans concerned at its nu-metal elements, McClain shrugged: "Pissing people off isn't a bad thing, you know? For people to be narrow-minded is bad. People [just] hear Ross Robinson and think 'Korn'. They don't even know... if they hear the record, they're going to [think] 'Korn'. Fact of the matter is, one of the first things we said to Ross is, 'We don't want to sound like Korn'. Those [nu-metal] bands... they're good, you know, but this is our third record and a lot of bands that go to Ross are new bands, and on your first record you usually sound a lot like your influences. And so those bands go to Ross and they want to sound like Korn, and that's cool because it's like their first record and whatever, and they want to sound like that. Just like probably seven or eight years ago, on their first record most bands were going, 'Dude, can you make us sound like Pantera?' to whatever producer did it. And we told Ross, we like Korn, we like Limp Bizkit, but you know, we have two records under our belt and people expect a certain sound... But people are still going to hear the record and still go, 'Oh, Robb is rapping on this part or that part', you know? I've heard people say, 'Oh, I hate Ross's mixes'... Ross didn't even mix our record. They just hear Ross's name and they automatically hear what they want to hear. Whatever. It doesn't bother us at all, we know we're going to piss people off with this record, but some people hopefully will actually sit down and listen to the whole record." Two tours, the Livin' La Vida Loco dates (named after the puerile hit by Ricky Martin of almost the same title) and the full-blown *The Burning Red* tour occupied Machine Head in North America and Europe until the end of 1999. Readers of a certain age may recall the atmosphere of slight panic that preceded the dawning of the new millenium: in most cases, there was no need to worry.

In Machine Head's case, however, the future was about to deal them a catastrophic blow. Several, in fact.

Chapter 5

2000–2002

In the mid-2000s, Adam Duce told the author: "We do one thing really well – we're heavier than fucking shit – and that's what we do. It's not going to be accepted by radio, and that's just fine. As long as we stay true to what feels right to us, it comes out great. What it needs to have is the feeling: when we wrote *Burn My Eyes* in 1993, we were going after a feeling, a hunger that we had. We didn't have preconceived ideas of what it was going to be. We just had a feeling, kind of a starvation, you know, and it translated like fuck through that record. That's the thing that keeps Machine Head, Machine Head. A feeling: way more of a heart thing than a cerebral thing – and people are going to feel that, because we're all made up of the same stuff."

Wise words, and ones that go a long way towards explaining the Machine Head ethos. When it comes to writing music, these musicians don't have a commercial plan, other than an awareness of how to write songs that intentionally sound big on stage and which stimulate their audiences. Machine Head don't write for radio: like all the best bands, they write for themselves and their fans.

At least, not any more. As Duce explained, "In the past we've tried to analyse the music business and try and think, 'This is what people want to hear', because we've got to do fucking radio, or we've got to do this, or we've got to do that." On the rare occasions when this has happened, as with 2001's *Supercharger* album, the results have been disappointing to say the least.

Let me repeat that this book is not going to take the standard approach of slamming the albums which Machine Head released during this uncertain period of their career, specifically *The Burning Red* and *Supercharger*. We've already seen that nu-metal ruled the airwaves between, say, 1996 and 2002, and that any metal bands who wanted to make big money were pretty much required to adhere to that movement's trademarks of hip-hop beats, baseball caps, lyrics based on sociopathic resentment and a generally snotty attitude. Machine Head didn't go far into this territory: Robb Flynn rapped here and there, and the band occasionally donned generously tailored trousers, but they retained enough of their Bay Area identity to make accusations of abandoning their roots groundless. Limp Bizkit they were not, despite legions of juvenile internet haters who have claimed otherwise.

Duce also said: "Writing music always seems to take us longer than it takes people in general. I'm not real sure why. We like to try things and try things until they feel natural – and if it doesn't feel natural, then we're not done with it yet," and although he wasn't referring specifically to the period between *The Burning Red* and *Supercharger*, it's easy to see how difficult it is for Machine Head to squeeze in songwriting sessions, given how much touring they like to pack into their available time. Most of the writing and recording for *Supercharger* was executed in the first half in 2001, after no fewer than 10 of the 12 months of 2000 had been spent on the road.

And what months they were. If you've seen Machine Head in recent years, you'll have been left speechless by the band's grasp of an audience and how all-enveloping the experience can be at its peak: an annihilation of the senses that no recorded album can capture. It was years on the road like 2000, merely one of many, that gave the musicians the ability to touch crowds the way they do. In that one year they swept through California, Arizona, Texas, Louisiana, Georgia, Florida, Washington (fortunately with a few days off between those last two states), New York, Massachusetts, Pennsylvania, West Virginia, Ohio, Michigan, Illinois, Wisconsin, Minnesota, Nebraska, Missouri, Colorado, Utah and back to the west coast states. Japan was next, before a quick run through Europe and some time off before more US dates. This is not a band that likes to sit around at home.

Things were changing in the Machine Head camp, though. Around this time the band signed with Rick Sales's management company, the organisation which also handles Slayer and other major acts. This didn't last long – Joseph Huston was back in the saddle by early 2002, where he remains today – but it certainly contributed to the general turmoil which was about to envelop them. Judging by the optimistic sounds of some of the material on *Supercharger*, which appeared on October 2, 2001, the live dates – which included the Tattoo The Planet-branded tour of Australia and a Roadrunner-badged US outing called Roadrage – had been a success. Machine Head must have felt that they were on their way to the next level.

Writer Brian Webb asked Ahrue Luster if he had felt any pressure when writing the material for *Supercharger*. The guitarist confidently replied, "With all the criticism that we got from the media with *The Burning Red*, it was still our biggest selling album: we sold twice as many tickets as we ever had, [and] twice as much merchandise as we ever have. When we play shows we talk to the fans afterwards, and almost every fan that we've met loves *The Burning Red*, and we have letters and letters of how it changed people's lives. We are more concerned with what our fans think than the media. Anything that's outside the four of us isn't really an influence on when we were writing the record, so there wasn't any pressure... When we were on *The Burning Red* tour, all those shows were amazing, and the energy between us and the crowd was incredible, and we used the electricity as an analogy to describe that. Coming off the tour we began writing almost immediately, so the feeling of the shows carried over into the writing process and that's where the title *Supercharger* comes from. It's a tribute to our fans."

As for accusations of pursuing a hip-hop-indebted nu-metal writing style, Luster was wholly in favour of it in a way that his band-mates were not: "We find that kind of amusing, because the hip-hop element has been a part of Machine Head since the beginning. The verses in 'Block' are basically hip-hop, as well as 'A Thousand Lies' and 'Colors' on the digipak of *The More Things Change...* album. *The Burning Red* comes out, and all of a sudden people are up in arms because there's rapping now – and we're like, 'When wasn't there?'"

Confidence levels were clearly high, then. However, between the Australian and American tours, the World Trade Center attacks took place, jolting much of America into hysteria and, as later became apparent, redefining the post-millenial era. Among the many, many catastrophic consequences of 9/11, one pertinent to the story of Machine Head is that the music industry took a major financial hit: international tours were cancelled and radio airplay restricted. Machine Head's lead-off single from *Supercharger*, 'Crashing Around You', was accompanied by a video depicting the group playing the song amid falling buildings. This proved too much for the music TV channels, now suddenly sensitive to any content that related to warfare or destruction, and the song received very little exposure as a result.

Dave McClain later told the author: "You know, when 'Crashing Around You' was cancelled after 9/11 happened, there were plans to bring that record back when the music business had recovered. But it just never happened… My honest opinion about *Supercharger* is that there are maybe four good Machine Head songs on there, and then the rest of them aren't really Machine Head."

Well, let's take a look at them. After a brief intro titled 'The Declaration', the album starts with 'Bulldozer', a slab of groove and heaviness in the style for which Machine Head had been famous for almost a decade at this point. Riffs were clearly not in short supply, as 'White Knuckle Blackout!' begins with a suitably twisty figure from the old school, even if the verses stray into more lightweight territory dominated by eerie wailed guitar sounds.

The single, 'Crashing Around You', isn't terrible by any means, but it's hardly Machine Head at their best. The sound is strangely weak – no walls of sound here, sadly – and the sung chorus lacks the adrenalised charge that make the band's best songs so compelling. The same goes for songs such as 'All In Your Head', 'Kick You When You're Down', 'Nausea', 'Trephination' and 'American High' (the last of which opens with a Tarzan wail and laughter, curiously) all of which are no better than average. 'Only The Names' and 'Blank Generation' go into more satisfactory territory, with deep, heavy layers of guitars the perfect accompaniment to Flynn's urgent vocals. At least the title track, a hardcore-influenced rant that gets the blood flowing at last, has energy to spare.

These points are merely one writer's opinion, of course, and Machine Head themselves wisely refuse to take much notice of critics' judgments to this day. Interviewed by the author in 2009,

McClain reasoned: "You know, it's all a matter of opinion, what's good or what's not. If that is the collective opinion of everybody, or most people, or some people... hey man, we just make music. That's why we started this in the first place – we wanted to hear music along the lines of what we're playing, and no-one else was doing it. For example, when we came out it was all grunge, and everyone wanted to sound like they came from Seattle and shit. I loved Alice In Chains and Soundgarden and Pearl Jam, it was really well done – but it wasn't us. We do this basically for ourselves."

The drummer added, reasonably enough: "However people reacted to *Supercharger*, it still sold pretty good for a metal album – 250,000 copies, or something. And fans kept turning up to the show, too, which means a lot. That gave us a whole new appreciation for it."

As Ahrue Luster told Brian Webb: "We didn't [record these songs] because we are worried about what anyone thinks. A lot of the time when we get interviewed, people think that what we do, we do because of what other people think. We do what we do because we are trying to be true to ourselves and do what we want to do... It's looser, and I think that comes from the comfort level the band has now. This is the first time Machine Head have had the same line-up two records in a row. We are the same four guys that have been through ups and downs together and laughed together, and we feel closer than we ever had – and with that comfort comes confidence. When we're around each other, most of the time we are joking around and that feeling came out on the record. Perhaps some of the stuff we were feeling would not have come out in the past... I think the lyrics on this record are the best [Flynn has] ever written. When I hear them, they move me more than I have been in the past. All Robb's lyrics in the past have been great but these lyrics, there's something special about them. I think they are more focused and when he's talking about something, I can totally relate to it."

American and European dates took Machine Head into 2002, the most difficult year they have endured to date. While audiences rewarded *Supercharger* with reasonable unit sales, the real enthusiasm on the part of the public was evident in their continued willingness to show up at Machine Head gigs, then as now the lifeblood of the band's activities. The 'Supercharging America' tour continued into March: along the way the band contended with the usual hindrances to their progress, among them the ending of a three-year trademark case against a Californian sound design company which claimed that it had been trading under the name Machine Head since 1991. "We peacefully co-existed for seven years, and now Dewey Global [owners of the other Machine Head-branded business] claims that – all of a sudden – there's some sort of problem. We've been defending our right to our name and our identity ever since," said Flynn. He added that "from the very beginning we were willing to and repeatedly tried to settle this so that we could both continue to co-exist. They didn't want any part of that, so it forced us to spend a ridiculous amount of time, effort and money fighting their meritless case." Still, at least the band won the day.

A more damaging issue arose when Ahrue Luster decided to quit. The reasons for his departure seem to have been varied, but primary among them was his desire to play a different kind of music. It's too much to say that a war of words was fought in the press after Luster's exit, but a few barbed comments were certainly exchanged, despite eminently reasonable explanations from Dave McClain in *Midwest Metal* such as: "As time went on and we wanted to start getting heavier, he wasn't into it – and rightfully so, as he wasn't that guy in the first place. Even during the recording and then mixing of *Supercharger*, votes in the band were always three to one and things like that. In the end, he then told us he wanted to do a side project yet he'd commit to one more album with Machine Head, and that's not at all what we wanted."

"The guy really wanted to take Machine Head in a mellower direction, we weren't into it," wrote Flynn on his blog. "He wanted to do a mellow side project, we wouldn't take a back seat for that. His heart wasn't into playing heavy music any more, and he wanted to leave. Whether it was now, or a year from now, he was going to leave... I wish I had more to tell you, some drama that would make it more exciting, but I don't. We wish him the best for the future."

"Me and Robb were talking back and forth for about a month about this side project thing and about how I was feeling about things," explained Luster, "and he confronted me with a question: 'OK, what happens if the side project gets signed and they ask you to tour?' And I hadn't really even thought about it myself, so I had to think about it, and I told Robb I would think it over and call him back the next day. And I called him back the next day, and being completely honest with myself and being completely honest with him, I said, 'Well, if I am being more creatively fulfilled doing something else and I have a chance to do something more with it, I'm going to have to do that'. So pretty much on that, that's when we realised that maybe the best thing was for me to leave the band."

Sad to say, it didn't end there. Luster read Flynn's comment and disagreed. In an interview with the Blabbermouth news site on June 22, 2002, he said: "That's not true. I wanted to be more melodic, I wanted to have more melody, but not [become] mellower. Machine Head is Robb Flynn, pretty much. I mean, he is the main songwriter, and it's kind of just a reflection of him. For someone else that has strong, creative ideas to try to be fulfilled in a band that someone else has most of the creative control [over], it's difficult... I definitely did get a lot of ideas out – but the final word was his on everything. I would have liked to have had equal say. [Robb] kind of wanted me to trust in his guidance on music – trust in his opinion of what was good and what wasn't – and that was OK for the other guys in the band, but I can't trust anybody else's opinion on music except my own... Ideally, I would like everybody to have equal say. More than anything, I wasn't creatively fulfilled – basically, because I wanted to have more melody – so I suggested me doing a side project to get fulfilment, to get my ideas out, and then I wouldn't feel pent up and have all this stuff that I had to get out. But [the rest of the band] didn't want me to do a side project, so I had to follow my heart and do what I thought was right. I didn't want to change Machine Head [or] to turn Machine Head into something else – I just wanted to get my ideas out."

In fairness to Luster, it should be stressed that he also clearly stated: "I love the music that we made – *The Burning Red* is still, to this day, the thing that I am the most proud of in my life. We played great shows, the fans were great... all in all, it was a great experience, and I still consider the guys in the band friends of mine. I'm not sure if they consider me their friend, but I hope that some day we can all have a drink together." He also hoped that the friendship would re-establish itself in the future, saying: "I'm sure that there are hard feelings, but I just hope that it's something that down the road will be all right with everybody." He also commented that he had never felt completely accepted by the *Burn My Eyes*-loving section of Machine Head's fanbase (although, what fan of the band *doesn't* love that album?) and that the relatively disappointing performance of *Supercharger* had not influenced his decision to quit.

A year or so later, the subject still wasn't dead: Luster, by now a member of Latino metallers Ill Nino, was reported to have described Machine Head as a dictatorship. The exact quote, taken from an issue of *Metal Hammer,* was: "I've known [the Ill Nino] guys a long time. Machine Head did two tours with them, and I actually had more fun hanging out with them than any other band I've toured with. I feel more comfortable now than I did being Machine Head for a year. Ill Nino's more of a group effort where everybody puts in. Machine Head was kind of like a third-world democracy – where it's actually a Robb Flynn dictatorship."

Dave McClain was the next to pick up the baton, so to speak, replying with an angry post on the Machine Head website and adding that the band-members routinely vote on decisions in a democratic fashion. Luster replied with, "First of all, the supposed 'quote' that Dave's post was based on was not even accurate. My exact words were, 'Machine Head is more like a third-world democracy where it's really more like a dictatorship'. Meaning that although we claimed to be a democracy, I never really felt like we were one… I have since called Dave, after reading the post, to let him know that it was based on inaccurate information and it seems that things have been cleared up between us."

Evidently weary of the endless sniping, Luster concluded, "I know that some people in the press like to try to start wars between bands or members of bands to have something to write about, but I have no desire to perpetuate any sort of childish press war between Machine Head and myself, and hope that the journalists who read Dave McClain's last post will read this one too, realise that and let this rest" – which is exactly what we're going to do, right here.

Back to 2002. Luster had left the band before a sequence of British and European dates, requiring Flynn, Duce and McClain to find a second guitarist quickly, cancel the shows or play them as a three-piece. Fortunately fate was smiling on Machine Head in the form of none other than Phil Demmel, Flynn's old guitar partner in Vio-Lence, who agreed to sign up on a temporary basis for the overseas dates. Flynn said of Demmel, "We have a lot of history, we grew up together, and we learned how to play guitar together. Our aspirations, even when we were kids, was to be that kind of guitar team like Gary Holt and Rick Hunolt of Exodus. Especially in the Bay Area and all those big guitar teams, the thrashers, when we were coming to see those shows."

Despite this, Flynn also wrote in his blog that he didn't expect Machine Head to tour again for another two years at least. Why such gloom? Because, after four albums and almost a decade as partners, Roadrunner had dropped Machine Head. That is, the American branch of the label: elsewhere, the band was still signed to their old label.

For any US band, to lose the ability to get recorded product into stores in their home country – by an order of magnitude, the state which consumes the most metal, as with all forms of music – this was a serious blow. In retrospect, it's easy to see that this obstacle merely impeded Machine Head's progress rather than derailing it altogether, but at the time the situation must have appeared close to terminal to the musicians themselves, especially as a permanent replacement for Luster had not been found. Many a band has given up under these circumstances. After all, it's hard enough to pay the bills as a musician even when business relationships are secure: without them, the concept of making a living through music is tenuous indeed.

Asked about this difficult period, McClain pondered: "It's weird. All the different territories of Roadrunner are kind of like their own little label. For the rest of the world, they all wanted us back. They were pretty much all on the same page, but Roadrunner US is a different place. They started trying to break all these bands. When Nickelback broke, I think they started getting a lot of bands that were like Nickelback or whatever. I think they kind of changed their priorities from where they were before Nickelback broke. They wanted to be a different kind of label. At the time, they didn't really feel like our record was what they were into."

Flynn put it differently, telling *Absolut Metal*: "After *Supercharger*, we demanded to be let go from Roadrunner... we severed ties with them back in April of 2002. At the time when we did it, the band was in a different place, and you know, we were pretty unhappy. Ahrue ended up leaving shortly thereafter. And also, we had a manager at the time who was dealing with most of the relationships between them and us, and he was definitely pulling this whole kind of 'us against them' thing. And you know, after hearing that for about six months we started believing it, you know?"

Asked if the band was talking to other American labels, McClain said, "Hopefully, we'll be announcing the American deal soon. We'll see what happens. The people that we're talking with right now, at least the main companies, we feel are almost where Roadrunner was a while back, like when we were first with them, around the time of *The More Things Change....*"

Flynn added, "At the time, we had all these labels blowing a bunch of smoke up our ass about how they were going to sign us. 'As soon as you're off Roadrunner, man, you're on blah, blah, blah Records.' Maybe it was naïve of us on our part to fall for it. That period was just the three of us in the band. It was Adam, Dave and I. We didn't really know what we were going to do, but we loved jamming together. We loved making music together."

This period wasn't all about desperation, however. Nostalgic fun was had when Duce stepped in to play as a guest bassist at a Vio-Lence show at the renowned Milwaukee Metalfest, and the European tour dates with Demmel on board were a triumph. A secret show at the Highbury Garage in London under the name Ten Ton Hammer sold out in 24 hours, and Machine Head's headline set at the With Full Force festival in Germany was a career high point. Despite the setbacks of this year, it didn't seem that anyone in the band was about to quit the rock 'n' roll business just yet.

Fortunately the band could maintain their bond with their fans via their website, MachineHead1. "We get two million hits a month," said Flynn later. "A lot of people go there and they watch the updates and they watch the stuff. It's becoming like its own TV channel... just being able to put stuff up there and have stuff getting out there in that way. A lot of our fanbase, they're younger kids and they're internet-savvy. We've started using the internet and doing video updates [online]... When we started doing them, it wasn't like 'Hey, there's this new, great technology'. It's like, we didn't have a choice. We were unsigned. No magazines would cover us. We didn't have a way to keep contact with our fans. We didn't have a record coming out. We started using that as a way to keep in touch with them. Lo and behold, five years later, that's kind of become the way that things are now. Here, being one of the forerunners of it, it's cool to have pioneered that and it's offered a massive amount of exposure to us and it's been pretty cool. The thing that's best about it is [that] it's not under some sort of radio programmer's control. It's not under a video station's control. It's our site. We have the final say over it and the creative control. It ain't like we're going to misquote ourselves, you know."

At the end of 2002, Flynn was asked if he'd be interested in taking up the vocalist's position in the Texas metal band Drowning Pool, whose singer Dave Williams had died earlier that year: he declined politely, knowing full well that the story of Machine Head was far from over. A wise move, as we'll see.

Chapter 6

2003–2004

Recording a demo and electronic press kit, and shopping them to every record company in America, Machine Head spent what must have felt like an interminable period at the end of 2002 and the beginning of 2003 reading rejection letter after rejection letter. Not a pleasant experience, whoever you are – and a huge slap in the face for a band who had spent the previous decade slogging through dozens of countries to maintain their profile. All those road miles, broken nights, stage injuries and empty bank accounts, all for this.

"Every single one of [the labels] – all 35 – turned it down," said Robb Flynn. "The first couple of rejections were difficult. Towards the end, it was almost comical: 'Oh, someone else has passed on us. OK, well fuck them!'"

Machine Head's tenure with Roadrunner USA finally ended with the release on March 11, 2003 of *Hellalive*, the band's first live album. Appropriately, given that the industry in their home country had effectively rejected the band, the album contained material recorded in England and Germany – with most of the songs taken from a show at London's Brixton Academy on December 8, 2001 and two songs ('None But My Own' and 'The Burning Red') from the With Full Force headline slot from summer 2002.

Of *Hellalive*, Flynn explained: "We really like touring Europe, and we just wanted to record a show. We knew the London show would be great, but it was just more electric then we could have imagined. We had a shitload of technical difficulties, but it was still a blast and hella fun. That vibe, that charge of electricity is what we wanted to capture." On the With Full Force songs – which featured Phil Demmel – he said: "After Ahrue left, it opened us up to thinking about the album in a different way. We headlined, which was the first time we'd been able to do something like that, and we decided to put a couple of the songs on from there – songs we hadn't played in a while. Sonically, it flows. I mean, you can tell the difference, but to me the sound coming out of the speakers is irrelevant to the heart of the music."

Label-free for the first time in a decade, Machine Head continued to write songs as a trio, performing odd jobs to pay the rent: as Flynn told *Kerrang!*'s Tom Bryant, he worked as a studio engineer from time to time. However, in April a huge change in the band's fortunes arrived in the shape of Phil Demmel, who rejoined the group on a permanent basis after a couple of years in the reactivated Vio-Lence.

Demmel was, and is, much more than just another metal guitarist. He is a genuine virtuoso on his instrument, with a picking hand like few others and a grasp of melodic soloing that is second to none. Years of recording and touring had given him the stamina to perform in a touring band at the level to which Machine Head had become accustomed, and of course his history with Flynn in Vio-Lence was an enormous bonus. The two men knew each other's playing styles and working methods, and made a perfect fit – not least because Demmel is as good or even better a player than Flynn, himself no slouch as a guitarist.

As Dave McClain, who also plays the guitar as well as the drums and knows what he is talking about, told interviewer Tom Trakas: "Getting Phil in the band was like getting another Logan in the band, only better. He's a killer guitar player, both rhythm as well as lead, and a good writer – and by that I mean a heavy writer too. When Phil started jamming with us, he wanted to play some of the songs off *Burn My Eyes* that we hadn't played in a long time: that's the shit he's into. So having someone like that in the band challenged us and in particular, Robb. For a while we didn't truly have a lead guitarist: yeah, Robb's a killer rhythm guitarist who's also an accomplished lead player, but Phil can really fucking shred! Right from the start they pushed each other to become better – and not only that, but attitude-wise it was great having Phil around as well. He's far from the 'Uh, I guess I'll do another record' kind of [attitude]. He was and is still super gung-ho, and it's killer."

Flynn himself added: "We've known each other for over half our fucking lives, ever since we were young kids... he's a guitar player's guitar player. And having a guy like him in, it pushes me and it pushes him. Our styles already complemented each other, so there's just a chemistry there between us that was there back when we were in a band before."

Demmel also meshed quickly with the other members: he had known Duce from the Bay Area and had become friends with McClain some years before. As he explained, "I met Dave at a Torque show soon after he'd joined Machine Head. We were opening for Sacred Reich in Berkeley and he was seeing them for the first time with their new [drummer]. I introduced myself and, knowing that he was a [San Antonio] Spurs fan, started talking hoops with him. I walked away from that conversation the McClain fan I am today. I've been pretty blessed to have played in bands with killer drummers: Perry Strickland [from Vio-Lence] had the hands and the fills, while Mark Hernandez (Vio-Lence, Torque and Technocracy] had the meter and the consistency. Dave has it all, the complete drumming package. Amazing ideas, writes riffs and just plain looks cool! I look at his kit and can't imagine how he hits those things. His kick drums are a mile apart, his toms practically flat. He's a frickin' freak! Personally, I'm voting for a 10-minute solo on the next tour. He's been a great friend, the only guy in the band I can really talk sports with, and he's the only guy older than me in the band."

Looking back on his previous tenure with Machine Head – basically a fortnight in the summer of 2002 – Demmel commented, "They needed a fill-in guy. I came and offered my services. Hey man, you know, I've never been to Europe… I said, 'I'll go tour with you guys. I'll fill in, you know, just as a temporary guy'. I played two weeks of festival dates with them [and] got to play with Slayer, Bruce Dickinson and Halford and some other cool bands. I came back home, and I had some stuff at home that I couldn't deny – I was married, basically. And uh, things changed [Demmel and his wife divorced] and I offered my services to the band and hooked up with them in 2003."

He announced his move to Machine Head from Vio-Lence with a statement that ran, "I'm a firm believer that things, good or bad, happen for a reason. I can't control what has happened the past year or so, only deal with it the best way I can. Ever since my fourth-grade talent show, when I performed the song 'Convoy' behind a cardboard 18-wheeler, I've known what I wanted to do. Going from tennis racket guitars and putting on my own Kiss concerts in the backyard, and my first original band On Parole (with [later Exodus singer] Zet [Steve 'Zetro' Souza]), to signing a deal with Mechanic/MCA and recording my first album at 21. Touring with my bros, losing drums off the roof of the van, wiping boogers on the ceiling, meeting the coolest people and tearing shit up with one of the best live bands on earth, I've known what I was born to do. So that being said… it's simply time for me step away from the band that has been my baby for the past 18 years. There's nothing I would love more than to be able to make Vio into a functioning, working band. But damn it, everyone went and grew up. Sean, Troy, Perry and Deen, thank you all for understanding and giving me your blessing. It's been my pleasure these past two years reinventing what we've had. No one person is Vio-Lence. I wish you all the best… I fully appreciate all the kind words I've received from everyone. I've been truly blessed with a lot of supporting friends, which all of you are."

Demmel's other band, a group called Technocracy, called it a day at around the same time, although they emphasised that this was not because of his move to a larger band. "Some of you might be thinking that the reason behind this decision is Phil joining Machine Head," bassist Chris Addison (not to be confused with the British comedian of the same name) wrote on the band's web site. "Well, it's not. Phil promised us that as long as Technocracy was an active band, it would be his priority. He kept that promise, and not once did he ever lead us to think otherwise. The fact of the matter is that we burnt out long before Phil ever made that choice. We worked our asses off these past few years. When you work that long and hard at something so passionately, with minimal results, it can really beat you down. Just when we were starting to break through, the economy took a shit, and we suffered. We're not alone either. Look around."

Demmel recalled that Vio-Lence had never really recovered from their decision to fire Debbie Abono as manager back in the Eighties. Furthermore, certain members of the group had gained a reputation for being troublemakers: as he related to Tom Trakas,

"We got into a fight at Foundations Forum. Perry [Strickland] and Sean [Killian] beat the living shit out of [the late singer] Shannon Hoon from Blind Melon. It was so fucking funny! Shannon and his buddies were there and they talked shit to some chick Sean was with. And Sean just started kicking his ass in the pool room, and we just death-patrolled them, there was like five of them and like 10 of us. I tried to stay out of it, because of all the business [dealings which he handled], I had a very good reputation with a lot of people and I didn't want to be a part of that unless I had to. I just stood near and made sure this one guy didn't jump in. Perry had this guy in a headlock and was kicking another guy in the face, and Sean's just kicking the shit out of Shannon – and this is happening at Foundations Forum! Everyone in the industry or business was there, and everyone gets word that Vio-Lence are starting fights and all that. We brought it all on ourselves, man."

While Demmel was delighted to be on board (as he said, "There's always been a chemistry between me and Robb, and with the rest of the band as well. Robb and I grew up playing guitar together, you know, we learned from each other and we're so compatible and similar in our styles that we draw off each other's strength. It's a brotherhood, I'd say") he knew perfectly well that Machine Head were in the most difficult spot of their careers at the point when he joined them. Music is the force that drives him ("I'm not really in this for the business, you know, I'm in it to make music and enjoy myself... It's all about the music and jamming. A very small part of it is business. There weren't a lot of lawyers involved at all. There was an agreement between me and the whole band, not just Robb, and that was it") but on his arrival in the band, he could see that pretty much everything to do with Machine Head was in flux.

"Before I joined they had a meeting," he said. "Everybody was pretty upset with each other. I think it was Dave who just said,

'You know what? We're a metal band. Let's be in a metal band and write songs for us. Even what we're doing now, we're writing for our label. Let's do it for us.' That kind of turned everybody into like, 'Yeah, that's what we need to do'. Every label they were speaking to wanted... the radio single. That's just not what this band is about. They just got to thinking, 'Well, maybe if we write the one single and then just have the rest of the album this way, maybe that's the lesser of two evils. Or we can just not be signed'."

"The momentum definitely wasn't there," he added. "They were on the outs with the label. The album sold well, but it was their lowest-selling to date. The fans have always really been there. It's not really reflective in the album sales, but the way they tour they draw some of the most dedicated fans. It definitely was very transitional."

The new songs, many of which had been written before Demmel's arrival, continued to take shape, propelled in part by McClain's contributions on guitar. "I'm just kind of a riff-writer," said the drummer. "We didn't have another songwriter in the band [until Demmel was recruited], so I started writing, if for nothing else to help Robb out a bit. So I just started writing as much as I could and would record things: even if I hated something, I'd still turn it over to Robb. He'd listen to it, and liked a lot of things and changed up a lot of things. So a lot of it was shitty, a lot of it was cool, and most of all a lot of it spawned other ideas."

Keeping true to their oft-stated statement that the fans were their lifeblood, Machine Head asked their fanbase at around this time to choose some cover songs for them to record. Nominations flooded the website, and from these the band chose a short list of 10 of the most interesting possibilities. An online vote was taken and three final choices were made – Faith No More's 'Jizzlobber', Exodus's 'Toxic Waltz' and Metallica's 'Battery'. All three were classics by San Francisco-based acts and had been recorded at a time when life must have been rather simpler for the Machine Head members, which might explain some of their appeal. The Metallica cover in particular was astounding, showcasing a faster, heavier version of the original epic tune. Point your mouse at the brief documentary on Youtube which follows its making: the playing speed and precision of all the musicians is a lesson to any aspiring metaller. Adam Duce, usually the least vocal member of Machine Head, delivered a bass part comprising lightning-fast, razor-precise picking, one of the trademarks of his technique.

In fact, Duce was going through something of a personal transformation at the time. Having spent years as one of the band's most dedicated after-hours party animals, he had decided to quit the booze on a permanent basis – a major decision for someone who spends his professional life in a tour bus. As he told the author in a 2008 interview, "I haven't been drinking for about five years at this point. Remember, we came out with *Burn My Eyes* and had this amazing success right off the bat when we were pretty much kids. We were like, what – you want my autograph? It's kind of an overwhelming feeling, and you don't really know how to act because you've never been prepared for it. And you end up partying a lot, and you end up acting like an asshole..."

Asked what had prompted him to quit the demon drink, Duce explained: "My last drink was a fifth [750ml, a standard-sized bottle] of Captain Morgan in under two minutes. I didn't throw up. I shit my pants, but I didn't throw up. I went through a four-hour hallucination, where I was arguing with some fat guy in a suit in a high-rise building. In reality I was walking around my girlfriend's ground-floor apartment, spitting on the walls and arguing with someone that wasn't there. And I woke up out of this hallucination, walking around and talking – and when I realised where I was at, I was like, oh my God, what was I just saying? Then I remembered the whole thing – even the view out of the high-rise building. I analysed that over the next couple of days, and I realised that I could be in a lot of trouble for something I don't even remember, with that kind of behaviour. I also thought that I wasn't having any more fun with it, and I was done. Just like that, the decision was made, and I stopped."

Duce doesn't attend AA meetings, saying: "I don't believe in that shit. I mean, I don't want to slag it, because I know a lot of people get help from it, but it's not for me. I see it more as a twisted pick-up scene, and I don't even want to go there. I don't need that. I have a higher power that lives inside of me that I can rely on, I don't need somebody to tell me about it at a meeting."

Asked if it's difficult to abstain when on tour, where the whole point is to party irresponsibly after shows, and he chuckled: "Well, the first 10 years was kind of like that! But it gets old, like anything that you do too much. For me, when I made that decision, it was black and white. It was on or off. I still have fun partying with these guys, and I don't even miss the alcohol not being in my system. I used to have non-alcoholic beers on the rider, but I can have just as much fun with a Diet Coke. I have fun with everybody as long as they're having fun, but when they start to turn stupid, then I go to bed! It's all good. I don't miss it at all. All of a sudden, everything just lined up and made perfect sense – I was like, it's over now. I've always been an all-or-nothing kind of guy and that's where it's always been. I went for all, and all didn't work. So nothing is good for me."

Fortunately for Duce, a self-confessed adrenaline addict who enjoys skydiving and dirt-biking in his downtime, the rush of endorphins delivered by playing metal shows never dries up. "That never stops," he confirmed. "You finish the show at 11 o'clock and the adrenaline keeps you going until the sun comes up. There's no other feeling like it."

Perhaps this, among many other factors, explains the amped-up nature of the new songs which Machine Head wrote in 2003. The arrival of Demmel, Duce's newfound sobriety, a determination to prove their doubters wrong – all these elements helped to make Machine Head's fifth studio album something of a milestone. As Flynn explained to a *Terrorizer* writer at the time, "We've definitely got a fire up our ass. I'm not going to say it's the heaviest thing we've ever done. It's not heavier than *Burn My Eyes* and I want to make that clear. I don't want to mislead anybody, because some people in the past did. It's not fair to our fans. But do I think it's the best stuff we've ever done? Yes, I do. Is it heavy? It's fucking heavy as shit! We've moved territory and expanded our horizons and we're happy with what we've done. For us, the goal is to take all the elements and meld them together. But there's a couple of songs on here that are full-on, rip-your-head-off-and-shit-down-your-throat songs."

While all this was happening, a feud between Flynn and Slayer guitarist Kerry King was ongoing. This has been written about so many times, and occupied so many column inches in the online and print media, that it's hardly worth revisiting in any depth here, especially since this book is focused on Machine Head's music. In brief, it appears that Flynn reacted badly to some negative comments which King had made about Machine Head's recent music, and a series of insults were subsequently exchanged in the press.

Chronologically speaking, we had Flynn saying on June 20, 2002: "The other day, someone asked me what I think of Kerry King from Slayer always trashing Machine Head and me. You want to know what I think? I think the guy's a jerk. I think the guy's a lard ass. I think the guy's eaten so many cheeseburgers lately his brain is starting to clog up, and he can't think straight any more. And, I think it's really hard to get offended when the guy who's talking trash about you looks like Right Said Fred with a beard, and wears ass-less leather chaps... Where I live in San Francisco, that'd be Kerry Queen."

The following month King shrugged this off, saying: "I don't have a problem with Robb. Let him talk some more if he's got stupid shit like that to say. He'll bury himself. But if I was a cartoon character, I'd probably put a fucking grenade in his gut" – adding, a month later still, "The last time our bands went out together was a Japanese festival last summer. I don't remember us having bad blood at the time... I don't mouth off about Machine Head. If somebody asks me if I like their last record, I say, 'No, I don't like the record'. But that's not slamming anybody. The first Machine Head record is one of my favourite records. What they've done ever since... I couldn't give a fuck about. It's my opinion. If he's so fragile that that was painful, sorry dude, you're in the wrong business." This went on, with rounds exchanged every now and then, for a few more years. When this was finally resolved, as we'll see, the feud seemed deeply petty with hindsight.

But in June 2003, Machine Head had more important things on their minds, laying down tracks for the new album, to be titled *Through The Ashes Of Empires* and set for release outside America only. Flynn was producing the album this time, a decision reflecting the maturity of the group and the musicians' confidence in their own vision. Which band needs an expensive outside producer to come in and dictate terms after trials such as the ones which Machine Head had endured?

Flynn explained, "I had produced the band's demos since 1996. We looked at this as a glorified demo. We tried to get other people to do it and they just weren't available. The main guy we usually use... was working with Funeral For A Friend and their sessions had gone way overtime. We started talking to people we really didn't know and we didn't really trust. They wanted to charge us quite a bit of money for not really anything, because we knew what we wanted."

The recording itself was done with the aim in mind of capturing the soul of the music, he said. "We wanted to create some great music and capture it. It's very popular right now to record everything to a click track and then go in and fix everything. It's very perfect. Everything is perfect. But you get to the point where you're just cut-and-pasting guitar riffs, cut-and-pasting drum beats, and you're sampling everything. It's almost like it really isn't even music anymore. Our trip was that we just wanted four guys playing music. We recorded it to Pro-Tools and whatnot because it's most cost-effective. We went in there and if we had to play it, we had to play it. There was no cutting and pasting. It was definitely our M.O. We wanted to make a heavy, musical, frightening record."

Flynn's own role was to gather the disparate talents within the band, he added. "[McClain] wrote a bunch of stuff for the record, all the real kind of key songs… Phil, the guitar player, he writes stuff. We all kind of combine it. Adam helps me out a little bit with the lyrics. I write the songs on my own and kind of bring them into the whole thing. I'm the co-ordinator of the whole thing. I do a lot of the final arrangements. I think my role is to take a bunch of good ideas and make it one great idea."

Against all expectations, all these goals were achieved. When *Through The Ashes Of Empires* was released on October 27, the critical reaction was almost universally strong. As a statement of intent, the album was Machine Head's strongest and most cohesive collection of songs since *Burn My Eyes*. The key impressions left on the listener were a newfound strength and confidence that seared through the songs, which sounded broader and deeper thanks to the band's all-out embrace of the thrash metal and straightforward heavy metal influences that had suffused their earliest work.

Nowhere was this more evident than in the opening track and lead single, 'Imperium', an epic moshpit anthem that remains a set staple to this day. The fast section towards the song's end is melodic thrash at its finest. Other high points include the monstrous opening riffs and ice-cold melodies of 'Elegy', the soaring, Steve Vai-style guitar solo in the middle of 'In The Presence Of My Enemies' and the immense 'Descend The Shades Of Night', which closes the album. This song, with its epic dimensions and exploration of new sonic territories, points directly at the ethos behind many of the songs on Machine Head's later albums.

Extrapolate this further and it becomes clear that from *Through The Ashes Of Empires* onward, the old rappin', frontin', leisurewear-sportin' Machine Head was dead and gone. The band that was now poised to regain a place at the top of the metal scene was a completely different beast, with a new sound based on old influences, a new agenda and a new path into the future.

Not that anything is ever completely easy for Machine Head. A voice of dissent amid the generally positive reviews of *Through The Ashes Of Empires* came from the British edition of *Kerrang!* magazine, which called it "a directionless mess of an album", and labelled it "the sonic equivalent of eating last night's delivery pizza, reheated today". Unsurprisingly given that *Kerrang!* was sponsoring some forthcoming UK dates, Machine Head were quick to pick up on the poor review, stating: "The review comes at a time when the international press is absolutely raving about Machine Head's *Through The Ashes Of Empires*, calling it a return to form, with every single major metal magazine in the UK and Europe decidedly praising the record, with even the Australian edition of *Kerrang!* handing out a staggering 5-K review... While we are all a bit shocked, surprised and disappointed that this particular *Kerrang!* journalist has decided to attack us with such belligerence, we have many friends, supporters, and allies within the *Kerrang!* organization. *Kerrang!* have been champions of this band... and as music fans, we have been avid supporters of the magazine since its early days. While some within our own organisation feel it would be completely justified, Machine Head have no intention whatsoever of severing *Kerrang!*'s involvement in our UK tour dates over something as petty and trivial as this. We hope that we can sit down soon, have a beer, a good laugh, and put this all behind the both of us."

The Through The Ashes Of Europe tour kicked off in October and raged through the usual Machine Head heartlands – Ireland, France, Spain, Portugal, Italy, Switzerland, Germany, Scandinavia and beyond – with particular focus on the UK, where the local branch of Roadrunner had done sterling work in promoting the album. Flynn, in particular, was becoming known as an Anglophile, taking time out to visit curry restaurants in London and generally making himself at home with British culture: an intense relationship between Machine Head and their UK fans had been in place since the Nineties, for reasons that can only be speculated upon. Let's just pat ourselves on the back and say that we Brits invented metal and, therefore, we know it when we see it, eh?

It came as a pleasant surprise, not to mention a massive sense of vindication, when Roadrunner USA re-signed Machine Head for the North American release of *Through The Ashes Of Empires* in February 2004, aiming for an April release. "We previously had a deal with the band that was only for a European/Japanese/Australian release of the new CD," the label's statement read. "But now, *now* is [the] time for the US to hear the new Machine Head... Currently, we are looking at an April 20 release of the CD. Oh, and here is something that doesn't happen every day – bonus tracks included on initial release. Usually territories abroad get the CDs with bonus tracks... but due to this unique situation, the

US CD release of this [album] will have bonus tracks. The band should be heading into the studio at some point in the coming couple of weeks to record two new tracks for this release (one original, one most likely being a cover)."

"We were unsigned, basically, for about a year," reflected Flynn later. "In that year we started writing as a three-piece, and started asking ourselves a lot of 'Why are we doing this?' questions, and 'What are we trying to get out of this?' At the end of the day it just became about creating music, and not being concerned about if it was going to get airplay, or if it was going to be whatever, but just about writing what we felt were great, heavy songs. If they were eight minutes and had 15 changes in them, you know, as long as we were still having fun with it, and as long as it was a good song still, we were like, 'Cool'."

Flynn differed from Kontos regarding the Roadrunner deal but revealed that the new deal was much better than the previous agreement. "We're the only band to part ways with Roadrunner and be re-signed to [the label] in the 25-year history of Roadrunner!" he laughed. "When we started with Roadrunner, we signed one of those horrible deals that bands sign: we had to give them all of our publishing, [and] all of our merchandising, you know? It wasn't a very fair deal, but when we finally came back to Roadrunner, it was under a lot more artist-friendly parameters. We own our masters, all of our publishing, all of our merchandising, how we present ourselves on the record, in the videos, who produces the records, the artwork that goes on the record – everything about the band is completely in our control."

The epic nature of the new songs was a factor in the original split, he added: "We had always intended to re-sign with Roadrunner in Europe, because we'd always had a good relationship with them. So we did that, and at the same time the American deal was supposed to happen, but then at the last minute they wanted to hear what we were doing. So we sent them some stuff and we're like, 'Yeah, the new songs are like six and eight minutes long, and the vocals don't even start until like three minutes in', and they're like, 'Whoa, hey, we don't know what to do with this'. And at that time, they didn't. So they ended up not doing that, and then the record came out over in Europe and it did just beyond what anybody could imagine it would do... and so they were like, 'Wow, maybe there is something here', and they reconsidered. We had a lot of offers on the table at that point, from American labels. But they came in and had the biggest belief in the band, and kind of understood where we were coming from, so we ended up going with them again."

"No-one in the industry gave a shit if we lived or died," concluded Flynn. "We just sat there and basically wrote a record for ourselves. And, you know, we're glad that we stuck with our guns and we're glad that things worked out the way that they did. Roadrunner, especially now here in the US, is kicking ass, so it's cool for us. The record came in at number 88, sold 11,000 records in its first week... the video [for 'Imperium'] didn't get played until the first week of release, the record has been out for six months for import and download. The fact that it did that many numbers was a miracle. It was fucking amazing that it did that. We've got to thank our street team, we've got to thank the killer Machine Head fans that we have."

While on tour on the USA in the spring of 2004, Phil Demmel added: "We're really happy with [Roadrunner USA] – we've kind of developed a better working relationship. So we kind of resolved our problems from the past... In America, they have the option for the next [album]. So we just have this one album deal with an option for the next, so we'll see – we're still touring on this one. We had a really good first month. And we have to get out and work for it on the road. That's what we're doing. Down on the pavement." He added with some amusement that his on–the–road

120

lifestyle was a little different to the all-out partying which he'd witnessed with Vio-Lence: "Everybody's married, nobody does drugs, we only drink a little. Everybody's grown-up and taking care of business. The biggest difference now is that I actually get to tour in a bus. And I get my own hotel room. Before I was sharing rooms. Yeah, I'm living large!"

A headline US tour called the 'Weapons Of Mass Destruction' jaunt followed. This time Machine Head were supported by God Forbid, 36 Crazyfists and Arch Enemy, and some sparring occurred between the last of these and the headliners when Arch Enemy decided to pull out. Initially it was good-humoured, as Machine Head's statement shows: "In what came as a complete shock to the Machine Head camp, perennial support act Arch Enemy have informed headliners Machine Head that they must pull out of the entire Weapons Of Mass Destruction tour because singer Angela Gossow broke a fingernail which had recently been through a vigorous French manicure... The members of Machine Head instinctively rushed to her aid, offering her mouth-to-mouth resuscitation, after which the ever-benevolent MH boys granted the openers permission to miss a handful of shows while she recovered from what the metal diva claimed was 'an extremely painful broken nail'. Unfortunately, word came from their management and booking agent today that the nail would need emergency manicuring and that only the best French manicurist in all of Sweden could perform the repair, thus resulting in the band's inability to complete the entire remainder of the tour."

It got a little more serious when Flynn said, in an interview with *The Metal Show* in May, "It's unfortunate that they've decided to do things the way that they have. They kind of made up a bunch of excuses about going out, you know, because [Gossow] couldn't get her visa... You know, whatever. If you buy that, I've got a bridge in Brooklyn I can sell you too. The thing is that they needed this tour more than we needed them, you know. No-one's asked for their money back, so... it's unfortunate that they had to go the whole lying route, but whatever. No-one's hurting from it."

The same month, Machine Head were obliged to cancel a show in Columbus, Ohio, when Flynn lost his voice, which might not have become relevant to the Arch Enemy issue had Angela Gossow not commented in a later interview with Holland's *Lords Of Metal* webzine, "I was surprised to see how unprofessionally Machine Head handled the incident. It was not me who actually stopped the tour, but another person who had a big problem in the band, and they obviously didn't have enough respect to let it go and say they were sorry. We were sorry and said so, it was very shitty for both bands. They lost some people coming to the shows and it sucked for us because we lost a hell [of a] lot of money, we had to pay for the tour bus that whole tour, you know. At the end of the day it is a business and you might meet that band you are talking shit about again. It always comes back to you. Rob Flynn actually lost his voice later that tour, ha ha ha."

Flynn reacted instantly, telling Blabbermouth: "It's funny that Mrs Amott [Gossow] brings this up now, after six months of silence about it. We were willing to let it drift away. We made our jokes about it, and left it at humour. But now, *we* handled things 'unprofessionally?' Now she's talking about my throat going out (for one show) as things coming back to haunt us? Now, let's talk about unprofessional. Arch Enemy asked us to go along with their 'work visa' excuse. We did. They then told us they'd be missing Philly and New York, but to keep going along with the work visa excuse. We did. The next day at Metalfest, their bassist and guitarist both confirmed they'd be starting the tour, but were very evasive. Then, after tracking down their manager, he gave us 'his word' that they would be doing the tour. The next day they had their booking agent call our tour manager to tell us they were cancelling 'the entire tour' because she had blown out her voice. This wasn't their manager calling our manager, which would have been proper etiquette… no, the first official 'statement' we got from your camp was your ham-fisted 'apology' to your fans on your fucking website, and that didn't even give anyone an explanation… Yes, Mrs Amott, bands do cross paths, and things do come back to haunt you, and one day, your four boys are going to pay for your big fucking mouth."

Capitalising on the success of *Through The Ashes Of Empires*, Machine Head stormed repeatedly through Europe and America for the rest of 2004, with high points including a slot at the UK's Download festival in June, a second Roadrage tour alongside Chimaira, and – most of all – the arrival of Robb and Genevra Flynn's first child. Their son Zander was born on June 21 and, although the mission of this book isn't to dig into the band-members' personal lives, fatherhood made an impact on Flynn (as it does on all right-thinking men) that was both profound and enduring. "I still struggle to wonder how I am going to explain my past to my kids when they are old enough to understand," he pondered, as fathers since time immemorial have done. "What am I going to say? Daddy was an asshole, so don't be an asshole. I don't want them to see their father in that way. I don't want them to hear all the swearing I'm doing now at the age they are at. Even as out-there in my beliefs as I am, I still have some of those very strong and simple desires for my children as they are now."

As he told the Earth Dog website, "Having a kid definitely makes you feel more like a kid again. You can act like a full-blown dork, and the more you do, the more they love it. Kids don't judge you, there's no scepticism, just trust, and love. A lot of times Machine Head can be an all-consuming beast. I could spend every second of every day doing and delegating things that need to be done for Machine Head. But in the end, it's no way to live, man. At least for me, I've found that if I don't have some other side to my life, I begin to resent Machine Head. My son is that other side. My wife and I also took up wakeboarding four years ago, and it was one of the best hobbies I could ever take up. You go to the lake, summertime, your friends, on the boat, a bunch of beer, the water, blasting some tunes, it fucking rules! We go group camping quite a bit as well… get that 7 a.m. wakeboard run in, when the water is glass. It's the best way to shake off the camping hangover too. Already took my kid to the lake, and went wakeboarding with him on the boat, he loved it."

In retrospect, then, 2004 was a year of relationships: new ones for Flynn as a parent, renewed ones such as the partnership between Machine Head and Roadrunner, and damaged ones such as the rift with Arch Enemy. Additionally, Flynn's issues with Kerry King were still unresolved, although to his immense credit the Machine Head singer had tried his best to draw a line beneath them by offering King an apology and a handshake in the backstage area of a venue.

Tragically, one relationship ended permanently on December 8 when Machine Head's old touring buddy 'Dimebag' Darrell Abbott, ex of Pantera and latterly of Damageplan, was murdered onstage at an Ohio venue by a psychotic fan called Nathan Gale. This terrible event, dubbed 'metal's 9/11' by various media commentators, deprived the scene of one of its few genuinely vivid characters. Flynn wrote a heartbroken entry on his personal blog, recalling the times that he had spent with Dimebag and how glad he was that he had taken the opportunity a few months beforehand to tell the slain guitarist how much of an inspiration he had been to Machine Head.

Difficult days, then. Better, albeit equally turbulent, times lay ahead.

Chapter 7

2005–2007

By 2005, Machine Head were far from millionaires, but the days of living on pennies were long gone. Asked if it was still tough to make a living, Robb Flynn reasoned with commendable honesty: "Well, I haven't had to work a regular job for 10 years now, though for the first four years of that, I lived well below the poverty level. But I agree that most people have no idea how little the artist actually makes. I think a lot of artists like to brag about how much they got 'signed for', which doesn't mean a dime if it went into their pocket, but makes it sound like a big deal. It also gives the perception, untruthfully, that they're rich, which to some people is impressive, I guess. Myself, I have a modest lifestyle, I own a house, a wakeboarding boat, a 4 Runner [a Toyota SUV], money in the bank, but again, it's pretty modest."

Ask yourself if you would put yourself through the lifestyle that Machine Head had endured for so long to reach this comfortable, but far from affluent, level, as they approached their forties. You probably wouldn't. I certainly wouldn't. These musicians deserve your respect, if that point hasn't been demonstrated thoroughly enough already.

The tribulations which Machine Head had been through were depicted in painful detail on a documentary, *The Making Of Through The Ashes Of Empires*, which appeared on the band's first DVD, *Elegies*, released on October 11. While most of the content was devoted to live footage filmed at a London show in 2004, this behind-the-scenes material attracted a lot of attention for its in-depth portrayal of how Demmel came to join the band, and the band's on-off-on relationship with Roadrunner USA. "It was a bad time for sure," said Dave McClain, interviewed by Tom Trakas of *Midwest Metal*, "but being able to look back on it now is a good feeling. A good feeling of 'Look what we went through', and what we did to survive. As Machine Head, we seem to go through some fucked-up shit: there's times it feels like, every record we do, we have things to get through. So watching the making-of [footage] and talking about that time, I'll say it again: everything happens for a reason. And it's up to the person going through the hard times to use that reason as a positive, or let it continue to be detrimental."

"For the four of us, it's a tough section to watch," Flynn explained. "It's brutally honest, with moments that I watch and I just cringe. It's tough… but we've always maintained an extra honest relationship with our fans. We wanted to have something we felt represented the band, that captured the band the right way. If we do something, it has to be done right. We want to be able to stand behind the things we put out. If we can't, we just don't put it out."

Vindication for the superior quality of *Through The Ashes Of Empires* came in the form of several high-profile tours, beginning this year and – apart from some breaks here and there – continuing more or less to the time of writing in 2012. The album had re-established Machine Head with a vengeance: Flynn was amused by the hypocritical reactions of some of the record companies who had refused it. "We were basically rejected by every label in the business. Thirty here in the States rejected us. For a while there, it looked like we would never be a band again," he said. "Four months later, a lot of the labels that passed on us were like, 'Hey. What's going on? That record is so good'. And I'm like, 'The one we sent you four months ago? Yeah, it is'."

In May and June, Machine Head toured the USA in support of Lamb Of God, who had come from apparently nowhere in the previous few years to dominate the modern American metal scene. European festival dates included a triumphant closing slot on the True Metal stage at the Wacken Open Air event in Germany – in front of their biggest headlining crowd to date, of no fewer than 40,000 headbangers.

The band's upward trajectory continued when Flynn was asked by Roadrunner to be one of four 'team captains' tasked with recording an album in honour of the label's 25th year in business. The album, titled *The All-Star Sessions* and released under the name Roadrunner United in October, gathered a stellar cast of musicians either currently or previously signed to the label: Flynn composed, produced and played guitar on four songs: 'The Rich Man', 'Independent (Voice Of The Voiceless)', 'Army Of The Sun' and 'The Dagger'. This involved a collaboration with the Canadian guitarist Jeff Waters of the band Annihilator, one of the most accomplished guitarists on the planet: some amusing interplay between the two shredders can be seen on a bonus DVD that accompanies *The All-Star Sessions*. "We never toured with Annihilator," said Flynn. "That was a little before our time. I actually met [Waters] while coming home from England. This guy standing in front of me at customs was wearing an Annihilator shirt, which is really rare. You just don't see it coming to America, so I was just like, 'Are you in Annihilator?' and he was like,

'Yeah, Robert Flynn?' And I was like 'Yeah,' and we just hit it off from there."

One of the Roadrunner United songs, 'Independent (Voice Of The Voiceless)', was based on an internet report that Flynn would use later, and to more shocking effect. "The whole concept of that song is loosely based around 'Dimebag' Darrell," he said. "Around the time of his death, this guy named William Grim put out an article on this extremely conservative website called *The Iconoclast* entitled 'RIP Dimebag Abbott And Good Riddance'. It basically called him a scumbag that brought this on himself. It was pretty vile and it was published the day after his murder. I copied it, and sent it to [Soulfly singer and fellow Roadrunner signing] Max Cavalera, who ended up singing on the track. So the topic of the song is a response to that, and [the final] three-part guitar harmony was just going for this big, epic guitar-oriented outro piece with piano and strings as a kind of tribute to him." A concert featuring many of the musicians from the album took place in New York in December 2005: Flynn and Duce both participated alongside members of Slipknot, Killswitch Engage, Trivium, Sepultura, Biohazard, Deicide and other bands. A DVD of the event appeared three years later.

All this activity didn't disguise the fact that Machine Head needed to come back after *Through The Ashes Of Empires* with an equally good, or better, album – or be faced with accusations that *Through...* had been a lucky fluke and that, in reality, the band was still mired in *Supercharger* territory. When the announcement came in August 2006, therefore, that a new album titled *The Blackening* would appear the following spring, public and critical interest was immediately piqued.

In between recording sessions between August and November, as with *Through...* executed at Sharkbite Studios in Oakland with Flynn as producer, the band-members popped up in interviews here and there, dropping hints about the new music. "It's a one-room studio," said McClain. "A band we know out here called Unjust told us about it. We wanted to record at home – before we'd always gone to LA to record, and there's always those outside influences. You know, at night you go to the Rainbow, and in the day you've got record company people coming over to the studio… it was awesome to have the studio literally 10 minutes from my house this time. We demo a lot of stuff in our practice room anyway, so by the time we get to the studio Robb already knows in his head how he wants the album to sound. He's the guy who has the whole crazy organisation thing down and the whole vision."

Asked about the songwriting, Flynn explained: "There's no grand vision, that's for sure! Wouldn't it be awesome to just sit here and say, 'Yes, I have this grand vision of a 10-minute song and here it is'. But it doesn't work like that. Basically it just builds, and we'll be in the rehearsal room and be totally Beavis and Butthead… 'Yes! that part rules, no, that part sucks'. It's as simple as that, kind of. After doing this for so long, we've also learned that initial impressions are not always going to be [lasting] impressions. There's some stuff on the album that I didn't like at all when it was first written, but that can change maybe as you get more familiar with it, or put something in front of or behind it."

A recurring theme was that the new songs would be longer than usual, reflecting the lessons which Machine Head had learned about the pitfalls of writing songs of radio-formatted length – in other words, about four minutes in duration. "They're long," said Flynn, "but in a lot of ways there's still a conventional song structure. It's still very much like a pop song in the classic sense of what a pop song is, where there's a verse, bridge, chorus et cetera. With us there's a lot of other parts and transitions, so instead of going back to what we did earlier in the song we try to interject something new. But while building the song we'll be in the practice room name-dropping bands left and right, like, 'We need a Judas Priest part here or an Alice In Chains part there,' and it usually doesn't work, but it gets us trying different things and seeing what works."

Fortunately, Flynn knew that it isn't enough just to write long songs: they have to engage the listener's attention too. "When you're writing a 10-minute song, for me the hardest challenge for me is to not make it all sound the same," he said. "You've got to add so many things in there just to break up all the parts: if not, it all starts to blur into one thing. I think if I have any songs like that, it's forced us down that road even more, like we have to challenge ourselves to mix things up. We wrote 26 songs for the album: some of them were half songs but we narrowed it down to the eight, because these were the eight that seemed like they had the best ups and downs. They ended the strongest, they seemed like they all went together. As a musician, it was cool to have so much variety on a record. I listened to it and was like, 'Jesus'. We would never have done some of this stuff like six, seven years ago. We never would have done it, and it's cool we're still evolving! We never really tried to make the same record twice and we've always tried to bring in new things, just to keep ourselves excited about doing this and continuing to do this."

The Blackening was mixed by the ever-reliable Colin Richardson, who wrote on his blog: "We are all happy with how the mix turned out and can't wait for you to hear it… Of course, the entire album features the most underrated drummer in metal – Dave McClain. He has really raised the bar on this album." This merely added to the expectation that *The Blackening* would be either the album that truly brought Machine Head back to the top of the metal tree… or demoted them to the position they had occupied five years previously.

January 2007 was the calm before the storm, although the arrival of Flynn's second child, Wyatt, doubtless caused a few sleepless nights. In comparison, the leaking of *The Blackening* by some unnamed journalist of erratic moral compass was received with relative equanimity by the band, not least Adam Duce. As the bassist told the author: "I'm actually looking at that as a good thing, because I'm so proud of it. I'm feeling it so much that I think it can only help us. It's an unmastered version, but that version sounds great! But I expect journalists to do what they say they're going to do, and not turn around and do that... I kind of feel that the one who leaked it must be jealous of our situation, jealous that the best job they could get in the music business is writing about what other people do – and he's bitter. And he's got a hard-on for us, so when we say don't leak it, he says well here you go – it's on the internet now, what are you going to do? All I can say is, it's probably going to help us anyway – fuck off! We'll find out who it was, for sure. We'll just turn that information over to the Hell's Angels and they'll take care of it. Ha ha ha ha! I'm just kidding..."

Elsewhere, Phil Demmel was equally sanguine, commenting: "I look at it like this. There are going to be those kids and people that are not going to buy CDs anyway. They are doing us a service by going, 'Hey, this album is great'. They are able to test-drive it and give us a good review. You got to have a good record for it to sell anyways. This is actually serving as a vehicle for us. There's a huge buzz off of this leakage of the record. Those kids aren't going to buy it anyway, but hopefully they will come to the show or they'll buy a T-shirt."

Flynn added: "It was leaked by an American journalist, unfortunately, who got an advance of the CD and who wanted to be a jerk and put it up there. You know, it's unfortunate that had to happen, but at the same time, it's really creating an unbelievable buzz on the record and on the band. And nothing like we ever had before, you know. It's pretty amazing. I guess in the one sense, you know, it's pretty much inevitable that's it's going to happen with every record. And I guess it's a great equaliser, you know, it's leveled the playing field. There's internet street buzz versus record company hype, and if the hype matches up to the street buzz, then you're seeing a lot of bands selling a lot of records in the first week. If the street buzz does not match up to the record company hype, you're not seeing that big first week and that success. In some ways, it's definitely levelled out the playing field, and especially for a band that maybe doesn't have a very big record company behind them, that doesn't have a lot of push or whatever, they're getting a huge buzz on it."

Machine Head, Flynn explained, benefit from their fans in ways that other bands may not. "I think of other bands that definitely have something to worry about, but with us, our fans are very loyal and very dedicated and you know they will go out there and buy that record," he observed. "You know, they'll test drive it, but they'll go out and buy the record because they know, a band like Machine Head and a band that plays the type of music that we do, a very extreme form of music, for the most part isn't going to get played on most mainstream radio and won't get played on most mainstream video stations. You know, this is the way that we have to survive… We're given this platform because the beast is fed, and so they go out and support us and you know, it's cool. It's unfortunate, but it is what it is and there's other things to worry about."

Asked what fans should expect from *The Blackening*, Demmel explained that it contained songs which commented on social ills such as the current conflict in the Middle East. "The world is kind of a fucked-up place," he mused. "There's a lot of things going on right now. Robb was writing a lot of personal topics on the last couple of records. He wanted to bring it back to the first couple of records that had more social issues, so we're talking about the Christian right-wing coalition that's going on. It's hard for the four of us to agree on a certain subject, be it politics, religion, sports, whatever. There are a couple of things that we do agree on, and that is we are all against this war. So that is where a couple of the songs came from."

He added that the band was fully aware of the importance of the new album to Machine Head's career, saying: "Every CD that we're going to put out is kind of risky, because in this genre of music your next album could be your last album, depending on what it is, so you have to be absolutely correct and sure in what you're doing. Our previous record, *Through The Ashes Of Empires*, was awesome to us, and now we needed to do something that was gonna stand out above that. We took the approach of the same formula of writing, but we also wanted to make an epic, classic-sounding record."

When *The Blackening* appeared on March 27, the first thing the buyer noticed was its monochrome gothic artwork – a far cry from any of its predecessors. Big deal, you might think. In fact, the grim, medieval images encapsulated a new, and much darker view of life, as espoused by the songs themselves. Flynn put it best when he said: "*The Blackening* partially reflects my vision of the world. Often music is a reflection of the times, and during the writing of this album, that's what it felt like. I felt the world was literally blackening. The name itself summed up my feelings perfectly, and I think the artwork that we chose reflects the title. The cover is a very crude metal carving from the 1600s. Essentially images like the church [used] as propaganda… It was saying that these are the consequences for crimes against the church. They were a deterrent [stopping] people from doing these certain things."

He added: "The particular image that we chose is one of a skeleton king. He's sitting on top of a throne, and his throne is on a bed of skulls. One of his feet is on top of the world, and his other foot is on top of a sand timer. But the most telling part is the mirror that he holds up. Written on the mirror is 'The Mirror Which Flatters Not'. For all of us, when we saw that, it was a huge revelation. Here was this 400-year-old image that captured exactly what we all felt. This album – lyrically, musically and phonetically – is about holding up a mirror to myself, and not liking what I saw. It's also about holding up a mirror to you, along with society, and also not liking what I see."

Right from the off, *The Blackening* is an immense piece of work. Its first song, 'Clenching The Fists Of Dissent', is the most ambitious song which Machine Head had recorded in years, a 10-minute collage of atmospheric tension and murderously fast thrash metal. The impression left on the listener was that Flynn and his team had been hit by a tsunami of riff ideas and somehow managed to arrange them into an economy-sized song of enormous presence and power, a concept confirmed when Flynn commented, "Recording this was the challenge. Everything became so epic that everything else needed to become epic just to sound right. We have songs with 10 tracks of just snare drum. Just the beginning of 'Clenching The Fists Of Dissent', that acoustic intro, was cut with 84 different tracks. Mixing this record was hell… We tried editing 'Clenching…' and it was just wack. I mean, where do you start? You literally have to cut out half the song. It just didn't make sense as a song any more."

He continued, "If you look at a song like 'Clenching…' there's a good five minutes in the middle of the song where it goes in a bunch of different directions. We bring it back to the second verse and that goes to the build-up and ultimately goes into the chorus, as that's the part where I finally say 'clenching the fists of dissent'… so it takes a while to get there. As arcane as it sounds, it's just what feels right. We started writing that song in May of 2006 and I was still working on things up until November, I mean there was a day of drum tracks done and I was still trying different things, having Adam play six different bass-lines, getting rid of things that didn't fit, extending things that needed extending."

Lyrically, 'Clenching...' was the most specifically targeted Machine Head song in years, aiming its vitriol squarely at modern warfare, with topical references to oil making it clear that it referred to current events. Flynn told interviewer Tom Trakas that he'd done "a lot of thinking about 'Do I really want to go down this path?', 'Is something going to alienate people, what are people going to think?'... That's what I do at least, [I'm] not sure if it's the same for everyone. Oftentimes I write lyrics that are from the heart. Maybe it's something about my personal life, maybe something I'm pissed at. So yeah, I do think, 'Do I want to put this out there, do I want to say this?' With 'Clenching...', basically all four of us are just fucking angry about what we're seeing, and we never bought into what was being told to us. I brought it up to the guys, showed them the lyrics I had, let them read them and tell me what [they] think. Good, bad or whatever, because if we go ahead and use [the lyrics], we all have to be able to stand behind them."

'Beautiful Mourning' is next, a solid slab of metal that doesn't quite have the impact of the opening track but which contains a similarly impressive plethora of ideas, as well as a career-best performance from Dave McClain. As he told the author at the time, "There's this middle section to the song which is full-on Keith Moon. When we were writing this song and we got to this part, Phil said hey, 'What's Dave going to do on that part?' And I said, 'Whaddya mean, 'what's Dave going to do?' I'll show you what Dave's going to do!' They were picturing this regular beat and I was like, no way man, I'm going for a full-on Keith Moon part. I'm not even going to remember what I'm doing, I won't play the same thing twice. Just go crazy. I asked myself, what would Keith do here? Maybe I won't play as cool as him but I'll have that freedom. I'm always totally methodical, so this time I said to myself, just fucking do something! Just go crazy! But it's actually controlled craziness, because I'll probably do the same thing I did on the record when I play it live."

A highlight of the album, and possibly even its signature song, is the explosive 'Aesthetics Of Hate', based on the anti-'Dimebag' Darrell feature written on the *Iconoclast* website (long since offline) back in 2004. As McClain remembered, "Robb called me up one day when we were writing, and said hey, I wrote a song today – it's a thrashterpiece!", and indeed that's the best way to describe this exceptionally fast and enraged song. "The thrash beat is the thrash beat. It's full-on," noted McClain accurately. "At the end of each verse there's these superfast double-bass things going on. The middle lead section is totally crazy though, it's the classic guitar battle. I'm playing fills on my ride cymbal and stuff, which is a trick I stole from Deen Castronovo who used to be in Ozzy's band."

Asked about the song, Duce explained: "It's about anger and it's about an extreme sadness as well, about that fucking tragedy that happened. There was this writer on an internet magazine called *The Iconoclast*, who is probably not even worth mentioning at this point because he's probably done nothing ever since – and the day after Dimebag got murdered, he wrote this article basically saying how pathetic we all are for mourning this guy who was 'an untalented possessor of a guitar'. And he went on to slag Dime, not knowing anything about the guy's character, not knowing anything about how huge that kid's heart quality was, or anything about him – just slagging him, and slagging all of us for caring about him, and basically calling all of us ugly, filthy, bottom-of-the-barrel motherfuckers. He was unable to understand why the conservative right was unable to teach everybody that heavy metal music is just worthless garbage."

He added: "Everybody's entitled to their opinion, but that infuriated both Robb and myself, and we wrote the lyrics to that song as a partial tribute to Dime and a partial 'fuck you' to that guy. He was probably not even worth it, but you can feel the anger. It's there. And it made a great fucking song. He didn't know anything about this, all he knew was what he saw on the news or whatever – the vigil at the parking lot of the Alrosa Villa [the scene of Dimebag's murder] in Columbus – and so he slagged all the fans for how they looked. It was an attack on us worthy of that song."

Asked about Dimebag, Duce concluded: "I got to tell you man, that guy had a heart as big as all outside. He played the rock star thing to what he was expected to do, you know? He was expected to be a certain amount of over-the-top – and he played that shit to a T – but that guy was a genuine friend of people in general. He was a stand-up guy and I can't say enough about him. He was the real article."

Flynn, whose venom towards the idiot who wrote the original piece on Dimebag is clearly audible throughout 'Aesthetics Of Hate', added: "We've been criticised heavily in the conservative community for being the epitome of what [the writer was] talking about. He calls us Neanderthal, dumb and immature. Many people have criticised the lyrics to that song as immature. My response to that is that, yes, they're completely immature. That song is a fucking gigantic burst of Neanderthal anger. And I'll tell you this much, it felt really fucking good!"

The Blackening continues its rampage through 'Now I Lay Thee Down' (listen out for Duce's tapped bass part and the guitarists' volume swells) and 'Slanderous', which features McClain doing his best impression of a certain British drum legend. "This song is pretty standard triplet stuff like Nicko McBrain, with a middle section that is full-on Mercyful Fate," he said. "One thing I do a lot is kind of transform myself into other drummers, like 'Alright, I'm Nicko McBrain right now!' I think you have to do it sometimes."

While these are respectable songs, the album takes its next leap into spectacular territory with 'Halo', *The Blackening*'s most-remembered song alongside 'Aesthetics Of Hate'. "This was the one song that gave us the green light and told us where we were going to go in terms of timing our songs," said Flynn. "The three songs at the end of the album, they're all around 10 minutes long, and this was the first one where we noticed that we were only at the middle section and it was already four and a half minutes long. It was like, fuck it: if it works, it works!"

He added that the song had gone through a troubled development at demo stage before it made it into its finished form: "We had a version of 'Halo' [but] the chorus we had at the time was horrendous, just awful – it said something like 'I want your soul' and it was in a different key. It was so horrible, I'd listen to it and obsess on how much I hated it. But man, thinking of that time it was a weird period, we'd be writing things and we didn't exactly feel that good about things. I mean we had a few songs, a few riffs, a couple of half-done songs, but none of it was really rocking us, you know?"

'Halo' was one of those tricky songs that seemed to refuse to fall into shape, he told the author in an interview for *Total Guitar* magazine. "The funny thing is that when we wrote 'Halo', it was so ridiculously difficult to play that we joked that we'd never play it live. We were serious, dude! It was way too complicated for us. We'd jam 'Halo' as far as the end of the second chorus, and then it would always fall apart. We never knew where to go with it. For about six months, that song wasn't going anywhere for us, and as we got close to doing the record – three weeks from going into the studio – it still wasn't done. It was almost on the chopping block, but I finally wrote the end parts and Phil came up with the extended lead bit at the end, and then I stumbled upon the mellow part. I wanted to have this kind of Coldplay-ish part – that's what I called it! – and once that fell into place, everything else got done. I'm glad we stuck it out. I look back now and I think, 'Wow,

'Halo' is a killer song' but it only fell into place at the last minute. It makes you think that you should really hang on to ideas and not let them go."

Like 'Clenching The Fists Of Dissent', 'Halo' is an attack on the establishment, although this time it was the American church which appeared in Machine Head's crosshairs. "Here in America it was such a different landscape to what it is now," pondered Flynn. "The war had just kicked in, and all of us were really against it. The Christian right-wing extremists over here were really making a lot of headway: I'd just had my second kid, and I was thinking, 'Is this the future for my son?' 'Halo' was an attack on that."

The lyrical vitriol continued with 'Wolves', a furious celebration of energetic music. "I had gotten to bed around 1 a.m.," recalled Flynn, when asked by Tom Trakas about the song's lyrics, "and for some reason was totally awake at around 4 a.m. and was pretty pissed off about a bunch of shit. I decided to go and write the most venomous shit I could think about right now. So out of that came 'Unleashing wolves and carnage' and when it really started to come together, I looked at the lyrics and said to myself, 'This isn't about us, the band – it's about our fans'. This is about the carnage we see nightly as Machine Head, and in that one hour and a half, I pretty much wrote the rest of the song in this huge burst – and it really felt like the weight of the world coming off my shoulders."

While the lyrics came easily, getting the song down on a studio hard drive proved to be anything but. Flynn added: "It was incredibly tough: we double-track all the guitars on both sides, so that shit has got to be tight as hell, and those thrash riffs caused a lot of tracking and re-tracking and tuning and re-tuning... we were running a little slower than we wanted to, so that [pressure] was building, right? We realised just how much more had to be done, how much more layering of things, and really we had a lot more to do than we thought!"

The Blackening roars to a close with 'A Farewell To Arms', a melodic song that winds up this superior album with a dignified presence. "This song has some of the best melodies Robb's ever written," said McClain. "It was super-easy to do a drum pattern for this song because the melody line was so commercial – almost poppy. So I just played this poppy, heavy rhythm over it and it added so much to it."

The metal world was quick to embrace *The Blackening*, to the relief – and slight bemusement – of the band. Asked why the album was being so well-received by public and press alike, Flynn reasoned: "To tell you the truth, I'm not really sure. I can only speculate at this point. But I do believe the metal scene is really strong right now. I also believe that the band had a lot of momentum going into this album from the success of *Through The Ashes Of Empires*. By all standards, *The Blackening* stands against everything that dictates what should be a successful album. I mean, we open the album with a 10-and-a-half-minute long song! *The Blackening* overall has four songs that are over nine to 10 minutes long on there, features somewhat controversial lyrics and features edgy artwork."

He added: "In our heads, it was almost like we were looking at the album as a piece of art. We definitely weren't expecting it to do the numbers that it has done throughout the world. All I can say is that we're really proud. We busted our asses and worked really hard on this album. We just tried to make a piece of art that would stand the test of time, whether people got it in 2007, or eventually in 2017. It was a musical statement that we hoped would change metal and make a lasting legacy for itself. That was really our only goal. Numbers, success and chart positions are not the sort of thing we were thinking about when we were writing this album. Those are only long-term projections you can hope for. And clearly, I think that shows. A 10-minute song doesn't stand that much chance of being played on the radio or MTV. In many ways, it's limiting. But in other ways, it's also quite liberating."

The sales of the album easily outpaced any of Machine Head's previous releases: Flynn marvelled that its cumulative sales in the two weeks after its release exceeded the units shifted by *Through The Ashes Of Empires* over the previous three years. It had occurred to Flynn that the length and complexity of the songs might deter audiences, he told one interviewer. "Dude, that was definitely a concern!" he chuckled. "We talked about it, but we decided we weren't going to do anything to change it. That would have been ignorant of us to do that. There was always going to be a proportion of people scratching their heads going, 'What the fuck is this all about?' *The Blackening* was always going to be one of those albums that took a couple of listens to get into, and to absorb all the information put on there. But for the four of us being kids brought up on groups like Rush, Mercyful Fate and even early Metallica, it was natural for us. All of those groups had albums where they had very long song structures and complex arrangements. Those songs took a few minutes to really absorb, but ultimately they were also the most rewarding. That was kind of the mindset we were in… The first two singles from the album had to be edited down, because radio dictates that five and a half minutes is just far too long for a song. We just let the record company deal with that. That's their problem! We think the longer versions are cool. That's why we made them the longer versions in the first place."

Some of the length of the new songs was down to the level of interplay between Demmel and Flynn, the singer explained: "Where he really contributes is in all of the detailed stuff that you hear between him and me. It's where we bounce those ideas back and forth to come up with all the crazy guitar runs, and all the shit like that. Having a person like him in the band really opens thing up. Ultimately, I am still the main songwriter in the band, but having someone like Demmel in the band, who has been with us for like five and a half years now, it just opens up so many possibilities. Most of that comes from the team stuff we used to do in our previous band, Vio-Lence. I think a lot more of that stuff is starting to come out more again... Demmel had a big say on *Through The Ashes Of Empires* as well. He was there for the last third of the writing process for *Through The Ashes Of Empires*, but he contributed a lot of that third. A lot of people don't know this, but Dave McClain writes a lot of the riffs for this band. I don't think a lot of people realise just how much music McClain contributes to this band. McClain wrote the main riff in 'Imperium', 'Halo' and 'Descend The Shades Of Night'. He writes a sizeable chunk of stuff that sometimes gets overlooked."

Flynn was all too aware of the importance of *The Blackening* as proof of the rejuvenation of Machine Head's career. "We kind of came back from the dead with *Through The Ashes Of Empires*", he admitted, "and the safest thing we could've done would've been to just stay in [that] vein and try to keep that formula, because it worked last time. Not that there was a formula, really: we started writing and the music that we were writing just started going in this far more complex, intricate and layered direction. It's not like we sat there and intentionally did it. It just kind of [happened]. Pretty soon we ended up having 10-minute-long songs. But the thing that's really cool about it is, we're not just jamming on three riffs for 10 minutes. This is molten riffage – 20, 30 crushing riffs per song."

Canadian prog-rock legends Rush had been an inspiration, he added: "The one thing that they did is that they'd have these long songs that constantly had a continuing theme throughout them. The songs always reverted back to this one melody or this one hook – and that kept it in the context of a song so that ultimately, it wasn't just riff soup for 10 minutes. It kind of had some things that took you on a journey and then brought you back to something familiar. And that's something that we really started to try and bring into the mix. We'd have these long songs, but then we'd go back to these choruses or these hooks, but in a different context. The more we did it, the more we got excited about it. For whatever reason, it's worked."

Evidence of Flynn's evolution as a lyricist was apparent in the space he had given his words to breathe. Clarity of communication was now a priority, he said. "I really wanted to just make ideas clear. That was kind of my main thing in doing it. When you start writing, you're writing for how it reads. You're looking at it from a literary point of view, because you want it to read well. You think if it reads well, of course it's going to sing well. It doesn't necessarily do that, so with this record, I would write lyrics, then I would go sing them, and I would constantly revise them. Basically, I started dropping out words that were just excessive and not important. While sometimes words read well and sounded eloquent in a sentence, they were cluttering up the verses or the chorus so much that they just needed to be stripped down. It's like purposefully dropping words out so that it worked better in the framework of the song. I started doing that on *Through The Ashes Of Empires*, and I feel like I got a lot better at it on this album. I'm like a fucking OCD lunatic, when I'm writing lyrics. I just constantly revise words. I'll throw a whole batch of lyrics out and start fresh…"

"I'm proud of it," said Demmel of the album, "because it was a long writing process and recording process… it seemed like nobody wanted us to finish this record. Problems just kept coming up with gear, the studio, ProTools and everything. I mean anyone who's an artist wants their art to be liked, so it's like redemption because I joined this band when it was at its lowest point. It's been like an escalator ever since. It hasn't stopped. I'm playing with the guys that

I've always wanted to play with. They're my favourite band, and to be able to make music like this makes me really proud."

A barrage of tour dates surrounded and followed the release of *The Blackening*, including the Crusade Tour through the USA and then a support slot with Heaven And Hell, the reformed Ronnie James Dio-fronted version of Black Sabbath. This second tour came about after a support stint had already been agreed with Megadeth, the main support on the Heaven And Hell tour. "We were up for supporting Megadeth," explained Phil Demmel. "[They] were going to go out and do a headlining States run. We were up for that and we were going to support them. Then the Heaven And Hell thing came up and they were going to take Megadeth with them. So we were [like] 'There goes our post-release States run'. Then we got submitted for it. I was like the pessimist, 'We're not going to get it; they're not going to take us out.' Dave, in particular, was going, 'Yes, they are, we're going to get it'. Sure enough, we landed it. We are all so stoked because we're such big fans of that Dio era. It's amazing. We're super-stoked."

Like the rest of his band, Flynn was in awe at the chance to tour with a band that was effectively the best parts of Black Sabbath. "Walking out of my dressing room and seeing [Sabbath guitarist] Tony Iommi was too much. It took me two weeks just to get my head around that. I used to write letters to Black Sabbath when they broke up with Ozzy [Osbourne, Dio's predecessor], pleading for them to get back together so I could see them play 'National Acrobat' before I died... It's fucking awesome. I mean come on, it's fucking Black Sabbath! They fucking rule. But having said that, it's been a strange tour for us. The crowds have been receptive sometimes. It's definitely an older crowd than we're used to playing to. We kind of have our 10 percent that are up front for us going nuts. They're the younger crowd. And then we have a lot of older dads with younger kids that are rocking out to us, even if they've never heard of us. But overall, there's definitely a proportion of the crowd that's going, 'What the fuck?' So it's been awesome. It's been a challenge for us, because were playing to a crowd that is completely unfamiliar with us."

He added: "I wouldn't be surprised if 60 percent of the crowd had never even heard of us before. And that's a cool thing. We're playing to people that have never heard us before, and we're winning them over. That's the best part. Within the first song, you can hear them thinking to themselves, 'Well, who the fuck are these guys?' During the second song, they're starting to think it's cool, but by the third song, you can start to see people standing up on the chairs and headbanging and totally rocking out. It's cool. Plus we're playing 12,000 to 15,000-seater arenas. That's pretty sweet in itself."

Backstage, Flynn found that rubbing shoulders with his heavy metal idols was even more surreal than seeing his band's name on the bill with them. "You're sitting down in the dressing room, and all of a sudden Ronnie James Dio pops in to talk sports to you. Or you could be walking around past the drum riser, and who do I bump into? Tony Iommi! I feel like we're in some alternate universe. Every night our dressing room is right next to Megadeth's, and we'll just sit there and talk to the Megadeth dudes all night. We're all like the fans who made it into the club. It's kind of funny, because the Megadeth dudes are kind of older. We have a lot of friends come in, and we party a lot. So they have a security line for us night after night between their dressing room and ours! A couple of our drunk-assed friends will see Dio and be like, 'Ah! Dio!' So we've been given the green room permanently... From a fan's standpoint, to be on tour with Megadeth and Black Sabbath is beyond words. To be on tour with the two bands that are the very reason there is a Machine Head today is an unbelievable honour for us."

Talking of honours, Flynn was awarded a Golden God award at *Metal Hammer's* annual ceremony of the same name on June 11, 2007. As if this wasn't enough, the evening also saw the end of his longstanding feud with Slayer's Kerry King, who told the author: "I'm the kind of guy that once I'm over it, I'm over it. Looking back, I don't know what [Flynn] thought I'd said, but the way he attacked me in the press, I was like, 'You're cut off, fucker!' That was it for me – you're cut off until I'm ready for you not to be cut off. Then I got to the *Metal Hammer* awards [in 2007] and I saw his manager, and I was fine with everybody in the band – you know, they never said anything about me; Flynn just went off that one time and said enough devastating stuff that I couldn't recover from. I saw all of them at the *Metal Hammer* awards and I'm like, 'You guys are putting out heavy music, it's time to put this to bed and go do some tours'."

This being Machine Head, the year couldn't pass without their good fortune being tempered by some bad luck – and so it proved to be, with a series of incidents ranging from the mildly irritating to genuinely tragic. In June, a festival gig in the Netherlands had to be cancelled due to the most trivial of reasons – a broken-down tour bus. The band issued a statement which ran, "Machine Head offers their sincerest apologies for missing their scheduled performance today at Fields Of Rock. Unfortunately, a pipe in the engine of their bus cracked and left the band stranded in Germany for hours until it could be repaired. The band made every effort to expedite the repairs, and even attempted to charter another bus in the hopes that they could still make it in time. Unfortunately, nothing could have gotten them there in time for their performance. Again, please accept Machine Head's sincerest apologies, and trust that the band are as pissed as you are that they weren't able to play."

In the summer Adam Duce broke his leg in a dirt-biking accident, leaving him unable to tour. Brandon Sigmund of the Bay

Area metal band Hostility was his temporary stand-in while he recovered. Duce lamented, "It sucks to be in this position, because we have such a killer tour set up for the end of the summer and now we'll have to find a replacement for me. I've never missed one show that this band has ever played up to this point, and I never thought I would see the day when Machine Head would be playing and I wouldn't be on stage." He was back on stage for Japanese dates in October.

The hindrances just kept coming. Two Machine Head concerts in California and Florida were cancelled in the autumn when the mighty Disney Corporation – the owners of the venues, both House Of Blues buildings – decided in their infinite, or should that be infantile, wisdom, that Machine Head were not welcome to play there. "It's pretty disturbing," said Flynn with admirable restraint. "We are shocked that in this day and age, in 2007 America, that bands can be pressured [and] that promoters can be pressured by a business and be removed from a venue because somebody doesn't like what your lyrics stand for, or think that your fans are crazy. We've played these venues before, and there was no indication that anything was going to be different. It's basically a form of profiling, and it's pretty shocking. A result of 9/11 is that you have people acting in a way they say makes the world a safer place. I just want to know, safer for who?"

"Never in a million years would I have thought our band would have concerts cancelled on two days' notice because of our lyrics and because of our fans," ruminated Demmel. "[Disney said that] we 'draw a violent element' and our lyrics were anti-war and anti-government. I mean, we moved to another venue and all the kids came out and it sold out and it was fucking awesome, but if anything, it's made us feel so justified about the things we sing about on *The Blackening*. So I think there is definitely something more to say, and I think we'll just have to see where it goes. We're still angry."

Flynn explained the lyrics for the benefit of those of dubious IQ, such as the Disney exec who took fright at them, saying: "I think it's spelled out pretty clearly. I work on my lyrics and refine and refine and refine for a long time – I've got three notebooks of lyrics for *The Blackening*. I think it's pretty clear where we stand on stuff; but that said, we're not a political band. We tried to make the lyrics not necessarily apply to this moment, but to be timeless. And in order to be timeless, they had to have a certain 'vagueity' to them, you know? I think our main thing was that we wanted to have a timeless record – and that in 20 years, when the next fucked-up president takes us into the next fucked-up war for whatever fucked-up reasons that weren't the truth, a song like 'Clenching The Fists Of Dissent' will still apply. Not to say that all the songs on the record are political, because there's plenty that aren't, but you do have to be conscious of that. And we tried to be vague in those terms, and it gives you poetic licence to not have to be so literal about everything. It gives you more areas to go, and it makes it more fun."

Dave McClain added, "It's unbelievable that that can actually go down today, still. It's frustrating to be singled out like that, and the music you love playing... We were all brought up on metal, and that's just lame that can actually happen in this day and age. We had heard that it was because of the lyrics on the album and they just didn't want our fans on Disney property. They're not admitting any of that stuff, they're just saying that they don't want certain types of stuff on their property. But the way they went about it, waiting two days before the show, you know we'll never get a straight answer from it. But we can pretty much figure things out."

He added: "It was fucking bizarre. We've played there for years and had great shows and had absolutely no problems with anything. It's not like our fans went there and drew fucking dicks all over Mickey Mouse's forehead or anything, you know?"

In this, he was absolutely right. Think about that next time you settle down to watch a cartoon, eh?

The year finished with long months of touring through America, Japan, Australia, the UK and Europe, but the latter dates were punctuated by the sad death of Phil Demmel's father Harry. Demmel wrote on his blog that he had experienced a fainting episode on stage in Milan (the result of a long-standing heart condition called cardiogenic syncope) at almost exactly the same time that his father passed away at home in America. The date was December 6, coincidentally also the birthday of Demmel's guitar idol Randy Rhoads.

Later, Demmel explained: "It happened to me when I was on tour. I was in Italy, and we were playing 'Descend The Shades Of Night'. It's a song about death. His health had been declining, and I would think of him during the song, and I cried during the song sometimes when we'd play... So we had gone on to play the show, and during the show I passed out on stage, during the song. So I kind of came to, and I've had a history of blackouts. So they take me out after, and we were on our way to Zurich the next day, and I felt weird on the way there. Woke up to a call from my sister. And it was a voicemail: 'Hey, we really need you to call home. We need to speak with you.' Called home, and she gave me the news that my dad had passed. It was kind of shocking. I knew that it was coming, but you're never ready. You're never ready to hear that news. So we decided to play the show and I was going to fly back home. Dave, my drummer, he kept asking me, 'What time did it happen? What time did he die?' And I said, 'Man, I don't know.' And I did the math. So what happened was that [my dad] got out of his dialysis, sat in his car, and he took the keys and set them on the dashboard and just went to sleep. So it happened at the same time I passed out on stage. And just knowing that he touched me in that way was just... it was a blessing, but it was still hard to deal with. It's amazing, but it's just really hard to know that and all the circumstances."

While Demmel was at home with his family, members of the other bands on tour with Machine Head stepped up to fill in for him. "We didn't think it would be possible," said Flynn afterwards, "but a lot of the guitar players on the tour rallied around Phil last night and volunteered to help out on guitar duties. We really can't thank them all enough. Adam and I spent most of our day off today teaching Corey [Beaulieu] and Matt [Heafy] from Trivium, Christopher [Amott] from Arch Enemy, and Frederic [Leclerc], the bassist of Dragonforce, the set. They will all be playing various songs throughout the rest of the tour." Demmel returned to play the tour's final night, a date in Helsinki on December 14, which finished off what was perhaps the most eventful year in Machine Head's career to date.

The most important point which we can draw from the rollercoaster series of ups and downs that made up 2007 is, perhaps, this. Machine Head had now endured pretty much everything that a truly iconic band will ever face, except the death of a member. Addiction, poverty, rejection – all these had come and gone. What does this do to a band?

The indomitable Adam Duce put it best, saying: "When you have the luxury of putting together a band with people that you know and that you are already real good friends with, you have a lot better chance of making it work. And that was the case with Machine Head. I don't think we would have been able to make it this far, had that not been the case. Robb and I have been really good friends for a lot of years – most of life at this point – and that was the basis. We've been through all kinds of shit: we've been on this super-long journey together where there's these incredible highs and incredible lows – and that kind of shit tears people apart. But we have a pretty tough resolve, and a pretty tough mental fortitude."

The legacy of 2007 was *The Blackening*, the album that had redefined and reshaped Machine Head. Looking back at this monolithic work, Flynn concluded: "When we were writing, we had these broad goals as far as what we wanted to accomplish, which was essentially to put together a timeless metal album. We had that goal. We wanted to have a *Paranoid* [Black Sabbath] or *Master Of Puppets* [Metallica]. That Metallica album in particular became our goal. That's not to say that we were writing the album that we think Metallica should be writing, or that we're trying to be the next Metallica. No-one will be the next Metallica. We're just trying to be the next Machine Head. We wanted to write an album that had the influence, the power, the epic grandeur and timelessness that *Puppets* had. That was one of the more wide-ranging goals that we had with this album."

Equally importantly, *The Blackening* brought a renewed sense of social relevance to heavy metal as we now know it. Flynn added: "Another goal that we had was to lyrically have something to say. We were so sick and tired of listening to [bands] sing about how their girlfriends were leaving them. When we grew up listening to thrash and listening to metal, no-one even thought to write about that shit. It seems like every fucking band that has a thrash sound is singing about this non-issue. In our eyes, and with all the fucked-up shit that's going on in the world today, the only thing they can find to sing about is their goddamned girlfriend [or] something that's really pathetic. They should open their fucking eyes."

Consider our eyes opened.

Chapter 8

2008

The appropriately-titled Balls, Volume, Strength tour of America kicked off 2008 and brought the new material from *The Blackening* to mass audiences for the first time. The band was playing larger venues, in the wake of the wave of appreciation that had greeted the new album, and with the larger audiences came gig-goers who had never seen Machine Head play before. As Robb Flynn explained, "It's cool to get up there and see the reaction of people freaking out to the new stuff. I mean, like going crazy. Especially considering that probably half of the audience hasn't seen us in a long time, or [is] hearing us for the first time. If we play LA, if we sell out the House of Blues, that's like 1,100 people. But, we just played the Wiltern in Los Angeles and that's 3,000 people, so you got to figure that 1,900 people are seeing us for the first time in a long time – or the first time ever. It's awesome, man... Live is definitely a different environment than when you're writing. You're getting that instant gratification, instant reaction, looking at everybody's faces, seeing jaws drop and you're like, 'cool'. Whereas when you're writing, it's your gut instinct going, 'Man, this is really fun and this feels right and this is really good'."

The differences between the new, expanded–horizons Machine Head – new in the sense of post-*Through The Ashes Of Empires*, at least – and the older band, which had been trapped in the shadow of nu-metal to a certain extent – translated instantly into their stage set. The vocal harmonies deployed by Flynn and Duce were more advanced than before, for a start. "I really started doing a lot of that stuff on *Through The Ashes...*", said Flynn, "and we definitely wanted to take that and build on that, just because it's kind of a new thing. Well, not a new thing – Adam and I have always done trade-offs and harmonies on the other records – but we just wanted to take it even farther than we had ever taken it before."

The same was true of the guitar parts. We've emphasised before that Machine Head's overall ability to write astounding music had taken a leap forward since the recruitment of Phil Demmel, but nowhere did this become more obvious than when the first full tours began after his first complete album with the band. Demmel and Flynn had become a guitar team to reckon with by anyone's standards, thanks to serious levels of motivation and hundreds of hours of work. As Flynn said, "Us spending the extra hours after practice jamming back and forth had a big impact. [Phil would] get there early, or we'd stay there late. Then we'd refine and work on parts. Just having someone to bounce ideas off of was huge. There's [a] chemistry between Phil and me. We learned how to play guitar together, when we were teenagers. Now I think, you still hear a lot of that. Our goal was to be a guitar team. It was never to have one guy be 'the solo guy' and the other guy be 'the rhythm guy'. It was always about being a guitar team, trying to model ourselves after Glenn Tipton and KK Downing of Judas Priest and that vibe."

In fact, Priest had played a definite role in the new guitar parts, Flynn added, whether they knew it or not. "There's a lot of Judas Priest jacking [hijacking]," he said. "Whenever we find a riff or we're inspired by a riff, we call it 'jacking.' We even had one song that we called 'Victim Of Changes 2', because we felt like we had borrowed pretty liberally from it. I met those guys in Priest when we did the UK. KK [Downing, then-Priest guitarist] came out to the show, we told him that, and he was super-flattered. He was like, 'Oh my God, that's amazing. That's my favourite song!' It was killer."

Despite their more ambitious song structures and performances, Machine Head were never likely to enter full-on progressive-metal territory along the lines of their Roadrunner stablemates Dream Theater. The brutality and heaviness of their Bay Area background was still an essential part of the songwriting – and just as well, or Machine Head's day in the limelight would have been over by now. "Sometimes there's definitely complex parts," noted Flynn, "but you always got to have that classic, Neanderthal, Machine Head breakdown where it's like the two heaviest notes ever. We try and keep a balance... granted, there are some riffs on here that are hands down the most technical stuff we've ever written. There's also something to be said about simple, stupid Neanderthal riffs, you know?"

In February, Machine Head missed out on what would have been their first Grammy award: at the institution's 50th annual event, the award for 'Best Metal Performance' went to Slayer's 'The Final Six', a bonus track from the reissue of the thrash legends' 2006 album *Christ Illusion*. The nominated Machine Head song, 'Aesthetics Of Hate', is easily the better song, but a Grammy award for a band as uncompromising as Slayer benefits everyone in the metal community, and Flynn accepted it with good grace.

"The Grammys have always voted for [relatively mainstream bands such as the Deftones and Soundgarden and Rage Against

The Machine in the past," he said, "so if they finally got it right with Slayer, at least they got it right with Slayer. Five minutes after it was announced they won, I got a text from Kerry King which said, 'I'll take the Grammy, but you guys should have won this!' It was very cool of him."

Meanwhile, Machine Head lined up for another back-breaking year of touring. For those not in the know, this is no picnic. Imagine being trapped in a bus, which is basically a metal tube that smells of socks and a chemical toilet, no matter how many lounges it has, with three guys on an intimate basis, 24 hours a day. Then imagine the junk food and its effect on your digestion, the irregular hours of sleep and the effect they have on your temper, and the scarcity of laundry facilities and the effect that has on everyone's personal aroma – especially as each of you is required to sweat in a red-hot club for two hours a night. Mobile phones often lack reception. The internet drops in and out. Guitars, and guitar strings and cables, break. Planes are delayed. You miss your family and friends. Fans endlessly ask you which amps you use. Journalists try to trick you into saying controversial things. You shouldn't drink too much, but the booze is free and ubiquitous, so you usually do. And you never know how big your pay packet will be at the end of the tour... this is the life of the midsize touring band. And it never ends – if you're lucky.

In Flynn's case, he also had two small children waiting for him at home. "It's tough," he sighed. "My wife and I planned having them close together in age, but we didn't expect for me to be on tour four weeks after having a kid, so it's a lot of responsibility that I've left her with. We'll get through it, and we'll get over it, and we'll keep on going." The Machine Head way, as we've seen, was the same as ever: to convert the people to the cause city by city, club by club, fan by fan if necessary. He continued: "We went about making our fanbase in a different way. It was a tougher way, there's no doubt about it. There's definitely a lot more work and there's still a lot more work involved. Ultimately, we've got one of the most loyal fanbases in all of metal. They stand by us and they pick up the record and they support the band, no matter what. It's pretty cool to have that freedom. The thing that's really cool now is, radio [is not] going to be receptive to this record either. Especially because we've got these five-and-a-half-, six-, nine-, 10-minute-long songs and clearly don't fit into any kind of video or radio format."

Family issues continued to affect the band at this time, with Dave McClain's mother passing away in the early spring. Machine Head soldiered on, even heading to Dubai in March to play the country's Desert Rock Festival. Amid the chaos, Flynn explained that there was still ample room for new and enlightening experiences. "It was completely shocking, to be honest," he told one interviewer. "It was us, Sepultura was opening [and there was] a couple of other bands, Within Temptation and The Darkness. It was like totally out of nowhere, and randomly The Darkness was headlining, but this was when The Darkness was worth something! It was kind of scary when we were going over there... you see all of this stuff on the media. We had never been there, so we didn't know what to expect. My wife was literally pleading with me the night before, 'This has got to be some kind of terrorist plot' and I was like, 'I don't think so'. They were paying us a lot of money and I don't think they would do that, you know. But I've got to say that it was in the back of my head... We got there, we were expecting to see nothing but mosques and turbans and camels. We drive out of there and we the first thing we see is Starbucks and Roundtable Pizza! We were like, 'What the fuck?' and the next day it was McDonalds and Burger King and Arby's and Nordstrom's and Cactus Jacks! They put us up in the Fairmont Hotel, they took us to the Hard Rock Hotel for a press conference. It was like Las Vegas on crack, but it was on the beach."

The gig itself was even more astounding than the culture shock, he added. "Five thousand people," he enthused, "kids from Iran... and all these crazy places like Beirut, and obviously Dubai and Saudi Arabia... and they were all metalheads [with] long hair, Metallica shirts, Machine Head shirts, Slayer shirts, Slipknot shirts... they were jumping and headbanging. They knew the 'Machine fucking Head' [chant]. We were like, 'What the fuck?' We were just so freaked out what it was going to be like to be [there]. You know how the media, especially here in America, really manipulates everything. We expected bombed-out cities, and it was one of the nicest cities you could ever be in, you know. But they hammer that perception into America and totally build that fear. It's total fear-mongering, and in the same [way] they expected us to be a certain way... and you know, it was this cool cultural experience that we got to trip off of."

Dates in Israel, India and Japan finished off the first, and highly multicultural, leg of Machine Head's 2008 road commitments before they began the ultimate tour, the one which would bring them greater exposure than any other since the Slayer jaunt back in 1995 – a world tour with none other than Metallica, then as now the biggest heavy metal in the world and indeed, the biggest there is ever likely to be. "Holy crap!" marvelled McClain. "It's pretty well documented on our DVD, *Elegies*, when we were talking about where we were as a band. There was a period where nobody wanted to really touch us. The band went through this weird dark period, and when we came out of it one of the things we said was, 'We need to get to a point where a band like Metallica says, 'We need to take that band on tour'... it's surreal. Metallica does not need Machine Head to open up for them to bring people into the arena. They are doing us the biggest favour that anybody could ever do for a band. It puts you in front of an arena full of people that potentially you can win over. That's amazing. That speaks volumes for the dudes that they are. We couldn't be more honoured. We couldn't be more... We're blown away by it."

Metallica, whose album *Death Magnetic* had been released that year to a sense of general relief because it was immeasurably superior to its 2003 predecessor, *St. Anger*, were about to spend close to three years on the road supporting the album. Determined to win back the critical ground they had lost and availing themselves of the world's biggest stadiums in order to do so, the San Francisco foursome were about to deliver an elaborate, hard-hitting show – and Machine Head had to step up to the mark in no uncertain terms to match them. Fortunately, Flynn and his band was on the best form of their careers – and, as Metallica frontman James Hetfield told the author in an interview for *Metal Hammer*, *The Blackening* had made a huge impact on him when he and his band-mates were considering options for support bands.

"What Machine Head means to me is the Bay Area," said Hetfield. "They've always been a well-loved and respected band in the Bay Area, ever since Vio-Lence, way before Machine Head: the guys have been around forever. It was great to have them out on the road with us, because we're of the same thinking and both bands struggled from the Eighties on, trying to deliver the best stuff possible. They still have an amazing drive. Me, Robb, Phil and Adam text each other once in a while and keep each other updated. They've got a really great sound: *The Blackening* is one of those albums that is so full and solid. It reminds me of our 'Black Album' [aka *Metallica*, 1991]. It's so full-sounding, and every track really has potency: they've got a mixture of a lot of different things, you know?"

He continued: "They go from being extremely fast and heavy to more slow and melodic: Robb has experimented with singing instead of just barking all the time. He and I have talked a lot about that in particular: him and I together, he reminds me of me when I was kind of a little afraid to take some chances and go with some different voices. I've heard him do an acoustic thing, which was unbelievable. It was great. When we were looking for bands to take out, *The Blackening* stood high above most of the other stuff. There is a lot of great music out there, but that album seemed to me to be very solid and very aggressive-sounding, but it also had depth to it. It had exactly what we thought we'd like to have our audience check out."

From June to August, Metallica's World Magnetic tour passed through Poland, Spain, the Czech Republic, Portugal, Russia and Germany before heading to the USA and Canada. Looking back on the tour, Flynn said: 'It's amazing to see how passionate those dudes still are about music. They don't have to give a shit about music at this point. They don't have to care about other bands. They're fucking Metallica. But there were times when I'd sit there and talk to Lars [Ulrich, drummer] or Hetfield and listen to them geek out on a band. Lars and I went and saw [first support act] The Sword, and he's singing every word and doing air guitar to all the right parts. I'm like, 'You know every fucking word to The Sword's songs?"

The popularity of some of Metallica's more complex songs also made an impression on Flynn, as well it might after the ambitious songwriting on *The Blackening*. "To me, one of the raddest things in the world was touring with Metallica and watching [the 1986 song] 'Master Of Puppets' – not [the huge 1991 hit] 'Enter Sandman'. I get why 'Enter Sandman' is so fricking huge, but to watch 'Master Of Puppets', this eight-minute song with a million parts in the middle of it with complicated choruses and off-time rhythms – to watch arenas every night sing every fucking word, that was amazing. There's this whole other part of music that can be well-written and well-constructed that can be somewhere [outside conventional music], and still translate to millions of fucking people."

Machine Head's setlist contained the expected signature songs from the Nineties as well as new material. Demmel noted that the headliners had a sophisticated system when it came to choosing songs for the live set: "We saw how they did it," he said. "They have a whole grid that they bring up with the last five times they played this city and a list of what they played. It's really thought-out. So we're trying to remember what we played [in each city] to try to mix it up. We have to play the current album, because that's what we're selling right now. But we also play some hits, if you can call them 'hits', that the people want to hear, so we've been trying to mix up the set list." Asked if he ever got tired of playing *Burn My Eyes*-era songs such as 'Davidian', he replied: "No, never, man. There's never been a Machine Head show without that song being played. It's just the staple... I've been a fan since the beginning. I saw their first show. Robb quit Vio-lence to form this band, and ever since then I've been a huge fan."

The year was set to continue with more support dates with Slipknot, and further Metallica dates had been scheduled for early 2009. Asked if executing perpetual support slots was a deliberate strategy on Machine Head's part, Demmel answered: "Well, since I've joined the band all we were doing was headlining tours, so to be able to get on support slots is what we needed to do. We were preaching to the choir every night before, so now we're out winning fans. We've got some good support slots on this cycle for us. This is what you need to do, unless you want to keep playing to the same old fans. [The old fans] are great, but if you want to win other people's crowds over, then this is the way to do it. I mean, if you're comfortable in what you're doing, and if you're Disturbed and [you've] got the Number One record in America, then you've got your own thing and that's cool, but we're not. Some nights we've got to work [for a good reaction from the crowd], but that's why we're here, man. Every night it's been rocking for us."

Still, the endless touring was beginning to take its toll. Demmel was asked if he was suffering from 'battle fatigue' and told his interviewer, "Yeah, dude. We had a little bit of time off, but I mean, this is what we signed up for. We're probably halfway through our touring cycle now. We've got shit lined up at the end of this year with Slipknot, and then we've just landed something real super cool [more Metallica shows] at the beginning of next year, we got summer festivals next year, and we want to do a proper headlining in America and overseas because we haven't done that. We've just done co-headlining. We're halfway through, man."

A keen sense of the absurd helped to keep Machine Head's collective sanity intact, Flynn added. Referring to Blabbermouth, Borivoj Krginy's renowned news website specialising in hard rock and heavy metal, whose visitors are infamously scathing with their opinions, he explained: "You just have to have such a good sense of humour – about your band, about your fucking life! You go on Blabbermouth and they take shots at you, and you just got to fucking laugh. I know all these people in bands who hate it, but I fucking love Blabbermouth. I think it's the funniest shit ever. We are a serious band, and we take every aspect of what we do seriously. But you know, this is an absurd life; it's a fucking gypsy's life, and to not be able to laugh at the absurdity of things… you have to, or you need to learn to. Shit happens. Once you've taken that step to be in a band, you no longer live your life in private – you live your life in public. You have to have a sense of humour." Asked to expand on the sacrifices needed to keep a band like his on the road, Flynn laughed: "I can't even begin to tell you all the things you have to sacrifice – time with your friends, time with your family, your privacy, sleep… there's thousands of things!"

But there were always the crowds, and their unstoppable enthusiasm, to keep the members motivated. Flynn noted that the Machine Head crowds were now younger than ever. "It's just teenagers – that's who we play to now," he said. "In fact, we're playing to a younger audience now than even when we started! Back in '94, metal was as uncool as it's ever been. It was so fucking uncool... and I think it's really rad now to see how popular metal is again. Even bands that aren't metal are calling themselves metal! And because of that, there's a lot more kids into the scene again. The kids are what keeps this scene alive. Thirty-year-old people don't listen to fucking metal. They really don't. They've moved on with their lives, they get jobs, they get girlfriends, they listen to what's on the radio. Kids are what keeps the scene alive, and being in a band that's, like, forefathers of the new underground, it's awesome to see this."

Late 2008 saw two equally unexpected events dominate the global headlines. The first was the election of Barack Obama, America's first black president, about whom Flynn commented, "Awesome, man. It's fucking killer. It's amazing, really. Historic beyond words. First black president in the history of America; it's pretty fucking unbelievable. The dude's fucking getting dropped into a giant pile of shit... with no paper towels to wipe it off or anything, so he's a got a lot of fucking work to do. And I get the vibe that he can do it. For the first time in a long time, I believe. And I want to believe."

Perhaps just as unlikely was the release, after many years of speculation, of Guns N' Roses' album *Chinese Democracy*, an album that had been so long in gestation that it had become a metaphor for delays or prevarication of any kind, at least among music fans. Sadly the album failed to repay GNR fans' expectations. Demmel dismissed it, saying with typical down-to-earth candour, "I don't care. You know, Robb just brought it up to me in the airport on the way over. He was talking about the new *Celebrity Rehab* show in America, and how it's got [sometime GNR drummer] Steven Adler on it, and what a mess Adler is, and he's talking about [GNR guitarist] Slash, and how he hates Slash because he didn't ask him to play on his solo record, and it's just the whole Guns N' Roses thing, man. I don't care, man. I really don't. I didn't really like [post-GNR project] Velvet Revolver all that much. And Axl [Rose, GNR singer] has got [guitarist] Buckethead to play with him? He's got the Marilyn Manson guy playing guitar with him too? I don't even know what's going on in that camp any more. But, I mean [Rose is] an amazing songwriter, so I'll listen to it... You mix endless amounts of money with, you know, drug addicts, and just the kind of individuals that they are, and that's what's gonna happen. Mötley Crüe, the same thing. I was reading Nikki Sixx's book, and it's just personalities and money."

Perhaps Demmel's impatience, justified though it was, was more pronounced because of the immense stress of the huge, post-*Blackening* tour. The dates had extended more than anyone in the band had expected, as McClain explained: "We didn't know that the tour would stretch out for that long. And the album snowballed into a big thing, something that all of the bands hope for, so we didn't think that it would cause a problem. When we went on the road with Metallica, the tour [lasted] an additional year, but to tell you the truth, it wasn't that hard, since we had two weeks on the road and two weeks off, so there was time to take a break and get back home. After all, the band wasn't constantly on the road for the entire period of time."

Despite McClain's optimism, an additional series of dates in support of Slipknot at the end of 2008 almost proved to be the undoing of Machine Head. A long string of shows through Japan, Australia and most of Europe ended badly when Demmel suffered another episode of cardiogenic syncope in Sheffield, England, and the band was obliged to cancel their last two dates. As well as the disappointment he felt about this, Demmel was also in deep mourning for his father. As he said, "This past year has been really hard for me. My father passed away a year ago. And the circumstances in which it happened… it was really hard for me and I'm still… I've spent the past year drunk. I quit drinking a couple of months ago to kind of deal with it."

Asked about the cancelled dates, Duce explained: "After considering the seriousness of Phil's health condition, we all feel that skipping these last two shows is the best thing to do. It's a bummer to end this tour like this after doing nine amazing weeks and three continents with Slipknot, but getting Phil back to the States to get checked out is the most important thing right now. Our sincerest thanks to Slipknot and Children Of Bodom for their support and understanding. We understand that it's a big disappointment to the fans, and Phil is very sorry about it, but we all feel that his health and safety is most important at this time."

The bassist was also going through an emotional time, telling the author of a particularly poignant moment he experienced on the road in Sweden. "When we were on tour with Metallica with Sweden, we stopped at the little monument which they made for Cliff [Burton, the Metallica bassist who died in a road accident near the Swedish town of Ljungby in 1986]. It was really heavy. I sat there and I cried for a while. I could never have been the bassist that he was at that age." More troublesome was the news that he and Flynn had argued to the point where the latter had even considered leaving the band, as McClain told an interviewer. "There was one time in particular in Paris during the Slipknot tour; Robb and Adam had some pretty serious problems, and after we got offstage that night, Robb was ready to call it a day and just end everything right there. But he and Adam did some therapy together and kind of worked things out."

Flynn wrote about the therapy sessions that he and Duce were undergoing on his blog, and later the twosome talked about the experience with *Kerrang!* writer Ian Winwood. It was brave of them, most people would admit, to go on the record with these most personal of recollections, especially as the therapy process was still ongoing. The two musicians even revealed the per-hour cost of the sessions and the name of their counsellor. As for the final straw which caused the rift in the first place, Winwood wrote: "Someone Robb Flynn did not care for was set to attend that night's show. The frontman believed he'd made it clear to Adam Duce that this person's presence was not welcome at the show or in the dressing-room. Duce, for his part, did not believe the issue was so clear-cut, and felt that were this individual to attend the show he could be kept out of Flynn's way. This proved not to be the case, and when Flynn discovered the offending person in the dressing-room, he went nuts. Duce swears that he did not permit the man access to the backstage area of the Amsterdam Music Hall to spite his band–mate, but the 'the way [Robb Flynn] reacted you would think that I had done so'."

The feature continued, "This is not the first time Machine Head had incurred trouble within its ranks. Some years back drummer Dave McClain abandoned his post in an unseemly squabble over money, hurt and offended that Flynn had referred to him as 'a one-percenter'. Today McClain says that 'life in any band can be difficult, and we're no exception'," adding that Flynn considered leaving the band during a period in which he and Duce refused to speak to each other. "I didn't book a flight," the singer told Winwood. "I was still in my hotel room. But I was up all night. I was too angry to eat or sleep, I was so angry I couldn't even go pee. In all of the time that I've known him, I've never been so pissed at Adam as I was at that time.'"

Asked why he chose to document these events on his blog, Flynn reasoned: "I look at it as being like a diary. I think about what's going on in my life, in the band's life, and I write it down. It's a snapshot of that. We're a very honest band that tells people what's going on, and we tell them to hang in there with us. And the part of the diary that concerns [what happened between the two bandmates] is only one paragraph long. But we played two shows in Paris, and by the time of the second show we'd had our fight and we were starting to work things out as best we could. He said that he'd never seen me as angry as I had just been, and that it was time to clear the air."

Duce explained that while he regarded Flynn as a friend, "I'd also describe him as being my brother, and brothers fight. We fight. Being in a band together and being friends for as long as we have, that's way more of a brotherhood... I think [Robb and I] have a very [problematic] communication barrier between us. And because we've known each other for so long, the way we talk to each other – or at least until recently – went from zero to 50 in no time at all. We'll be talking like you and I are right now, and then two seconds later we'll be yelling at each other. The thing is, he's not trying to press my buttons and I'm not trying to press his, but they've been pushed so many times that if you push a couple of them, then the 'fuck you's start to fly."

Flynn explained that band life sometimes makes a schism inevitable, something we discussed earlier when we examined the claustrophobic existence of the touring musician. "If you've been in a band for 17 years, and if you've been friends for as long as we have, then there's lots of things that can happen," he pointed out. "But the things that make [Duce] mad, I would never think would make him mad. And the things that don't make him mad are the things that I assume would drive him crazy. So it can be very difficult to gauge. It can be like a minefield, and I'm sure it can be for him as well. I'm not saying it's his fault, or all his fault, because it's not. I want to be very clear about that... Adam and I are both alpha males, and we are both better at fighting than we are at talking."

When Winwood asked Flynn if control lay at the heart of the problem, he mused: "Well, I would say that I definitely have control issues... I think my guys deal pretty goddamn good with the attention I get. I'm the singer and so a lot of attention goes onto me. But I think I could have done a better job at deflecting that [attention], though. I try and share the credit out, but I might have done better with that. But I'm a control freak, I'm not denying that. I'm not saying I don't like control, I like it and I tend to take a lot of it. I think that's a good thing in some ways, but in other ways it's a bad thing. There's a line in there somewhere."

Duce, a tough-looking dude by anyone's standards, pointed out that his uncompromising appearance didn't mean that he was unsuited to the therapeutic process. "You shouldn't judge a book by its cover," he said. "People tell me I'm intimidating to talk to, but that's not the way I mean to present myself. All I want is for people to listen to what it is I have to say, and to look me in the eyes when I'm saying it. But growing up the way I did, this isn't the first round of therapy that I've gone through. Between the ages of 11 and 18 I spent two four-month periods at home with my parents. The rest of the time I was in drug rehab, juvenile hall, group home, mental hospital... It's quite a list... I definitely had faith. I definitely wanted this to work. These sessions are costing me 75 bucks a fucking hour! I want to get to the truth as quickly as I can!"

Flynn explained his side of the story, saying: "Adam is a really strong dude, and I really respect that. He's got super-strong convictions, and those are qualities that I admire. He quit smoking cigarettes, he quit smoking weed, he quit drinking alcohol – he's a very different person to the guy he was when we started. He used to be a really difficult person to be around when he was so fucked-up all the time. But he cleaned up and straightened up. But sometimes it seems that he gets consumed with stuff at home that supersedes the band totally, you know. A lot of it had to do with trust issues, and him honouring, or not honouring, the things we agreed to. He doesn't like touring, and that's a hard thing to get your head around with a band that tours as much as we do. I was pretty sure he was going to quit in 2007 not long after [the Download festival], he just seemed miserable. When he broke his leg and we toured without him for the one tour, I think it helped him appreciate the band more, and it made me appreciate him more and what he brings to the band."

Whatever the pros and cons of the situation, Duce concluded that quitting the band now, after the lows they had endured and the work they had put in to bring themselves to the top again, would be the ultimate failure. "Well I'm pretty big on winning and losing, and I don't like losing. I'm not fucking good at it and I don't try to practise it. Quitting at this point would just be one of the biggest losses that my life could possibly have. And I'm not going to play a part in that. I'm not just going to say, 'OK, well, I lose'. To me quitting and losing are brother and sister. To quit something that I've been a part of for almost two decades is simply not acceptable."

He added that the therapy sessions were yielding positive results: "I can already tell that we interact with each other with more compassion than we did prior to therapy. Before, Robb and I were really quick on the draw, and now we speak a lot softer towards each other. How much longer is it going to take? I don't know. It took us a long time to get [to this point] so it might take a while for it all to unwind. But I do know that every time we go [to therapy] it feels as if we're accomplishing something. It feels like a good thing."

Flynn concurred, saying: "I think therapy has already taught us both that we don't want to lose [the group], that this is worth fighting for. I have my wife, my kids and the band. But the music business is where all the rejects find a home, you know? Both Adam and I are both pretty fucked-up. We've both had very fucked-up childhoods, [and] similar childhoods in a lot of ways, and we're two guys who are used to not giving in. And we've been living on a bus together for much of the past 15 years – there were bound to be problems. It's a very dysfunctional way to live, and we started off as dysfunctional people in the first place. So there is stuff that we have to work through, and right now we're working through it. And that is a good thing."

And so another hellishly turbulent year ended. While Demmel didn't make the following statement with reference to any of the above, he made it at about this time and it seemed to fit perfectly, not only with the trials endured by his bandmates, but with Machine Head's newfound strength in the wake of their finest album in a decade and a half. "Be honest, man. Honesty is so important in every walk of life. Be it with your parents, be it with your friends, your girlfriends, your bandmates, your music. Just be honest and be true to yourself. And I don't think that you can fail."

Chapter 9

2009–2010

After a year like 2008, Machine Head needed a well-deserved break. Of course, they didn't get one. If you want breaks, get a normal job.

Asked by Anthony Morgan of *Ultimate Guitar* if he'd expected Machine Head would still be in business after 15 years, Robb Flynn said: "Never in our wildest dreams did we think that we'd still be here in 2007. There were people that told us, 'Hey, you'll probably last about five years'. They told us that when our first album came out. 'Yeah, I can see you lasting about five years.' No-one had us lasting much longer than that, let alone ourselves. The fact that we're still here, hitting creative highs, and probably doing the best we've ever done on a worldwide scale, internationally – as well as America – on one of the coolest tours you could be on, it's incredible. It's really cool. That's kind of due to the fact that we just write from the heart. We've been consistent at doing that one thing. Our goal has always been to never have a record sound the same."

Writing from the heart is all very well, but let us be very clear that Machine Head were also continuing to pursue a deliberately businesslike strategy of supporting bigger bands in order to play in front of new fans. It had worked when they supported Slayer back in 1995 – and how! – and so it made sense to do it all again. This meant a lot of hard work, of course, but by now the members of Machine Head knew no other way to operate, even if it threatened their collective health and sanity.

In early 2009 the band headed out with Metallica again, this time across the USA, the UK and Europe. Three months of touring went smoothly until Duce dropped out of a show in Stockholm, Sweden, to undergo emergency root canal surgery after his jaw became infected. He remarked, "Apparently I've had this abscessed tooth breeding infection just above my mouth for a couple of years. The pain was tolerable, and I didn't think to have it checked out. I went to the doctor to see if it was OK to fly, and she told me to go get some X-rays. My dentist found the abscessed tooth as soon as he looked at the X-rays, and sent me to another dentist that could fit me in immediately for a root canal procedure. The dentist also informed me that I couldn't fly with that condition because, believe it or not, it could be fatal due to how close the infection is to my brain. I apologise to all the fans in Sweden for not being able to be there for Monday's show. Thanks for your understanding and I'll see you next time." His temporary replacement on bass was Patrik Jensen, one of the guitarists in the Swedish thrash metal band The Haunted.

Considering what Machine Head had been through in previous years, the small matter of emergency dentistry was unlikely to derail the band. In fact, this run of dates had plenty of lighter moments, such as the occasions when Metallica singer James Hetfield played with the band. Flynn recalled that the decision to do so came after Hetfield showed up for an impromptu jam in the Machine Head dressing room on May 16, although the Metallica leader chose to play drums there rather than the extra guitar part he supplied on stage.

"He said, 'Do you know any 'Tallica?'" Flynn remembered. "I'm like, 'Do I know any Metallica? Fucking call it'. So we did 'Master Of Puppets'. Then he goes, 'Do you know any Maiden?' And I'm like, 'Fucking 'Wrathchild''. And then I realise, 'Oh my God, I'm jamming with Hetfield and he's on the fucking drums, playing it killer'. Then he says, 'Let's jam 'Aesthetics Of Hate'.' I'm like, 'You know 'Aesthetics Of Hate' on the drums?' He knew every fucking drum beat, every part, and that ain't an easy song to play. While we're playing, Dave [McClain] comes in and goes, 'He's playing my drum parts. This is amazing!' To see a band at that level and think, 'Wow, man, those dudes are still fans. They still love music' is kind of a revelation… I think I might have thought they'd be different now, because they're huge and they're Metallica."

Demmel added: "It was one of the highlights of my musical career, having him approach us. He originally came into our dressing room and played it on the drums first, and then he was like, 'OK, maybe I'll play this one with you live', or something like that. So he came up and did it twice and it was awesome – very amazing and very surreal."

It wasn't all fun, as indeed it never is. In May, the legendary Black Sabbath, Dio and Heaven And Hell singer Ronnie James Dio died of stomach cancer, followed soon after by Flynn's old manager Debbie Abono. These two losses, firstly of an idol with whom Machine Head had toured only three years before, and then of a woman whom Flynn described as one of his family, hit the band hard. In tribute to their passing, he recorded an acoustic version of Sabbath's classic 'Die Young' and released it online.

"Yesterday was a very sad day for metal. I am devastated at the passing of Debbie Abono and words aren't coming very clear for me right now," his statement read, followed by his memories of touring with Abono when he and Demmel were members of Vio-Lence. "Thinking back on it now," he added, "touring with a bunch of snot-nosed thrash metallers for two months at a time in a van, playing crummy clubs, isn't the usual course most 55-year-old ladies take in their lives, but she was no ordinary 55-year-old lady. She was fiery, feisty, charming, funny, and could look a person over in about two seconds and find something to joke about/roast them about should they wanted to test her. She was one of the biggest forces behind the thrash and early death metal movements than I think most people will ever realise. I dated her daughter Gina, and I lived at her house in Pinole on and off in my late teens, and even after Gina and I broke up, she gave me an incredible amount of belief and advice once Machine Head started. She was so proud of what we accomplished. Most importantly, she believed in me, even right up until the end."

An obituary published in the *Contra Costa Times* read, "Debbie was in her mid-fifties when she plunged into the Bay Area's heavy metal/thrash metal music scene. She quickly [started working with] some of the Bay Area's strongest metal bands... Many of these members who have gone on to further success with their careers with Debbie's constant guidance. She is known around the world not only for the work she has done for countless musicians, band crew members and their families, but more so for her heart and generosity and her ability to uplift, motivate and empower all those around her to always be honest and to be their best."

The sense of loss among the Bay Area's metal alumni was widespread: a concert in Abono's honour duly took place in Concord, California, with members of many bands with whom she had worked in attendance. James Hetfield dedicated a song to her during a Metallica show, and Testament guitarist Alex Skolnick echoed Flynn's words when he wrote, "In the mid-Eighties when most folks over 40 were afraid of metal, there was Debbie Abono, a kind, sophisticated woman in her fifties. She saw right through the pentagrams, upside-down crosses, leather and spikes and recognised that some kind souls lay underneath... By doing so, she helped us realise that older people weren't so bad either."

After no more than a few days off after the Metallica dates, Machine Head joined yet another high-profile tour, this time the Canadian Carnage dates co-headlined by thrashers Megadeth and Slayer. Strangely, a full US headline tour had yet to take place in support of *The Blackening*, a fact that had not escaped Machine Head's fanbase. Phil Demmel took to the band's website to address the issue, explaining that the number of shows which Machine Head had actually played in North America since the album's release far exceeded those played in Europe. "*Blackening* Europe/ UK shows: 117; *Blackening* US/Canada shows: 155," he pointed out. "I was wondering which support slot we should've turned down to go out and headline? Lamb Of God? Heaven And Hell? Hellyeah? The Mayhem fest? Metallica? Slayer/Megadeth? Any suggestions?"

"Timing is a huge factor in picking tours," he continued. "I feel bad for the US [fans] but everything we're doing is setting up what comes next. We only headlined up until this record, and when it came out the biggest names in metal wanted us out with them. Finally. If we don't take support slots we're confining ourselves to playing the same clubs and theatres forever. Yeah, the setlist was pretty similar for a lot of the runs in the US. We had to put together songs that would be best for people who'd never seen us before. We've been better and [more] cognisant about mixing it up this past year. That will continue. I understand the frustration. We haven't 'forgotten' about North America. We've just been made offers that we (or any metal band) couldn't/

wouldn't refuse. Europe/UK is simply more crazy for this band. In a sense, the US has been the priority, raising our profile and reaching new fans via support slots was the vehicle to do this. We've been killing ourselves (almost literally) out on the road just so we can still be a band. Things are done for a reason. We've always been one of the fan-friendliest metal bands out there and always will be."

Asked if he'd wanted to headline in the USA, Demmel explained: "We wanted to, but then the Megadeth thing came up. How can you deny doing Slayer and Megadeth? And then the Metallica shows came up. We headlined so much in the States. So it was better off doing this. We're doing a proper headlining [tour] of Europe, which are more deserving in my eyes." This last comment was telling: then as now, Machine Head are fully aware that – for reasons which still aren't obvious – they are most popular outside their home continent.

As he'd been in Vio-Lence, Demmel was proving himself an invaluable asset to Machine Head on multiple levels. As a guitarist and songwriter, his contributions were obvious, but as a business partner and morale-booster, he worked wonders behind the scenes. Sadly, he continued to struggle with his grief in the wake of his father's death and this made him more susceptible to episodes of cardiogenic syncope, one of which occurred during Machine Head's set at the Finnish Sonisphere on July 25.

Robb Flynn commented about Demmel's previous collapses, "It had been happening a bit on this last tour, most dramatically in Paris where, for no apparent reason, at one in the afternoon, he collapsed face-first into a wooden table and broke two glass ashtrays on his chest and had to go to the hospital. For the most part, none were public or onstage, so they weren't publicised, but we're very concerned, worried, and a little scared about what's going on. It's confusing. And because it's so random, frankly, it seems dangerous. The doctors he's been seeing, in my opinion, haven't been doing enough, and the advice they've given him is ridiculous. But he seems to be feeling good, and it hasn't happened since then, which is a great sign. He's working to change his habits and to be a little healthier – eating, exercise, stretching – but other than the first few days out, his habits haven't really changed much."

The British Sonisphere event, launched this year at Knebworth House in Hertfordshire, was subject to a dose of controversy. The festival, at which Machine Head were set to appear on August 2, had initially booked them to play third on the bill, but later inserted Limp Bizkit in that slot, pushing Machine Head down to fourth. What was interesting for our purposes about the public battle which followed was that the event organisers obviously valued Machine Head's presence but had felt obliged to include Limp Bizkit above them, although the rap-metallers' recorded output had been negligible for some years.

"It is with the utmost disappointment that we must announce that Machine Head will not be playing the Sonisphere date at Knebworth in the UK on August 2," ran Machine Head's official statement. "In a turn of events that has left us absolutely baffled, the promoter of the UK Sonisphere festival recently placed, unbeknownst to us, Limp Bizkit in our third slot on the festival. Seeing as the running order was a significant part of the negotiation and agreement between us and the promoter, and the fact that we had been advertised in that slot since the festival's announcement, you can imagine our surprise when we were 'told' that we would now be playing in the fourth slot, under Limp Bizkit, and bizarrely, it was actually expected that we would quietly move down the bill without issue. We will not."

The other fascinating aspect of the disagreement was the instant polarisation of the British metal scene once Sonisphere appeared.

Download was the reigning festival in this country and had been for some years, both in its current incarnation and as its Donington-branded predecessor in the Eighties and Nineties. Faced with a serious competitor, Download now had to compete for fans' ticket money, which also meant bidding for the bands themselves. "Machine Head turned down the UK's Download festival," continued the band's statement, "a festival we are very fond of – which, incidentally, had us above Limp Bizkit – to commit to the Knebworth festival, as we felt a closer kinship to the bands performing this year. In an effort to make this situation in Knebworth work, we have spent more than a week striving to resolve this issue in a proper manner. Unfortunately, that did not happen. So we have regrettably been left with no choice but to cancel our appearance rather than stand for the disrespect and indignity offered by a promoter who won't honour our agreement. While we know that our fans will be furious about this situation – as are we, beyond words – we trust that you will all understand our position, and we encourage you to voice your opinion about it as loud and clear as possible. The rest of our festival dates across Europe, including the other Sonisphere dates, as well as our headline of [Germany's] Wacken festival, remain unchanged."

The Sonisphere organisers shot back: "We regretfully confirm that Machine Head have made the decision to pull out of Sonisphere Festival Knebworth. We have spent close to two weeks talking to Machine Head to try and keep them on the festival, including offering them higher billing on the [second] stage, so that they would be performing immediately after Limp Bizkit and before Nine Inch Nails. They would also get a longer time slot and were offered an increase in fee. Unfortunately, the band did not find this agreeable. We have strived to make Sonisphere a great festival in our debut year, with one of the strongest line-ups out there. Our main priority is to give the fans a great weekend full of awesome bands, and it was only recently that Limp Bizkit became available. In the process, Machine Head have been upset, and despite our best efforts, they have made the decision to cancel their appearance."

Despite all this hot air, Machine Head did in fact play the festival after all, taking the stage before Limp Bizkit. Flynn said, "After the promoters of Sonisphere begged us to come back onto this thing last week, the only consideration that we made it for is for all of you fucking fans, man! It wasn't for Sonisphere, it wasn't for Limp Bizkit – it was for the fucking lunatics of this fucking country that have treated us so fucking good, man. It is an honour to play for you, guys. It is a privilege to play for you, guys. We are so fucking lucky to have a fanbase like you."

A minor, and it must be said fairly juvenile, exchange of shots came before and after the show: beforehand, Flynn wrote, "We're going to fucking crush Limp Bizkit!" on the Machine Head website. After the show, Bizkit member DJ Lethal wrote on his Facebook profile, "Just finished playing at Sonisphere festival in London with NIN and Metallica... As for [Machine Head], hahaha, the only thing crushed was your egos... Suck it!"

Elsewhere on the site, he is said to have written: "I am a fan [of Machine Head] too; they just got pissy about some promoter stuff then got personal... I even wore a MH shirt on stage... They still played after crying about the whole thing. We would have gladly played before them; no big deal. But whaa whaa whaaaaaa..." His singer Fred Durst also added, "[I] love Machine Head [and] always will." These posts prompted a final diatribe from Flynn, in which he labelled the Sonisphere set 'unbelievable' and added: "Apparently [Lethal] forgot to mention the 'unprompted' three-minute-long 'Fuck Limp Bizkit' chant today from all 45,000 people at Sonisphere. Tonight was one of the biggest ego boosts we've ever had! Not that we had shit to do with it, but it was funny how the crowd chanted 'Machine fucking Head' in between every song that Limp Bizkit played tonight... By the way, we had 21 circle pits today!! That is a new record for the UK. Today we made fucking history, Sonisphere! If there's any doubt, footage from both sets will appear sooner or later."

Flynn was quizzed on the subject of inter-band feuds later that year, when Machine Head toured in support of Megadeth on that band's *Endgame* tour. By that point in his career, Megadeth singer Dave Mustaine was a reformed character when it came to slagging other bands, but for many years he had been known for the long-standing disagreements he had nurtured with bands such as Slayer and Pantera, and most of all with his old band Metallica. He and Machine Head rarely if ever met on this particular tour, reported Flynn: "We haven't seen Mustaine at all, it's like he's a ghost. It's kind of trippy to be on tour with the band and you never see them... [but] it's going good, man. We're about a week into it. Most of the shows have been sold out. It's pretty awesome. Tours and metal have been getting crushed lately, so it's been cool. It's trippy. [Mustaine is] a smart dude. This is a business arrangement. We aren't friends or anything. Machine Head is worth a lot and he knows it. It's good to have us on, and it's good to be touring with Megadeth. It's a business arrangement, so it's cool. It makes it easier in some ways."

Like most metalheads, Flynn was a fan of Megadeth's current album, *Endgame*, their best in years. As he said, "It's rocking, man. It's really good... it's probably the one we play the most in rotation. We toured with them on the last record too. There are only a couple of songs off [Megadeth's previous record, *United Abominations*] that I like. This one is solid. The production is amazing. It's probably the best-sounding, heaviest Megadeth record in a long time. [Guitarist] Chris Broderick is ripping it, good songs, nice thrash beats, and Mustaine's riffing out again. It's cool."

Flynn had played a part in relaxing the tense relationship between Megadeth and Slayer when Machine Head had opened the Canadian Carnage dates earlier in the year. He recalled, "We're friends with some of the Megadeth dudes and we're friends with the Slayer dudes, and that was the first kind of squashing of the [bands' mutual antipathy], if you will. I was hanging out with Kerry [King] on the last night of the tour. We did five dates or whatever, so on the last night we're hanging out and getting hammered. I walked over to Shawn Drover, the drummer of Megadeth, and said, 'Hey, come on and hang with us'. He's like, 'I don't know. I don't want a weird [vibe]'. I'm like, 'Just come on with us'."

He continued: "So I walk him into the Slayer dressing room, and I introduced him and they were like, 'Oh, hey, how's it going?' and he was like, 'Oh, hey, how's it going?' They were just meeting for the first time. They've been on tour for a week and a half, and were just meeting for the first time. It was an interesting sight. It's been a great feud. It's lasted for so long. You still see [Slayer drummer Dave] Lombardo making comments like he wants to give Lars [Ulrich, Metallica drummer] lessons or something. I was like, 'Maybe Lars can teach you not to blow smoke up your own ass in the process'. To me, I don't see Metallica needing to make those comments. It's not like Lars is out there taking shots at Lombardo for slopping up the 'Angel Of Death' roll. I don't think he has to care." (The author of this book admits to being the writer who reported that quote from Dave Lombardo, but wishes to make it clear that Lombardo was speaking in jest...)

Talking of bonds being renewed, rumours abounded at this time that a festival bill featuring the original 'Big Four' of thrash metal – Metallica, Slayer, Megadeth and Anthrax – might take place in 2010. This did take place to vast acclaim and public support, making it hard to believe how unlikely the concept first seemed.

All four bands had been through enormous trauma over the years, with incessant bickering going to a greater or lesser degree in all directions between them: the fact that several Big Four dates took place in 2010 and '11 is testament to Metallica's diplomatic skills and enormous international presence. It's relevant here because of a comment which Kerry King made very early on in the process.

"I've heard people referencing Lars," said King, in the interview with journalist Terry Bezer of *Metal Hammer* which first revealed the whole Big Four idea to the public. "I don't know Lars that well and I haven't heard it from Lars, but apparently he's talking to somebody about it. Maybe us, Metallica, Megadeth, I think he even threw in Anthrax, and I said, in this day and age, I know we had that time together, but how do you leave out Machine Head? There's better options than Anthrax, and that's nothing against Anthrax, but they've just been in pieces for quite some time and that doesn't make as much sense to me." Now, when Kerry King regards your band as a seminal player in the thrash metal movement, you know you're doing something right.

In late 2009, five years after the death of 'Dimebag' Darrell, *Metal Hammer* magazine released a CD of Pantera cover versions, one of which was Machine Head's version of 'Fucking Hostile', originally released on 1992's *Vulgar Display Of Power*. One of Pantera's most popular songs, thanks largely to its exhilaratingly violent speed and liberal use of expletives, '… Hostile' took on new life in the hands of Machine Head, who played it tuned down for extra heaviness. Asked why they chose that particular song, Demmel explained that the choice of cover version had come down to this one or 'Five Minutes Alone', from Pantera's *Far Beyond Driven* album of 1994. "We decided to go with 'Fucking Hostile' because the song sums up where we were at that time – it's really fast, and really aggressive," he said. "Ours is downtuned, so it's a step and a half lower. We recorded 'Fucking Hostile' in

C# to see if Robb could sing in that key. We patterned ours after the [live 1997] version, so there's some picking differences. The solo is patterned after the solo that Dime did on the live version, but other than that, we tried to keep our rendition as close to what they did. When we do cover songs, we try to do that; we try to play them note for note like the originals."

Asked if Dimebag was an influence, Demmel mused: "He's a huge influence. He's the most influential heavy metal guitarist there was. He created sounds and styles that hadn't been done before. I mean, yeah, he patterned a lot after Eddie Van Halen, but Eddie Van Halen was a rock guitarist. Dime brought it into the metal world, so he was a huge influence. [I met him] in 2004, actually, roughly pretty much [just] before he was killed. We did the Download festival, and were playing the main stage. Slayer was late, for some reason. [Dimebag's post-Pantera band] Damageplan had pulled up, and they had been up for a couple of days. Dime was pretty hammered – this was right after *Through The Ashes Of Empires* had come out. He came up to me, and just praised my playing on the guitar. He called me a shredder, and said he thought the leads on our album were great, and that I was such a good player. Coming from Dime, it was just one of the compliments that I'll always remember. It was really cool."

It seemed that 2010 was rapidly filling up with dates. A tour alongside Hatebreed, Bleeding Through and All Shall Perish, dubbed the 'Black Procession' tour, was announced in the summer. In the wake of his recent health issues, and with this serious commitment lying ahead of him, Demmel was asked how he was progressing when it came to managing his fainting episodes on stage. "I can never be sure that it won't happen," he said, "because three out of the four times I was pretty surprised that it did. Health-wise, it's been better. It's more a head-space thing than anything else, you know, so it has a lot to do with depression and has a lot to do with stress. Ever since my father died two years ago, it's been tough. So it's hard to gather all those emotions and keep things in check. So I can't be sure. But I feel better these days for sure."

He also looked back on a period of illness that had made the previous year's run through the Middle East tough to endure: "That was the last time I've been really sick. That was almost two years ago. I was deathly ill, I had pink eye [an eye infection] and my equilibrium was really fucked up. So I couldn't go and see all the cool things that everybody was doing, but the show in Dubai was amazing. Awesome festival, and then from there we went into Israel [with] crazy kids just aching for metal, and it was so good. Then we went to India to play this festival with Megadeth. We were staying in this plantation [style] hotel with amazing amenities and it was really cool. Then 40,000 kids show up screaming and having a great time. [They were] really exotic places and each one of them was really cool. In India, we remember walking in on this red carpet and they had this procession of people dancing and drums and everything. When we stopped, they stopped. They were kind of following us and gave us a coconut. It was so cool."

He also enthused about that year's headline slot at Wacken, by some distance the most popular metal festival in mainland Europe: "So many cool things have happened to this band. There's been so many benchmarks made and achieved, bigger things and bigger venues. [But the best] would have to be playing the festival weekend. We headlined Wacken and there were like 85,000 people there. It was one of the best shows in Machine Head's history, if not the best show, and we then hurried off to a private plane that was booked for us to fly to Sonisphere UK to play with Metallica, then to wake up and have this really cool hotel. That whole weekend was the highlight of 2009 for me. Then the *Kerrang!* awards [at which Machine Head won an 'Inspiration' trophy] on the next night… It was a really cool weekend."

When the three-month Black Procession tour began in January, Machine Head were firing on all cylinders: years on the road will do that to a band, if it doesn't kill them first. A strong bond between the band and their fans had always existed, but it was strengthened along the way by incidents such as one in Vienna when Flynn invited a fan on stage to play his guitar parts on 'Aesthetics Of Hate'. He told the fansite Take My Scars, "About one song before 'Aesthetics…', I noticed a kid upfront with a banner which said, 'Let Me Play 'Aesthetics Of Hate' On Guitar, Robb. I'm Fucking Serious!' We both made eye contact, and both laughed it off. So when 'Aesthetics' came up in the set, him and a bunch of his friends start screaming, 'Please'. I'm like, 'Dude, you better not be fucking around,' he's like, 'I can do it'. So I told security to bring him up. His name was Peter. He did fucking killer! Knew all my parts [on guitar]. I had to slow him down in the beginning a little; he was playing it at 100 miles an hour. But once the band kicked in, he got it. It was really, really cool. Super-fun. It was an incredible moment in an even more incredible show. We brought him and his buddies back after the show to say 'Hey', and I asked how far the crowd surfed him after he stage-dived back into the audience. He said all the way to the bar, where three people bought him beers, and he proceeded to cry. Amazing stuff!"

In years like this, executed largely on the road between album releases, Machine Head – and many touring bands like them – had one mission in mind: to reach as many members of the public as possible and, if possible, stay alive and sane at the same time. When a band as committed as this one comes to a city, that city needs to repay that commitment – or face disapproval on a biblical scale, as happened in San Diego. Interviewed in February, Flynn said: "If we're playing in San Diego, we're not going to go on a radio station and [say], 'Oh, yeah! San Diego crowds are awesome' – because they're not. They're beat. That's Machine Head slang for

'We don't like them'... They don't come to a show and, like, rage and go crazy. They come to a show and they're like, 'Oh, OK, this is cool. Oh, I like this song'. That kind of vibe. So we're not into that... I don't know why they come to a rock gig with that kind of attitude... They're fired."

As always, downturns in the road awaited, one of which was the unexpected death of Slipknot bassist Paul Gray in May (the band's statement read: "We are extremely saddened to hear of Paul Gray's passing. Slipknot are longtime labelmates, peers, friends, tour mates and metal brothers. Paul was a great songwriter, bass player, and a genuinely nice person... He will be missed by all of us") and on September 7, by a serious break-in at Flynn's house in Martinez, California.

Having returned from picking his son Zander up from school, Flynn entered his home to find theft and damage which he later estimated at $20,000 to $30,000. "We walked in and I realised we had been robbed," he said. "Our bedroom was ransacked, my tools were on the [living room] floor because they had used them to pry the TV off its corner mount. I definitely feel we were targeted, it was a team of people and in fact I think I was followed the moment I left the house until I got home, because they stopped halfway through for no apparent reason and just dropped everything, like someone alerted them I was coming. It wasn't a teenage smash and grab, they knew what they were doing."

Initially, Flynn said, he had been unimpressed by the efforts of the local police department until the case was assigned to a cop who knew his metal. "I don't feel they did a good job at first. I had to insist that they take fingerprints, and even then they only reluctantly agreed and just fingerprinted the three acoustic guitars [that were handled by the thieves]," said Flynn. "I didn't hear from the police for the next two days... but then Officer Leong came on board... He's been extremely helpful, he knows [of the band] Pantera. But the police [never did take fingerprints] of the doors and windows, it was that bad."

He added, "The hardest part for us, besides feeling the sanctity of our home has been violated, is that we're paranoid. My wife wants to move and my son asks me at night if the robbers are going to come in and kill me. I tell him, no, I'm not going to let that happen. On Friday we had the top-of-the-line security installed."

Flynn's livelihood as a musician was directly threatened by the theft not only of computers and cash, but also of four precious guitars. One of these was the black Ibanez Stratocaster with which he had recorded in the early days; another was the Washburn Dimebolt prototype given to him by Dimebag back in the mid-Nineties; and sadly, another was his older son's miniature guitar. He immediately offered rewards for the return of the instruments. "Items include my wife's jewellery, laptops, wakeboards, cash, and most importantly four of my guitars, including the guitar that I recorded *Burn My Eyes* with," he said. "Also stolen was a guitar that is priceless to me, that was a gift from Dimebag Darrell. The cocksuckers even stole my son Zander's mini Flying V I got him for Christmas."

Within two months, members of Machine Head's forum had donated enough money to replace Zander's guitar. Now that is special. Can you think of another band of this size whose fans are so connected to them?

At the end of the year, Machine Head began to consider their next album. If the task of following up *Through The Ashes Of Empires* had been tough, imagine the pressure that faced them when trying to outdo *The Blackening*, one of the decade's most acclaimed metal albums. Initially, the band was taking small steps towards new music – with only a riff here and a chorus there. As Demmel explained, "We wrap up our touring commitments in March, and that'll make *The Blackening* pretty much a three-year touring cycle. We've started writing a little bit, but not [much]. Dave brought a few riffs to the table, and Robb has a few. I've had a couple, Adam brought a couple. There's no songs or nothing yet. We're not a writing band as such. We just lock ourselves up in a room, and hash it out that way. It could be a while before you get another Machine Head record... I don't know when it will be ready and when we're going to record. We're not setting any time. When it's ready, then we'll go in."

As is always the case, the band-members were asked to describe the new music before it had even taken shape – a painful process for both interviewer and interviewee, but one that magazine and newspaper editors often insist upon in order to steal a march on their competition. Demmel was a trooper, doing his best to evoke the new sounds: "From the stuff that we've written, some of it could've been on *The Blackening* and some of it couldn't have. The thing about being involved in the band's writing process for the last album-and-a-half is that I could pick out a song like 'All Falls Down' or 'Wipe The Tears', songs from *Ashes...*, and then compare them to 'In The Presence Of My Enemies' or 'Imperium', and you can tell the state of mind that the band was in at the time. You can then go from 'Slanderous', which was one of the first songs written for *The Blackening*, to 'Clenching The Fists Of Dissent' or 'A Farewell To Arms', and there's a difference in what our state of mind was at that time. It's going to be where we are."

He added: "We're in a state of euphoria. Those albums were written when the band was at a pretty low point. We're riding this nice wave of success now, so I'm just hoping that we remember the hunger, remember the starvation that we had at that point. We didn't have a deal: we didn't have a record label. All of that justification that we were striving for, we have now, so we want to remember the fire that we had."

Asked if he felt under pressure, given how immense *The Blackening* had been, Demmel laughed and said: "An extreme pressure, yeah! There's a lot, but it's the same that we felt with *Ashes*, too, though. After we came out with *Ashes*, and it was reviewed so well and held in high praise, we felt, 'Fuck man, we got a hell of an album to follow up'. I said after *Ashes*, 'The next album is going to be the one', and I'm saying it again: the next record is going to be our best record. We haven't hit our writing peak. Dave McClain is bringing a ton of stuff – he wrote 'Halo'. He wrote some of the best riffs on *The Blackening*. Dave is the unsung hero of that record. Adam's taking lessons, and he's really learning his instrument, really getting into it. With the four of us all just really pouring ideas in, this is going to be the most complete record."

Obviously scenting battle ahead, Demmel exclaimed: "Screw the radio play, screw the labels, and screw everybody else – let's write songs that we enjoy to hear. As long as we adhere to that formula, which we did for *The Blackening*, we know that we'll be all right, and at the end of the day, we'll be OK with ourselves. That's all that matters. It'd be different if we just wrote with a different agenda, and it failed, and we thought, 'Wow, fuck. We can't even look at ourselves in the mirror.'

Flynn, by now the producer of two successful Machine Head albums, was ambivalent about whether he would tweak the faders on the new album, saying: "I don't know. We haven't discussed it. I know that they [the band] are happy with the production and I'm happy with the production. I'm not set in the idea that I'm doing it, but I know everybody's had a good experience with it." Demmel, however, was adamant that his bandmate was the man for the job. "Robb produced the last two records, and we're really so comfortable with him doing that, and then finding an engineer. We don't know where we're going to record it or who's going to engineer, but Robb's going to produce again, I'm pretty sure. Robb knows the Machine Head sound better than anybody; he knows the tones, and he knows the structure of what it should sound like. We trust him with that. He's got such a good musical ear, and such a good phrasing, that we all lean on heavily. We were kind of hesitant when we did *Through The Ashes Of Empires*, and by default we didn't really find anyone available, so Robb took over and it worked out really well. We're not going to break that."

Either way, Flynn was straining at the leash to begin work. "We're going to jump right into it," he promised. "We just had three months off, which was the first big break we've had for this album. We have a month off after this before the Europe stuff. We're ready to get into it. We took those three months off and started writing a little bit at the end. I totally got the bug. The *Blackening* cycle has been such an amazing moment for the band, [but] it was cool to say we're moving on from this. When we started writing, it was on to bigger and better things. As much as this moment meant, it's cool to see what we can accomplish next. I'm super-excited about writing this new record!"

Once more, and again this is not generally the case for other bands whose trajectory has been uninterrupted, the new album was a make-or-break moment for its creators. The spectre of those lonely, label-free months back in the early 2000s has never fully faded, and it's for this reason that each album since then has been an epic work. Flynn knew this, as ever, and had pondered what he wanted to achieve with the new songs. His aim was not merely to write an album, it seemed: this time it was to redefine music itself.

"I've been thinking about where to go with the new record, and the mindset," he said. "I was talking to Lars [Ulrich] and James [Hetfield] about their mindset when they were writing *Master Of Puppets*. Who were your rivals? Who did you have to be better than? What was driving you to write this insane music? There wasn't a template to follow. They had their influences, but what they did was take it and make it 10 times more extreme. I'm trying to put my headspace into what it would have been like for Slayer or Metallica or Rush or Black Sabbath, people who created a style of music out of something that wasn't there." Those, friends, are the words of a brave man.

Chapter 10

2011, 2012 And Beyond

The downside of hitting the best form of your career when you're a musician is that people seem to expect you to fail – even your most loyal fans. This depressing fact of life is doubly intimidating in the heavy metal arena, an oversaturated field in which bands come and go every few weeks, it seems. Perhaps there's no way to win: if you release a great album, people whisper that you'll be on your way down again before too long. If you release a poor album, on the other hand, you won't hear people saying the opposite – that you'll be on your way up again any moment now. This would be enough to make most of us give up, get a haircut, buy a tie and get a job in a bank.

But not Machine Head – as you'll have figured out by now if you've read this far. They took the endless adulation which was laid upon them in the wake of *The Blackening* as their cue to redouble their efforts, rather than an encouragement to slack off. Not that the endless queries about how they could possibly outdo their last album didn't grate after a while: as Robb Flynn recalled,

"For the whole last six months of *The Blackening* tour cycle, all that we heard, every day, every interview, first question: how are you going to top *The Blackening*? At first we didn't really know because we hadn't started writing yet. After a while it just got so fucking irritating hearing that. In some ways it lit a fire under our ass – like, all right, we're going to show you!"

Adam Duce was more sanguine, as always, commenting: "I think we did what we had to do on that record and then it was done. We had to kind of move forward from that and just get that behind us. When you're so widely critically acclaimed, if you let any of that shit go to your head, it makes the next thing that you do harder... like from after *Burn My Eyes*, we had huge success on that, then we all kind of freaked out, like 'What the hell are we going to do now?' But then we wrote *The More Things Change...*, which was not that much of a departure from *Burn My Eyes*. That was a product of feeling too much pressure. Then we tried to predict what the world was wanting at the time, and in comes *The Burning Red*. And that reacted in a good way in the United States, but I think it alienated a lot of fans just because of the production, really. Had we had Terry Date record and mix the entire thing, I think it would have been looked at completely differently, but we didn't, and it is what it is."

He continued, "Then again, we go trying to basically figure out what the world wants with *Supercharger*, and we end up getting dropped. And we just decided, 'Well, look, if this is the last fucking chance that we might have to make a record, then let's hoist our middle finger flag in the air as high as we can fucking get it, and go down like that on our own fucking terms! This is how we're going out!' But as soon as we did that, of course, it reacted. And that was kind of a fucking hard pill to swallow, just to know that the only fucking thing the world wanted from us was whatever *we* wanted to do. It was like, 'Jesus

Christ, we just wasted how many fucking years?' So it's been a giant learning process. Of course, after *Through The Ashes...* came *The Blackening*. We were calling the next one from *Through The Ashes...* when we were sitting here doing this press and stuff, it was like, 'Well, you know what? We're just gelling as a band right now. Wait until the next one. The next one is going to be the one!' And we hadn't written one fucking note for it, but we knew it. It's a basic continuation of just making music for the sake of it, because it's all that anybody wants out of us anyway. They don't want us trying to 'figure out' what they want. We're not that fucking smart, we're a fucking handful of musicians. We do one thing and we do it well. So I think that Machine Head fans, if you're a fan of our back catalogue, then you're going to feel this one. It's undeniably Machine Head and there's new, fresh ideas and new, fresh songs that deliver what a Machine Head fan's looking for."

At this point in early 2011, Machine Head could collectively look back and know, no matter what happened next, that *The Blackening* had been as thoroughly promoted as it is possible for any album to be. Three years of more or less non-stop tours had stamped the identity of this colossal record firmly onto metal communities in dozens of countries – show by show, pit by pit, interview by interview. Asked what the high point of recent times had been, Flynn promptly replied: "Having this incredible opportunity to open for Metallica and play arena shows – and watch our music take an arena full of 15,000 people who have no idea who we are, and watch it ignite in little pockets, until at the end of the show we've captured this arena crowd." It was, to say the very least, a job well done: a job that had taken three years.

Of the huge tour, the ever-unflappable Dave McClain shrugged: "*The Blackening* kept doing better, so it just snowballed for us. Seven years before, we didn't know if we were going to be a band, so we were just soaking it in. Then Metallica came around the last year and a half of our tour, so we did some random dates with them, and then it turned into a full-blown tour. Now with record sales the way they are, it is all based around live shows, so it's good that we can keep touring and keep it going."

At the end of it all, Flynn could review the stellar cast of bands with which Machine Head had travelled and say with confidence, "Most bands are pretty chill. They are a lot more chill than most [people] think they are. They like to hang, they like to drink. I mean everybody likes to have fun. I'm sure little things come up here and there. I find that in metal, there is a lot more camaraderie." However, he noted with the accuracy of a seasoned observer that a whole swathe of supposed metal bands are anything but, naming no names of course. "There was a period," he added, "when we were touring with a lot of radio bands, or we would end up on these radio shows. A lot of these bands that are pop bands, they are a pop band that are trying to differentiate into metal. They don't really know much about it. They don't have the background. They're not legit metalheads. They are more like, I don't know, something else. Those bands are the hardest to deal with, because they have the radio mindset. We don't really get along with them."

The *Blackening* tour would, he added, be chronicled in a DVD at some point: "We've been filming this whole four-year period. It will come out next year, probably at the end of the summer. It's going to be the four-year journey of the band, from writing the record to recording to touring, to all the ups and downs and everything in between." Meanwhile, Flynn had moonlighted as a remixer for the German metal band Rammstein, tweaking their song 'Rammlied' by adding more extreme beats. "I think our old publicity person in Germany is now their publicity person," he commented, asked how the project had come about. "They offered me a lot of money, and I was like, 'All right!' Over there they're massive. It's ridiculous how big they are. I'm stoked. It was fun. They told me to go crazy. They wanted it as brutal as possible. It had some cool riffs, and I added some thrash beats and blastbeats. I love a lot of old-school hip-hop, so I threw in some of those beats. I had a blast with it."

Machine Head finally got around to completing the writing sessions for the new album in early 2011, although songs were being assembled as far back as the previous spring. Dave McClain, then as now an underrated member of the band when it comes to his songwriting skills, explained: "I think we started [to put ideas together] in May 2010, when me and Robb got together and finally we entered the studio in April 2011 so, I'd say it probably took us 10 months to have all the songs for the album completed or, I'd say, almost completed – since a song is not completed until the last day just before it gets recorded. Robb always changes lyrics or adds new melodies, so we're constantly working on different arrangements or trying new ideas. Even if we have the basic structure of a song, there will be changes in the last moment, before getting in the studio to commence the recording sessions."

"We didn't want to write *The Blackening Part Two*," said McClain. "We weren't going to write a bunch of 10-minute songs or three-minute songs; we just went into it blind. We have this musical freedom that we have enjoyed on the last three records, starting with *Through The Ashes Of Empires*, as we don't have any outside influences – nobody looking over our shoulder watching what we're doing."

The band knew full well that while the *Blackening* approach had sounded fresh back in 2007, it might not be so novel four years later. "The thing that was on our minds," said Flynn, "was that in [the] years since then, a lot of bands have come out and started doing that sound. If we were going to stick with that formula, it probably wouldn't be as fresh. So we really needed to challenge ourselves and make something extraordinary. Even though the safer thing to do would have been to just play it safe and stick with the formula, we were like, 'We can't do that. We've got to take this some other direction'. We're trying to bring something new and exciting to the table, kind of get out of the safety zone and do and try some scary stuff!"

Once again, this meant casting off any concerns about commercially acceptable song durations: long tracks were definitely going to be the order of the day. "We have two 10-and-a-half minute songs and two nine-minute songs, and we were actually wondering if our fanbase or other bands could wrap their heads around what we were doing," said Flynn. "I think that in the end they do believe in us and they can get it around it. It's not like pop music, where you've got to have just one riff for three minutes. We can do a lot. I think our fans have learned to always expect something a little different on each record. I think, in many ways, they kind of demanded it of us as well… In the end, it was a great feeling, having that kind of confidence. For many, many parts, we were just kind of writing and seeing where things were going. When we finally sat down, we were as surprised as anybody to find out that we had two 10-minute songs."

He continued: "When we're writing, we're not timing how long the song is. We're just going with the vibe of it and going with what it feels like it needs. I think the beauty of music is that it can take you on a journey. I think that there is a theory in the music industry that three- or four-minute songs are the only things that are going to connect with people, but that sells people short. I think people's minds can take them on a journey. I like all the ups and downs of the longer songs. Our [influences] are Metallica's *Master Of Puppets* era and the Zeppelins and the Sabbaths, the seven-minute songs and that kind of vibe. That's what we grew up on and that's what we like. 'Victim Of Changes' by Judas Priest is eight minutes long and totally awesome."

Inspiration flowed quickly, said Flynn: "We took a three-month break and after the second month, I was chomping at the bit to get back to writing and so was Dave, our drummer, so he and I started jamming. After two months, I was ready. I felt I had taken a break and I had musical ideas already going. But it was nice to be home for a while... it was a good break that we had. After taking that much time invested in the band and touring, it was good."

In fact, the time spent away from the band was essential, added McLain. "We toured for three years on *The Blackening* and when we got off the road last year we went our separate ways. We needed some family time and to decompress, or do whatever, before we got back in writing mode. When we did get back together, it was for a few days a week to see what we had going on, and as the songs started building we were practising more. We wanted to get in and write the record, but we didn't want to rush it... We gave ourselves a deadline to get into the studio and get it done, so we got pretty busy towards the end of last year."

Once the songs were ready, or at least as ready as they were ever going to be given that Machine Head's music often changes during the recording process, the band commenced recording sessions, this time at the Jingletown studio in Oakland owned by Green Day. As with the previous album (you'll recall the troubles that plagued the writing of 'Halo', for example), some songs were completed faster than others. McClain said, "It kind of depends on the situation: some songs come together really fast and it seems like they write themselves. And then you have other songs where something doesn't feel right and we have to try to find the missing piece. In the end, it's just a feeling that tells you that [a] song is ready. Still, Robb is a guy who constantly has new ideas and always thinks how to make a song better. To really understand what I'm saying, I'll tell you that he was changing vocal melodies while the album was being mastered and mixed. Thank God that you can't change something that's already done, because probably he'd be changing stuff to make things better after the album had been released!"

Flynn produced the new album, titled *Unto The Locust* and – as early pictures showed – adorned with black and green artwork depicting the eponymous ravening insects. He recalled, "For the most part, we recorded it the way we did the last few. We got a new jam room, which was cool. During *The Blackening*, we moved jam rooms so we decked it out and made it more like a clubhouse than a jam room. We put up posters like Pink Floyd's *The Wall*, Maiden and Sabbath – more the album art than pictures of band-members. It just gave it a vibe, and made it a cool place for inspiration."

Surrounded by the right vibes both at rehearsal and during recording at Jingletown, which Flynn described as possessing a "cool vibe", each member of Machine Head was able to perform at his absolute best. Dave McClain anchored the album with tremendous reliability and power, and while there's nothing new there, he also laced his drum parts with great inventiveness. "Man, McClain is on fire!" said Demmel. "Some of the BPMs (beats per minute) on these songs are almost too fast to play along with. There's some burners on here."

The drummer himself added, "There's a lot of stuff on the new record that's super, super fast – easily the fastest bass drum stuff I've ever done. We're talking sixteenth notes at 230, maybe 235 bpm. There are parts that are just flying. It's crazy. There's songs that are like 'Aesthetics Of Hate' on crack. There's a huge, wide spectrum of stuff, and it's challenging for everybody. When we started writing, Robb came in with a song that was right-hand mania – his picking hand was huge and my right hand was doing the thrash beats super fast. I was like 'My God!'"

As well as contributing drum parts of demonic speed to the album, McClain had also written some unorthodox material for it. As he said, "We actually have two songs that didn't make the album, even though musically they were done. But Robb wasn't happy with the lyrics and some of the vocal melodies. Maybe these songs will be released at some time in the future, and I really hope they will. There's one that I wrote the music for, and has Robb on the piano and some of the orchestra stuff that was on the album... I would really like to see the song with the piano be on an album instead of coming out on a special edition. The second one is a heavy song and can be a bonus track, but the first one is really special for me; I wrote the music some days after my mom had passed away, so it has a special meaning for me."

Duce was also playing at his very best, and excuse us for a moment while we geek out a little over the specifics of his bass technique, but his precise playing is an essential part of Machine Head's sound, so here we go. Over the years, Duce had refined his picking hand to machine-like levels of accuracy, he explained to the author when the new album came out. "I hold my pick with the index finger and the middle finger on the bottom side. That reinforces the pick, although I don't know the exact physics of it. When you're doing fast picking, especially on a bass, you can get really sloppy, but with the extra finger reinforcing the pick, it makes the upstrokes tight. For any kind of galloping stuff, or just fast picking, it tightens it right up and you can hear everything.'

Asked how he'd built such levels of precision, Duce added: "By acting like it matters! Being on time and tight with the drums is quintessential to good bass playing. You can't be sloppy: you're half of the rhythm section and you're most of the low end. In Machine Head we do so many intricate things, and it's got to be right for it to sound good. If it's not tight, it's going to sound terrible."

After years as a composing and recording musician, Duce knows what works for him. "I don't know anything about theory: I barely know the names of the notes that I tune my bass to," he chuckled. "I've tried to go back and learn theory, but it's insanely boring to me. I play with feel. I know what feels good and sounds good. Those guys who understand theory and are able to employ it to add to their playing, more power to them – but it's not me."

This eminently sensible approach also extends as far as basses, of which many have come and gone through the Machine Head camp. "I've recorded with five-string basses, but I turn them into four-strings," he explained. "*The More Things Change...* was recorded with a five-string Alembic. It was amazing, but I only needed four strings, and it was easier to play the fast stuff without having to contend with the extra inch of baseball bat that they call a neck on that thing, ha ha! If you're going to tune down really low, then a greater string mass is in order, unless you put an extra inch or so on the scale. That way, you can get away with a lower tuning and stick with the same set of strings, which I personally prefer because it stays tighter without having to push down further. Heavier strings can sound muddy and they're also more difficult to play."

Nowadays his gear is reliable, versatile and solid, as you'd expect from a player with such presence. "I play a Yamaha BB," he said in 2011. "I borrowed one from Jack Gibson, the bass player from Exodus, and I really liked it. He had a five-string BB series and I compared it with all the other basses that I had. I tried all my Zons out, and some Fender P-Basses, but the Yamaha smoked everything. I also had a Musicman, which didn't work out either: although they've got a really full tone, they weren't what I was looking for. I've got my setup to deliver exactly what I need. The tone pots just take out the clarity, so I removed it, cranked it and covered it up. I don't use many pedals, apart from a DOD bass chorus-flanger, which I've used on a few different things in the past and on the new record. I also have a delay pedal in line for the parts where I need to mimic a cello. It gives you that bow kind of sound."

OK, that's enough bass… Phil Demmel, too, was on fire during the *Unto The Locust* sessions, playing with a melodic approach that was relatively new to him. He explained, "I surprised myself with a couple of things that I did on this record. I kind of developed another style to what I'm doing. I'm trying to pick my notes a little bit better and write memorable solos. I love it at Metallica shows when everybody hums Kirk Hammett's solos: they're songs within the songs, and that's what I've been aiming for with *The Blackening* and this record. I'm slowing down a little bit and going for better phrasing and better melody." He also took off his metaphorical hat to Flynn's superb rhythm playing, adding: "Robb did the vast majority of the rhythm tracks on this album, as he did on *The Blackening*. He's such a better rhythm player than I am. His picking hand is better and his timing is amazing, so it makes sense for him to do those. I do my leads and the ambient pieces."

Demmel also praised Flynn's production skills, saying: "If anybody knows what Machine Head should sound like, it's Robb. So I love having him in the producer's chair. He's got the best vision of what this band should sound like, he's got a great ear for notes and tones, and I think we'd all prefer to have him there instead of some outsider that comes in and says, 'Well, what about this?' Robb gets good ideas from outside sources, but he eats, sweats, shits and breathes this band 24 hours a day. He does tell us what to do, but he mostly suggests it. 'Hey, how about we try this?' And if we have ideas, he's open to trying them. Ultimately, at the end of the day, if he wants something done, it's probably going to get done that way, and we've learned to kind of trust him on that, kind of lean on him in that regard."

The results spoke for themselves, he said. "These are the best songs that this band has [ever] written!' he told the author during a break from the recording at Jingletown. "The new stuff is melodic as hell – and at the same time, some of the most brutal riffs we've ever written are coupled with the most beautiful music we've ever played. It's the next step for Machine Head. The new album is not *The Blackening 2*. There's a lot of music coming out of all of us, and it's the next chapter. It's a progression. There's nothing under six minutes long on there."

Asked if *Unto The Locust* would be as full of rage as *The Blackening*, he pondered: "The new album is dripping with emotion. When people read the lyrics and hear the songs, they'll understand what I'm saying. It's a different emotion now: there's still some of that anger that *The Blackening* had, but there's some angst and a lot of heart-strings being pulled on with this one. Music is a way of purging and releasing, and that's what this album has turned out to be."

On June 14, an advance single titled 'Locust' was released to keep fans on edge. McClain explained the choice of song: "We chose 'Locust' because it is, against the other material, middle of the road. It is between the dark stuff we do and the fast brutal stuff. 'Locust' just turned into a song for us, just like 'Halo' did. We fell in love with the song and when it came time to pick the single, it was just the obvious choice."

"The song is about locusts," added Flynn – perhaps obviously, but hold on. "Locusts are a metaphor. The story of locusts when they fly in swarms. They can fly but they can't control the direction they fly in. They kind of float in the wind, and then they land and cause all this havoc and destruction. They fly away and leave you in the aftermath. The song is a metaphor for a type of person who sometimes comes into your life and has a similar effect."

The Rockstar Energy Drink Mayhem Festival 2011, always the most irritatingly-titled event for anyone who has to type its name out, took up Machine Head's time in July and August, while dates in Australia and South America continued after that into the autumn. *Unto The Locust* was released on September 27, and by God, it was another almighty album: a worthy successor to *The Blackening* and a killer third strike to anyone who still thought that Machine Head might slip back into their mid-career doldrums.

Asked if the problems which Machine Head had had with Roadrunner were now in the past, Demmel replied: "I would like to think so, yeah. We're pretty deep into this touring cycle... I think there's people at the label who really believe in the band, and really hold us in high regard. Shit, you know? If you look at where Machine Head started to where we are now, and how many bands that've come and gone... [All these] years later, we're more relevant now than [we] were back in the day. That's a real testament to the band, and to the people that work for it."

The UK's *Metal Hammer* magazine released the album as a limited-edition cover-mount before the standard CD and download, a cunning new business model which guaranteed that a large number of albums would be quickly sold to the exact demographic which wanted it most. Edited by long-time metal writer and Machine Head expert Dom Lawson, the special *Unto The Locust* issue celebrated the long and diverse career of the musicians, examined their collective rise, fall and rise again and contained many new insights into the band.

Lawson, asked to contribute his thoughts for this book on why Machine Head still matter after so many years in business, told the author: "Huge, life-affirming tunes. Massive, crushing riffs. Heart-rending solos. Integrity. Honesty. Passion. Power. There are numerous reasons why Machine Head are one of the greatest heavy metal bands of all time, but for me they stand tall above the vast majority of their peers because they connect on an emotional level that most metal doesn't even attempt to reach.

I've loved them from the first time I heard the opening seconds of 'Davidian', way back in 1994. Since then, they have been an omnipresent and invaluable part of my musical and, dare I say it, spiritual life. Getting to know them on a personal level has been one of the best things that's happened during my career as a music journalist; but beyond that, their music provides me with cherished armour against life and its disappointments, cruelties and frustrations. I strongly believe that there is no other band in metal that believes so fervently in what they do, and that's why the bond between Machine Head and their fans is so intense and unwavering. When I listen to 'None But My Own' or 'Down To None' or 'Imperium', I feel 10 foot tall and bulletproof. When I listen to 'Descend The Shades Of Night' or 'Darkness Within', I always fight back tears because those songs, almost uniquely in heavy music, express my truth. I fucking love Machine Head and feel honoured and blessed to have them in my life. So. Fucking. Heavy."

The author's own review, which appeared in the regular edition of *Metal Hammer*, ran: "Make no mistake, that's what *Unto The Locust* is: the most accomplished album that Robb Flynn, Phil Demmel, Adam Duce and Dave McClain have ever recorded, alongside their two career-framing records *Burn My Eyes* and *The Blackening*. Like the former, *UTL* boasts a sonic palette overflowing with box-fresh ideas; like the latter, the album is a storm of complex arrangements and riffs, compiled by musicians who have gained absolute command of their vision. It's a breathtaking work.

"Right from the off it's obvious that Machine Head are out to take chances, and consequences be damned. The three-song 'I Am Hell' suite begins with a minute of choral vocals before breaking into one of the huge, fully-leaded groove riffs that the band have made their trademark since 1994. Oh, that's predictable, you say? Well, less than three minutes later your jaw will have hit the floor, because Machine Head are now playing murderously fast thrash metal. Your favourite metal band, no matter who they are, would find it a challenge to match this immense song, not least because it devolves into harmonised acoustic guitars and strings. 'Be Still And Know' follows up this epic opener with an amazing, Joe Satriani-style guitar loop loaded with delay. This song is a beast: the only track under six minutes long on this vast album, and even then, only just. Shredders extraordinaire Flynn and Demmel are on fire here, layering multiple guitar solos just like they did on 'Aesthetics Of Hate' last time out.

"You've heard 'Locust' by now, and doesn't that central riff remind you of 'Black Album'-era Metallica? But there are way too many ideas flying about for that reference to stick for long, with the song going in multiple directions. There's that huge, audience-levelling groove at 3'16" and 6'40", which you'll play again and again until your ears bleed – and then there's Flynn's sweet, choirboy tenor. Told you they had a lot of ideas. This applies to 'This Is The End', too, a meaty thrash tune for the pit jockeys which features a classical guitar intro.

"The core of this fully-evolved album is 'Darkness Within', which the MH bandmembers have been reluctant to define in interviews – and with good reason. The first couple of minutes are Flynn as Bob Dylan, with lines such as "I'm just a broken man" ripped from him while the song builds with agonising slowness. This is emotion at its rawest, and utterly different from anything we've heard from Machine Head to date. After that, the upbeat 'Pearls Before The Swine' sounds almost pedestrian, and indeed it is the closest this album comes to filler. *Unto The Locust* winds up with 'Who We Are', an experimental blend of children's choral vocals, strings and an infectious chord sequence. At 4'13" there's a maddeningly intense high-speed riff – but it only lasts 10 seconds, the swines…"

Other press and fan reviews were also generally in favour of *Unto The Locust*, something noted by the band. "We're all just super proud," said Flynn. "I mean, we worked our butts off. I feel like we delivered something really special – something the metal world needed. We just did a bunch of listening parties in LA, New York, Chicago and Oakland and got to get some first-hand fan reactions, sitting there in the same room as them and talking to them. People seem to be really stoked… It is the logical-follow up to *The Blackening*, but it is not *The Blackening 2*. It's definitely part of the evolutionary chain of Machine Head records, but it's still has all the things that you've grown to know and love about Machine Head. It's got the patented harmonics, heavy vocals [and it's] fast [and] grooving."

Asked about his singing style, which – as in 'Darkness Within' – often ventured into cleaner territory than on previous albums, Flynn said: "The melodic vocals that we brought more to the forefront later on were the result of just feeling trapped as to what we could and couldn't do. We felt like we'd backed ourselves into a corner, and wanted to try some new things. We made a conscious decision to change, and when you do that, you run the risk of making some mistakes. But the way I look at it, for the most part, every record after your first record, you're going to be crucified one way or another. If you never change, you're going to crucified for always sounding the same. If you change, you're going to be crucified for changing. But to me, never changing is boring. So if I'm going to be crucified, I'd at least rather be crucified for changing."

He continued: "With this record, even from the first song that was finished, we knew we had something special. The first song that was done was 'This Is The End'. We knew we had something different, something special and something unique, and that was inspiring. It was really inspiring to have such a strong start, and that helped spread into the rest of the work."

'This Is The End' is indeed one of the more hard-hitting songs on *Unto The Locust*, combining modernised thrash metal sounds with ambitious musicianship. "That was the first song that was written for the record," recalled Flynn. "I wrote the riff, the main chorus riff, in Auckland, New Zealand on the Slipknot tour. That's the first riff I remember writing for the record, and I wasn't sure if I was going to bring it to Machine Head at that point. And then the classical bits happened, and then the other stuff happened. The thing that was really cool about it was that because that was the first song written for the record, it just set the bar so high, right off the bat. It was like, 'Wow, man, this is a hard fucking song to play'. I mean, we could have sat there and been like, 'We're the fucking dudes who wrote *The Blackening*. Everyone can suck it'. But we went in and we came up with that song right off the bat. It was a pretty humbling experience, like, 'Jesus Christ, man, we've got to fucking step up our game here. This is really some fucking tough shit to play!' It was a really positive mind frame to write from, this very vulnerable place to write from, to try to better ourselves and constantly push ourselves to be better and tighten up our playing and improve ourselves. That was a big motivator for this record, to push ourselves and challenge ourselves as we were writing the riffs and the arrangements."

The neo-classical elements that he mentioned came from a newly educated position these days: Flynn had studied classical guitar in preparation for the new album. "It really works well in metal," he said. "When we went in to do the record it wasn't like, 'Oh, let's write some classical stuff'. But the first things that I wrote were these classical bits, and I was digging it and I started writing riffs around it, and I was like, 'Hey, this is pretty cool'. And I knew, I could tell that I was just doing it wrong. So I thought that before I started getting into some bad habits, I should really try to break them early."

He added: "I actually took classical guitar in high school. It was an elective [academic module] I had to take, and I mainly just smoked a lot of weed and played Black Sabbath songs. I got a C-minus, which isn't a very good grade. It's below average. I guess I showed that teacher, huh? But it really got my mind into that mindset of playing it, and once I really started playing I always leaned towards classical players. Like, I always liked Ritchie Blackmore, and Randy Rhoads in particular was a massive influence. Randy Rhoads on the first two Ozzy albums brought a lot of classical vibes and that was a huge influence. So between that and Jimi Hendrix and Black Sabbath, those were pretty much my main masters."

The song is also unusual for a metal band in that McClain lets loose in its midsection, delivering a largely improvised drum part that sounds positively vintage. "McClain's definitely channelling his inner Keith Moon, for sure," said Flynn. "It's just that chaotic anything-goes thing that I love, y'know? He adds this chaotic vibe. Granted, we're not playing rock music like The Who, but if you apply that same theory to metal it really just makes it more random, and that's what I like about it. We're really bummed out by a lot of metal bands right now. Every band plays to a click track, every tempo is the same, they snap all the drums to a Pro-Tools grid, they record the guitar parts and fly them all in. And it just all sounds perfect, and everything is perfect. Every roll is perfect, every hit is perfect, everything is just perfect. And that sounds like shit to us. Because to us, part of the charm, and maybe this comes from our punk rock roots or our hardcore roots, but there's something about when it isn't perfect, and it's feeling like it's about to run off the tracks, and the drums are speeding up and the vocals are starting to crack, and you're just getting that fucking chaotic energy – that is what sounds perfect to us."

Flynn added of McClain's performance, "When it came to the drums, the drums were the easy part. We basically got all of the tracks done in about a day and a half, and then we went back in like three or four days after and just tried the craziest idea. [We] tried different fills and all this crazy shit, that we would fly in later. The basic tracks, the basic drum parts, [McClain] laid down in about a day and a half. He and I had been working on a lot of pre-production prior to that. He was coming down on his own, pretty much for the last year. He'd get there about three hours before we would even show up, practice for three hours by himself and then we would show up and he would practise four hours with the band. He was busting his ass, man, and it really shows. His drumming on this record is a whole other level that metal has yet to see."

"The last four years is the most I've ever practised, and I've noticed more improvements in myself," said McClain himself. "My double bass is much faster than it was. I've totally changed my style: you see a lot of these death metal guys who are playing completely differently than I did when I was learning. It's different muscles, and much more effortless: some of those guys play super-light. That's great for them, but for me, I have to play with full aggression and full force. My kit is set up super-flat. I want to see the drummer fucking rocking when I go to see him live."

Curiously, one writer suggested to Demmel that 'This Is The End' sounded like a metalcore song, metalcore being an oft-maligned modern metal style involving clean and death metal vocals as well as hardcore breakdowns. As always, the guitarist remained diplomatic, reasoning: "There's not a lot of new bands that I really listen to consistently. Unearth's a band that I'll listen to, Trivium's a band I'll listen to, Killswitch [Engage] and the new Times Of Grace record's really good. But yeah, we're influenced by stuff like that. Those guys are all great musicians, so we kind of take something away from that. We're a band that's always evolving. We're always trying new things and listening to current stuff. That's something that's necessary. But I think that you'll hear just as much Judas Priest, Iron Maiden, early Metallica and some Slayer on this record as well. We draw from our influences all across the board."

Another eye-opening new song was 'I Am Hell', the third part of the opening suite of cuts on *Unto The Locust*. This was Demmel's concept, as he explained: "I had the concept of a pyromaniac, an arsonist, who's writing in his journal about discovering the sickness that's taking him, and Robb had the music and the title for a song called 'I Am Hell', so I emailed him a couple of verses and [explained] what I was going for, and he said that it would work. So from there we'd kind of sit down – before he would go in and sing, I'd come to the studio and we'd sit down on the couch and throw ideas back and forth to each other, just phrases and words that sound cool and stuff like that. We'd bounce off each other that way and as songs came up – as we worked on 'Locust' and worked on 'Be Still And Know' – it just worked. We had a good vibe. We have different writing styles; I'm really descriptive in my writing, but Robb likes to write in the first person – I, you, me – and I'm more about describing situations without using those pronouns. So it's a good mix." Now, how many musicians know what a pronoun is?

'I Am Hell' was more than just a song, explained Flynn: it was the beginning of the division between the *Blackening* cycle and the *Unto The Locust* cycle, two equally significant chapters in Machine Head's story. "We actually attempted writing in November of 2009," he said, "and nothing much came out of it. The actual beginning of 'I Am Hell' came out of it, but it was more just a symbolic moment for us, like, 'Wow, we're really moving on from *The Blackening*'. I wrote the end outro riff while I was in Norway, the tremolo picking, again geeking out on classical. And then for a while that song just kind of hung around, with those two parts connected with nothing in the middle. That intro had been on a few different versions, and I had written that guitar melody probably around the same time as I'd written the very beginning, and I had always heard it as this *a capella* thing with all these layers and all these different vocals, and I thought, 'Man, if I can ever get a goddamn song around this, it's going to be really cool!' But for about a year, a good year, it didn't materialise. I just kept those riffs because I liked them and they were really cool, but I didn't have anything else to go around it. We rarely played it at practice. At one point it was actually the beginning to 'Who We Are'."

Finally, a moment of temporary trauma provided the necessary impetus to complete the song, Flynn added. "About three weeks before we went in to record the album, I was demoing a bunch of songs because I was going to play stuff for the label back in New York, and the Pro-Tools rig went down and I was like, 'Fuck!' I was super-pissed. So I sat there and I was like, 'Y'know what? I'm just going to play guitar and see if I can write'. So I started messing around with ideas, and I stumbled on that thrash riff, and then I thought, 'Maybe if I take that end part and use it as a chorus...' And in 45 minutes I wrote the rest of the song. I brought it to the dudes and they were like, 'Holy shit!'"

Duce experienced a similar moment of epiphany of his own during the writing of *Unto The Locust*. He remembered: "The song 'Be Still And Know' from the new album has a guitar riff in the chorus and believe it or not, I was sleeping when I wrote [the accompanying] bass-line! I woke up at three o'clock in the morning and I was like 'That bass-line is killer' and I got out of bed, figured out what it was, wrote it down and played it a bunch of times. Then I went to practice and it didn't work..."

However, serendipity was at hand. "Although that part hadn't worked in rehearsal," he continues, "when we went to record the song on the studio, I said to the producer 'I want to try something here' because that part was still in my head and I wanted to see if I could use it. Guess what? Between the time I brought the part to practice and actually recording it, the rest of the band had changed up the beat – and now it fit exactly with what I was doing. I was like 'This totally works out!' It was nothing like what the riff was doing, so it brings a musicality to that part that makes it, for me. It really grooved. It was just one of those things: an example of the luck that goes into being a successful musician. It was magic."

The 2011 Rockstar Energy Mayhem Festival featured Machine Head opening the main stage for Megadeth, Godsmack, and Disturbed. It made sense that they supported the mighty Megadeth, who had been among the leaders of the thrash metal scene for 25 years, but it was curious that they were placed beneath Godsmack and Disturbed, two highly pedestrian bands whose music possessed a fraction of the energy and emotion of Machine Head's songs. A more sensible bill came when Machine Head accompanied Brazilian thrashers Sepultura to South America. That band had received endless complaints over the years since their founding frontman Max Cavalera had left them to form Soulfly in 1996, and indeed their recent recorded work lacks the immense power of the Cavalera-era albums, but live they were still a powerful proposition and one much more suited to Machine Head than, say, Godsmack.

Flynn described himself as "super excited" about the South American dates, and rightly so, as crowds on that continent are the largest and craziest anywhere. "We played Argentina one time, but we've never been to Brazil, we've never been to Chile," he said. "To go out and have Sepultura co-headline with us and let us close is amazing. It's huge. It's killer, we're really stoked. The response to the tour has been phenomenal; we're very much looking forward to it. I've seen so many of the Rock In Rio [festivals] with Rush and the Maiden thing... I've just heard so many amazing thing about it; I can't wait."

…Demmel, Robb Flynn, Adam Duce and Dave McClain, the band most likely to inherit the heavy metal crown if they're still together 10 years now. JOHN MC MURTIE/RETNA UK

Nowadays Adam Duce is a man of sobriety and serenity, but if you spilled his pint a decade ago, you might be in for a little surprise. JOHN MC MURTIE/RETNA UK

Flynn, delivering the goods. GETTY IMAGES

Demmel, the most musically accomplished member of Machine Head. His arrival in 2003 allowed Flynn to embark on more complex musical orations than before.

The bad old days. The McClain, Duce, Flynn and Luster line-up: interesting beards were evidently the order of the day;

Flynn on the mean streets;

Logan Mader in full flight.

...ther town, another gig, again they will explode (to paraphrase Machine Head's frequent touring partners Metallica). ROSS HALFIN

...n Duce, whose devastating picking hand makes him one of metal's greatest bass players. CORBIS

He added: "When I was at NAMM [the annual music-industry trade show held in Anaheim, California], I went to see Sepultura play. We've never toured with Sepultura before, but we knew the guys. Obviously they were a huge influence to us. They were one of the main reasons that we wanted to sign with Roadrunner. We felt whoever Sepultura was with, they knew what they were doing. I was just talking to Andreas [Kisser, Sepultura guitarist] at the show and it was kind of like, 'We should tour, man'. They were getting ready to release their record, we hadn't been there, it was a great opportunity to get together. They were like, 'You guys can headline, and it'll be fucking awesome'."

Sepultura, continued Flynn, had been one of Machine Head's earliest influences. "Sepultura, I think, gave us the thumbs, [along with] Napalm Death, Slayer... Biohazard, who was also on Roadrunner at the time, definitely were big supporters of the band. They were really hot at the time, they had that video on *Beavis And Butthead*. They really backed the band, even from before, I was seeing them open for The Exploited, like super-hardcore punk rock shows. We loved them."

The big metal dates of 2011 were, of course, the Metallica-headlined 'Big Four Of Thrash' events, which happened sporadically throughout America, having debuted in Europe the previous year. Flynn had heard that Slayer's Kerry King had suggested that Machine Head should be on the bill, and said: "I was blown away when he said that. I don't know if we felt like we should be involved. Those were the classic bands. Those were the bands that we looked up to." He also revealed that he might have had something to do with the genesis of the Big Four dates: "For my part, being on tour with Metallica, it was cool to play this little role in putting that all together. I kept on asking Lars [Ulrich], 'How come Metallica and Slayer have never toured

together? You guys should tour. We'd be all hammered.' Then in
LA, I introduced Kerry and Lars and said, 'Hey, man, you guys
should tour together'. I kept on sprinkling some seeds. I didn't
play any big role in it or anything, I was just sprinkling seeds here
and there… watered it a little bit. To see it finally happen was just
incredible; it's such a cool thing."

Asked if he thought that any of the original Bay Area thrash
bands would be a serious commercial force, Flynn added: "I never
thought any of them would be huge. It was so brand new and
heavy, and so different. When I was in high school everybody
was into Def Leppard and Poison. I thought it sucked. I hated
it. I liked Mötley Crüe because they had an edge, and you'd
read these crazy stories about them. It just seemed so unlikely
that any of them would be huge. The Bay Area thrash scene back
then was brutal. It was violent, it was dangerous. There has been
a romanticising that has happened, where thrash was fun, and
some bands played that up a little more. But when the real stuff
was starting with Exodus and Metallica and Slayer, those shows
were dangerous. It was super-violent. I came out of pits with
broken ribs and sprained arms. It was intense. To think that would
go big or mainstream, seemed absurd. The fact it did was amazing.
It connected with people on so many different levels."

The year ended with the Eighth Plague tour of the UK and
Europe – Machine Head's first headline tour of arenas. Supported
by Bring Me The Horizon, Devildriver and Darkest Hour,
Machine Head and their music filled these giant spaces with ease.
It was a little odd to witness this most intense of bands on these
huge stages, but then that is their future, if there is any justice in
the world. Apart from an incident where Phil Demmel walked off
stage after being hit by a shoe (well, you would, right?) at a show
in Brussels, the tour went smoothly: another notch on the band's
collective bedpost.

"We always make an effort to bring out a big show," Flynn told an interviewer from the *Quietus* website, "but you have to remember that within that big show there's still four people playing music, and that ultimately we're all there not to watch TV or pyro or fucking chicks dancing or whatever, we're all there because of this music. And as long as you remember that the connection that is there is because of that, I think that's how you can keep that intimacy. Never let the show, or the effects, or whatever, overshadow the fact that we're all here because we love music – even in a big venue."

Asked if he thought that Machine Head could fill still larger venues in the future, he enthused: "I think we can go bigger. Much bigger! I mean, we're really happy with this run and it seems like a milestone in the band's career, but I want to headline the O2! I want to headline Wembley Stadium. I feel like we can still bring this to a larger audience, we still think there are a lot of people out there that can get turned on to the music we create and can connect in the same way as so many other people have."

In early 2012, Machine Head executed a headlining tour of North America, with Suicide Silence and Darkest Hour in support, finally giving the fans what they so urgently needed. There was a sense of homecoming about all this, and indeed this is the perfect point to end the story, which is now up to date at the time of writing, apart from Machine Head's forthcoming slot on the UK's Download bill.

What to conclude about this courageous, complex group of individuals? Well, it turns out that they have several conclusions of their own about the world and their place in it. For a start, Adam Duce revealed that the best shows are the ones where the fans are close up and personal, rather than the huge stadium gigs which Machine Head had recently been playing. "I prefer playing in the parking lot, just because it's crazier," he said. "You've got the fans that could only afford the lawn tickets, and in the parking lot they can fight their way to the front. The people who want to be at the front are the ones that are at the front. The people who are in the pit want to be there. You've got the craziest fuckers down there responding to it, that's what they came for. And when you're on the main stage, these guys are about 100 yards away on the lawn up there and you're looking at a bunch of seats. Now over the years, and we've been doing this for 20 years, we've gotten good at being able to transition from one thing to the next and being able to work the seats people and stuff. It's just not the same. You don't see the visual response of what they're feeling. You go out into the parking lot and it's a goddamn hurricane in the middle of it, and it's fucking awesome."

Warming to the theme of contact with his fans, and specifically the endless meet-and-greet sessions which Machine Head execute with competition winners and suchlike, Duce explained: "I remember Michael Anthony of Van Halen talking about this. You can either be a super-cool guy that your fans talk about, or you can be a jerk that they talk about. I've personally had band-members ruin it for me because they were so up their own asses with themselves – so much so that I don't even like their music any more. I wouldn't want to do that to somebody that likes me that much, or likes what we collectively do that much, and go ahead and be that idiot that turns them off. Sometimes it's unavoidable: like if you just quit smoking two days ago, you're going to be rude to everybody you talk to. It's unavoidable! But when you have an opportunity to be cool to a group of people for just five minutes, why not make the most of it?"

As we've seen, the rigours of touring can get Duce's goat from time to time. He explained: "One of the things that's the worst about being on the bus is the fact that I'm fucking 39 years old, and I've achieved a certain level of lifestyle that I don't really want to do without when it comes time to get on fucking tour. It's like, 'OK, leave your motorcycles and your fucking airplane at home and fucking get on the goddamn school bus'. And it would be awesome if we could just do whatever we wanted to do, but you can't. You're fucking stuck. You don't have transportation, you're like a little kid." Modern music doesn't impress him either: "We get a lot of stuff on the bus all the time and most of it's just crap. I mean, I appreciate their enthusiasm, and I remember being that kid, so I try to be as nice as I can to everybody, but at the end of the day usually it's not very good. I mean, what's coming out this year that I'm really anticipating?"

He had a point. In the last couple of years, the most impressive non-extreme metal albums had come from Machine Head and Metallica. Asked about the latter's comeback album, *Death Magnetic*, Demmel was positive, saying: "I think it's their best record since the 'Black Album' [1991's *Metallica*]. I like half of it, that I really like. I think it's great ideas. I love that they're playing fast again. I think the songs are a little long, but I think it's such a step in the right direction for me with that band. [Because] *St. Anger*, I heard a couple of tunes, and it was just like, 'Fuck...' I didn't buy it. I hadn't bought [a Metallica album] since the Black record. I think it's something that they should be doing. Just them getting the fire back. We did four shows with them last year, and seeing them just having fun playing – they're playing 'Damage Inc.' and 'No Remorse' and all these great tunes – I think that they're back to just really having fun and being a band again. I think they're on the right track."

Other things that bug Duce include the record industry, which has been on its knees since someone invented CD-ripping software back in the Nineties. "The powers that be have not done a very good fucking job at being able to work within the new digital media," he said, with remarkable restraint given how much revenue he and his band have personally lost as a result. "They've always had this product that was a bag full of something that they're selling, and now it's this cyber idea and they failed miserably at being able to capitalise on that. So there's a huge breach in security there, and there's no guard at the door. It's just, 'Oh, there it is. Grab it!' You can steal shit in the privacy of your own home. If it's that easy to get, I can't really blame some kid that doesn't have a job for fucking taking it. Does it suck for us? Fuck yeah it does, but you got to roll with it. When the record companies fail as miserably as they have been with selling records, then you got to concentrate on making money in other places like tickets and T-shirts. And then in comes the fucking record company again with a 360 [degree] deal. Are you fucking kidding me? Really? We figured out how to continue to make money, and you want more of ours? Fuck you! 360 this, motherfuckers... I'm not saying that we're not going to do it because that seems to be the way that it's going. But it's going to have to be sweet as fuck to put my name on anything. I'd rather fucking put it out myself personally, but that's going to be another fucking Machine Head battle [and] war of attrition there, ha ha!"

Make no mistake: Duce is far from your average long-hair, but a man with deep thoughts about stuff that normally eludes the average headbanger – perhaps because his mind has been clear of booze for many years. For starters, he explained recently that in his opinion, a complete revision of Western religious doctrines might be in order. "I would like to see the total annihilation of the Jesuit society," he stated. "Religion is controlling; organised religion is totally controlling, and the Christian conservatives all went the other way when Jesus came around... Jesus showed them the new way, the whole thing that Jesus had got totally turned around, the doctrine of rebirth got omitted from the scriptures, which was originally there up until 543AD. The doctrine of reincarnation was part of the scriptures until then, but it didn't work out with their controlling theory so they got rid of that shit. Most organised religions, like Roman Catholicism, are straight in-line with just control… and that's controlled by the Jesuit society, which is how you can get rid of that from the top down."

He added, "I'm in church right now, wherever I'm walking around – I'm thinking of God every single day. I never darken the doorway of a regular church, never, ever! Because I think it is bullshit. I don't want to listen to some guy who's getting paid to tell me about what he read in the fucking book, and tell me that I'm going to go to hell if I don't think the way that he thinks – I hate that. It's such a waste of life to have this stuff going continually in your mind about, 'Oh, I better not do that, or I'll burn in hell for eternity' – that's not the way it is. Hell is right here on earth and so is heaven, and then we come back and review the whole thing and come back to do it again. It's always a progression forward, there's never an end to it. You don't end up in this 'great suffering place' if you don't listen to that faggot on the podium… Those guys don't think what I think, no. I don't see it as my business to tell anybody how to think."

Ultimately, and many will find this Duce's most attractive feature, he's grounded enough to know that success in any line of creativity is not a given – perhaps the very rationale that underpins Machine Head's work ethic. "We're really lucky to have our fans," he told the author in 2011. "Being in a successful band is not a matter of how talented you are: it's a matter of having a lot of different components come together and the stars and the planets aligning. There's a lot of hard work too, but for most bands that hard work goes completely unrewarded: they don't make it as far as we have. There's a lot of luck involved in remaining a heavy metal band for 20 years or whatever."

Phil Demmel, too, has a keen awareness of where Machine Head fit into the world of music. Asked about his favourite touring spots, he mused: "The best part about Europe is we're so much bigger over there. The shows are always three times the size of the shows we do in the States. So it's just the crowds and the reaction we get… I mean, I love the conveniences of America, I really do. I love being able to stop at a truck stop at two in the morning and be able to get my favorite microwave bean burrito or a Slurpee [slush drink] or something. Over there you can't, it's probably a good thing, but it doesn't mean I like it… [in Europe] I think they're more intelligent music fans as a whole. They're more accepting of all music genres, instead of, 'Oh you can't like Slayer and Blind Guardian'. You get kids over there in corpsepaint going to the death metal show, but then are going to go to [a] Darkness show. They just love all types of music out there, they appreciate it. So I think over here you get too cliquey with [clothing retailer] Hot Topic and MTV telling you what's cool and what's not cool."

Looking back over his career, which it would (for once) be appropriate to describe as 'rollercoaster' as if we were some Saturday tabloid, Flynn remarked: "I would love to say I had this grand vision, but if you sat in the Machine Head jam room, it's just so *Beavis And Butt-Head*. It's like, 'What do you think of this riff?' 'Oh, that's cool.' 'What do you think of this riff?' We just try stuff, and sometimes I get these crazy ideas. I just try and write it out, and the dudes just let me go with it, thankfully."

He was being modest in saying this. The reality is that despite their lack of formal training, each of the musicians in the band is a virtuoso on his instrument. Flynn explained that the complex elements of the songs usually came about through intuition rather than design: "There's a lot of musicality. The neo-classical influence coming in really opened up a lot of doors that we could have. You know, as opposed to your having just evil notes… that's how schooled I am. I call it evil notes, or sad notes, or happy notes, or you know, like, 'Go to the third fret, go to the second fret'. I don't know any theory, I just hear it in my head. But, to me, having those – as opposed to evil notes, a little more of the sad minor notes – in the classical context, it really opened up melodies, and then you could build things on top of it. And the more that we went, the more ambitious we were, like, 'Fuck it. Let's just fucking pile it on, and see what happens'. Better to go too far and then pull back, than never go far enough."

As for the oft-repeated question about Machine Head's later songs being particularly long, he shrugged: "We've always had long songs. I mean, on *Burn My Eyes*, 'A Thousand Lies' was seven minutes, 'A Nation On Fire' was seven minutes, 'Death Church' was six minutes. You know, on *Supercharger*, 'Trephination' was seven minutes. With that record, the first four songs that we wrote, there was no indication that the songs were going to be long. The first four songs that we wrote [for *The Blackening*] were the shortest songs on the record – 'Beautiful Mourning', 'Slanderous', 'Aesthetics Of Hate' and 'Now I Lay Thee Down'. The first four months of the recording, it was just where we were going. And then, at some point, 'Clenching The Fists Of Dissent' came along. We've never written for the radio. We've never timed our songs, and gone, 'Is this going to work?' We just write until we feel it's done. And when we timed 'Clenching...', we were all fucking shocked. Like, 'This fucking song is 10 minutes fucking long, and it's killer!' It doesn't feel like it's 10 minutes long... some bands write a four-minute song, and it feels like a 10-minute song, you know? I've always wanted to write a song in the classic sense and structure of a pop song."

Flynn summed up the essence of his songwriting technique, saying: "Verse, chorus, verse. Yeah, I want hooks. I want things that repeat. I don't want to write riff soup. I've never wanted to do that. Even my favourite bands – you know, Mercyful Fate, Metallica – there was still a song in there. Maybe in between that, they took all these turns and twists, but eventually it came back to the song. And I still feel that's very important. Sometimes they're shorter, sometimes they're longer. You can plan all you want to, but at the end of the day, more often than not, the music will only go one way. You have to let the music take you where it's going… We really set out to challenge ourselves, both musically, lyrically, with storytelling, with arrangements, and try some stuff other bands aren't doing. Really be daring. Dare to fail. And we're stoked on the results."

The most recent two, and arguably three, Machine Head albums are similar in that they're epic in nature, inventive in structure and also headspinningly good. As Flynn explained it, however, the ambition behind each album was progressively greater each time. "When we wrote for *The Blackening*, we had pushed ourselves to the extent of our abilities. There's some really intense, dynamic stuff on there. Then we toured it for three years. At some point, what was the limit of our abilities became the new normal. So when we got done touring, it was like, 'I don't want to be stuck with this box around what we can and can't do. Let's just go for it and see what happens'. And we did… There were a lot of people telling us we should just play it safe. We got Metallica tours and Grammy nominations, and if it ain't broke don't fix it. Maybe it's just our attention spans are really short, I'm not sure, but that just didn't appeal to us. It had been almost five years since the last writing session."

Unto The Locust, in particular, was an album so expansive in sonic territory that it came close to being a progressive metal album, although the aggression of the riffs and vocals kept it from falling into that particular abyss. What it most represented was a declaration of identity, and a newfound confidence with that identity. Flynn: "We really wanted to make a statement. Not that *The Blackening* wasn't a statement. It wasn't about bettering

The Blackening... For us, it's not about comparing the two. We just wanted to make a record that will allow *The Blackening* to stand on its own legs, and make another record that could be different and stand on its own legs. And that's what we shot for. Whether we achieved it or not, that's for the world to decide. But we feel that we challenged ourselves... with *The Blackening*. The accolades: it's amazing, it's humbling, but we still have this challenge, this desire, we want to go out there and change things and shake things up and make a statement."

The band had matured as people as much as they had as songwriters, explained Flynn. "There's a lot less fear-based decision-making, you know. For instance, we [used to] refuse to play the song 'I'm Your God' off *Burn My Eyes* for the first five years that we were a band, because we thought, 'Everyone will think we're pussies'... so we never played it until like 1999 or 2000 or something like that. Everyone just went bananas for the song... it's like, 'What the fuck were we thinking?' you know? We wrote the song. It's a great song, you know, but [there's] a lot of that. *The Burning Red* [has] other melodic passages and bringing out influences like The Cure... even though they are a band I've loved forever, we just never would have brought them out because of people thinking we were pussies or doing too much melodic stuff. And now there's a lot less of that, you know. We're just going to go for it and if it feels right then it feels right."

In 2012, Machine Head are in a position where they can do more or less whatever they like. Their songwriting and performing skills are at a peak, and a generation of younger bands is now queueing up to pay tribute to them. Like all musicians who are fans at heart, Flynn finds it hard to accept that he is an idol to many of his contemporaries – which is good, because it means that he doesn't believe in his own publicity. "We paved the way for, and inspired and influenced pretty much a whole generation of bands, and that's

225

just such an incredible feeling," he said, "[but] I read James Hetfield saying that *The Blackening* completely influenced *Death Magnetic* and then when he told me [that] to my face, I was like, 'What the fuck!' My fucking brain imploded, y'know? This is a band that was a huge inspiration to us, and to have it come around full circle is just incredible. And to have the likes of Trivium, the Killswitch Engage guys, Disturbed and Lamb Of God in existence? It's pretty cool. I guess, if I had to pick a 'Big Four' of our generation, I'd say Slipknot, Machine Head, Killswitch Engage and Lamb Of God."

Flynn and the rest of the band still live like normal metal fans, which is to say, they walk the streets and stage without the benefit of security, at least most of the time – an issue that became relevant after Dimebag's senseless death in 2004. "I can't go around living my life in that much fear," said Flynn, asked if he ever feared for his wellbeing after spending so much time in the public eye. "I mean, that's not to say that we don't need security – we need security, obviously – we're happy to have security, and there's obviously times when there are security threats that we have to deal with. A lot of the time those things are completely spontaneous, it's not like it's a regular occurrence, it's something random, really; it's a lot to do with getting lost in the moment, and sure, in the wake of the Dimebag thing, most bands have taken steps with security, but you can't live your life in fear like that."

The future should, in theory, be bright for Machine Head, on personal and professional levels. Phil Demmel became engaged to Bleeding Through keyboard player Marta Peterson in early 2012: as he said, "I met the girl of my dreams in Australia... One of the greatest things that has ever happened to me was on that run. I have very special memories of Australia and knowing that I was in love for the first time when I was in Brisbane." This stands in stark contrast to the three-year *Blackening* run, a period riven by tragedy and despair, despite the concomitant rise in Machine

Head's fortunes: as Demmel explained about the forthcoming DVD, "We toured on *The Blackening* for three years, [played] almost 400 shows, [and] we have footage from everything. So much happened on that tour – our drummer's mom died, my dad died... So much happened to us. We almost broke up, we went to therapy... All this different shit happened. So we're trying to put all of this together. It's just too much. So we want to whittle it down and create a cool story."

Unto The Locust was Machine Head's most commercially successful album in chart terms, hitting Number 22 in the USA in its first week – an amazing coup for a band as aggressive as this one. Machine Head hadn't enjoyed such fortunes since the mid-Nineties, when the first rush of fame threatened to overwhelm them, recalled Adam Duce. "We came out with *Burn My Eyes* and had this amazing success right off the bat when we were pretty much kids," he said. "It's kind of an overwhelming feeling, and you don't really know how to act because you've never been prepared for it. And you end up partying a lot and you end up acting like an asshole. And then we got hit with the curse with the label of 'the new Metallica'! And look at everybody who gets hit with the curse of the new Metallica: I call it a curse, because nobody has ever been called that and pulled it off. If you get branded as the new Metallica, you have some hard times ahead of you. We certainly did – and it seems like it took three records to pass the curse. Then you see guys like Trivium, who are in the middle of that curse – I don't envy them at all... That's a hard thing to deal with. We've done tours with them and they're good guys. Call it a superstition or whatever, but it's a hell of a thing to deal with as a musician! Anyway, at this point I don't think they're going to call us the new anything, ever. We've established ourselves as Machine Head."

"It was a different time," said Flynn, thinking back to the band's beginnings. "Going back to when we started, we were four long-haired white dudes living in a predominantly black neighbourhood. We were sharing a rehearsal studio with four punk rock bands. It was a different vibe; it was a different mindset, too. I think that we were still figuring out where we wanted to go back then as well, and along the line we found our lane and we've been riding that lane. We've been able to block the outside world out and just continue to do our thing, which is a really good place to be."

It's beneficial for all of us that Machine Head have come back with such a vengeance, for several reasons. It proves that metal can command a fanbase and still be powerful, uncompromising music that doesn't pander to the mainstream while still being able to pay the bills. It also shows that there is still fire in the belly of popular culture, albeit on the edge of it. And it also keeps the members of the band off the streets: as Flynn revealed, there is no backup plan in case this all fails. "We don't really know anything else," he laughed. "I've been playing in bands since I was 15 years old. I've been on tour since I was 18. I don't really know anything else, so I've never had a Plan B – this kind of had to work. I think when you try and tackle something with that much tenacity, you make it work. A lot of people told me how I should get a Plan B, but I don't want a Plan B: this is what I want to do."

Flynn's old comrades salute him to this day. "I'm very proud of him," says Jeff Stewart, his first guitar-playing buddy, adding: "Robb always had that mental vision. I always knew that he was going to make it." Harald Oimoen adds: "I can't say enough about Robb. I'm so happy for his success. To this day, he is the nicest, most helpful, friendliest, coolest, down-to-earth guy ever in the whole Bay Area scene. He goes out of his way. He went out of his way to walk me backstage at Metallica shows when I was having trouble getting aftershow passes. They're still like that. Joey Huston's role in their success can't be overstated, either. He's like a fifth member of the band."

Craig Locicero of Forbidden also pays homage where it is due, saying: "I have immense respect for Robb, let's make that very clear. He was an integral part of a band which became a branch that everything grew out of, and he should always have been proud of it. Adam is pretty damn brilliant. He's smart and he does a multitude of things: he knows that the music business is not the be-all and end-all of life. I have the utmost respect for him and he's very honest. Logan Mader has gone on to be a great producer these days. Chris Kontos is one of my best friends and we've had many great times together. He also played with me in my band Spiral Arms."

The writer Paul Brannigan, who edited *Kerrang!* for many years and under whose editorship the two key Machine Head features which are quoted in this book were commissioned, writes on the same subject: "I think Machine Head have the capability, the ambition and the talent to carve out a place among the true legends of metal. They've always been an important band in our world, but since Phil Demmel joined the band they've ascended to a new level. They've always had the riffs and attitude, but now they also have soul and heart and a raw humanity that sets them above their peers. *The Blackening* and *Unto The Locust* are *incredible* albums, but I believe that their true undisputed masterpiece may be still to come. Robb is so steeped in the history and mythology of metal, but those world tours with Metallica have really opened his eyes to the potential his band have yet to realise. I think Machine Head have a hugely important role to play in the development and growth of metal in the next decade: they're the last truly vital band of their generation – and they're actually getting better with age."

"I think we can appreciate just how far we've come," mused Flynn. "I don't think about it all the time, but every once in a while I'm talking to the kids onstage and I sit there and I go,

'Yeah, man, our first record came out 17 years ago'. I mean, this is not the trajectory of a band on their seventeenth year; most bands are kind of [fed up] with it at this point and many of our peers have fallen by the wayside, and almost every band that was going when we started is defunct. The fact that we're still here and we're doing better than ever... we know that we're lucky, incredibly lucky, to have a fanbase that's so passionate and so intense about our music. I mean, our fans live and breathe this stuff; it's amazing. Every single day on this tour, I've signed kids that have our lyrics tattooed on their arm or the Machine Head logos and then they want to get our autographs, which I always think is crazy. You don't want my stupid autograph tattooed on your arm, but they've [also] got things that actually mean something, like lyrics. You hear these incredible stories and these heartbreaking stories, and you hear just how much it helps carry them through, and it makes us believe."

Trends come and trends go, but metal will remain, and Robb Flynn with it, he says. "I can't even imagine not being in a band," he told interviewer Tom Trakas. "I get that question, the old 'What would you be doing if...' and I have the same answer each and every time. This is all I was ever going to do. I've sacrificed everything in my life to do this. As cold as this sounds, but I used to tell my girlfriend, who is now my wife when I went on tour – and even when I say this now, it's like 'Jesus!', you know – but basically, I was like, 'Machine Head is number one and you're number two'. I know when I say that I sound like such a dick, but music is such an obsession with me. It's something that I have to create, something I have to listen to. I fucking love music, it's just such a huge part of my life. It got me through tough times as a five-year-old, a 15-year-old, a 20-year-old... it's never-ending."

Finally, Flynn concluded in that particularly powerful interview with *Kerrang!*'s Tom Bryant in 2007, "You need the valleys to appreciate the peaks. You'll learn more from your failures than you ever will from your triumphs. I wouldn't change a thing."

Who better to end this book than the mighty James Hetfield, who said on the subject of Machine Head: "They're great guys and a lot of fun. They deliver the goods, and they're very powerful. They love touring and they love the hard work. They love putting in the effort – and they love the passion that they get from it."

Is it too late for them to take over the heavy metal world, I asked him? "You know, it's never too late," said Hetfield. "They've certainly paid their dues. Their music kept them on the road for a lot longer than they actually wanted to be, which is similar to us as well, ha ha! It happens when it's supposed to happen – and they deserve it." Wiser words than that – at least on the subject of the unsociably violent music which sustains us all – have rarely, if ever, been spoken.

Machine Head Discography

All releases by Roadrunner

Albums

Burn My Eyes	1994
The More Things Change…	1997
The Burning Red	1999
Supercharger	2001
Hellalive	2003
Through The Ashes Of Empires	2003
The Blackening	2008
Unto The Locust	2011

Singles

Davidian	1994
Old	1994
Take My Scars	1997
Ten Ton Hammer	1997

From This Day	1999
Silver (Take My Hand)	1999
Crashing Around You	2001
Imperium	2004
Days Turn Blue To Gray	2004
Now I Lay Thee Down	2007
Aesthetics Of Hate	2007
Halo	2007
Locust	2011
Darkness Within	2012

DVDs

Elegies	2005

Machine Head members' appearances on other artists' albums

Robb Flynn
Forbidden
Forbidden Evil (1988; Flynn wrote material for this album, but didn't appear on it)
Vio-Lence
Eternal Nightmare (1988)
Oppressing The Masses (1990)
Nothing To Gain (1993)
Roadrunner United
The All-Star Sessions (2005)

Phil Demmel
Vio-Lence
Eternal Nightmare (1988)
Oppressing The Masses (1990)

Nothing To Gain (1993)
Torque
Torque (1996)
Technocracy
Technocracy (2001)
Roadrunner United
The All-Star Sessions (2005)
Dublin Death Patrol
DDP 4 Life (2007)

Adam Duce
Roadrunner United
The All-Star Sessions (2005)

Dave McClain
SA Slayer
Go For The Throat (1988)
Sacred Reich
Independent (1993)
Heal (1996)
Roadrunner United
The All-Star Sessions (2005)

Logan Mader
Medication
Prince Valium (2002)

Chris Kontos
Attitude Adjustment
American Paranoia (1986)
Out of Hand (1991)

Grinch
The Blacking Factory (1992)
Konkhra
Weed Out The Weak (1997)
Various Artists
A Tribute To Judas Priest: Legends Of Metal (1997)
The Servants
Mostly Monsters (2002)
Anti-Trust
Guilty as Charged (2005)

Ahrue Luster
Ill Nino
Confession (2003)
One Nation Underground (2005)
The Under Cover Sessions (2006)
Enigma (2008)
Dead New World (2010)

Sources

All interviews with Robb Flynn, Phil Demmel, Adam Duce, Dave McClain, Tony Costanza, Chris Kontos, Craig Locicero, Perry Strickland, James Hetfield, Harald Oimoen, Dom Lawson, Paul Brannigan and Jeff Stewart (www.reverbnation.com/envirusment) were carried out by the author between 2007 and 2012 except where indicated.

Quotes from issues of *Kerrang!* dated July 7, 2007 and April 4, 2009, others from *Ultimate Guitar,* and still others from *Midwest Metal* magazine, have been reproduced with the extremely kind permission of Tom Bryant (www.tom-bryant.com), Ian Winwood, Anthony Morgan and Tom Trakas (http://deathstar330.blogspot.co.uk) respectively.

Other sources: Aaron Yoxheimer (*The Morning Call*), Ben Richardson (*San Francisco Bay Guardian*), Rock Sound, Full Metal Jackie, Borivoj Krgin (Blabbermouth.net), Tom Trakas

(*Midwest Metal*), Tom Bryant (*Kerrang!*), Absolut Metal, *Bass Guitar* Magazine, *Music Mart, Total Guitar, Rhythm*, Sheila Rene, Brian Webb (PRP), Live 4 Metal, Ultimate-Guitar.com, *Metal Hammer*, Vassil Varbanov (Tangra Mega Rock), *The Flint Journal, Contra Costa Times*, That Metal Show, Machinehead1.com, Lords Of Metal, Earth-Dog.com, MTV, Austin Powell (*The Daily Texan*), Scott McLennan (*Worcester Telegram & Gazette*), Justin Donnelly (Metal Forge), Pete Richards (ChartAttack.com), Colonel Angus (Wormwood Chronicles), Patrick Douglas (The Culture Shock), Artistdirect, Karma E. Omowale (FourteenG.net), Artisan News Service, Vince Neilstein (best pen name ever: Metalsucks), Mick Stingley (Shockhound), Mia Timpano, *Revolver*, Dimitris Kontogeorgakos (Metal Kaoz), Headbangersblog.com, Chad Bowar (HeavyMetalAbout.com), Aniruddh Bansal (Full Metal Rock), TakeMyScars.com, David 'The Captain' Grant (Rock Radio), *Martinez News-Gazette*, Amy Harris, Jeffrey Easton (Metal Exiles), Bram Teitelman (Metal Insider), Zach Shaw (Metal Insider), Greg Pratt (Exclaim.ca), Roadrunnerrecords.com, Alternative Zine, Garage Radio, Peter Hodgson (I Heart Guitar), Loudwire, Bob Zerull (Zoiks! Online), The Quietus, Hardrock Haven, Anne Sciara (Bay Area Music Scene), Don Kaye (*Metal Edge*), Doug Gibson (Metal Underground), Terrorizer.

Index